BANGKOK
BEYOND THE BUDDHA

SCOTT SHAW

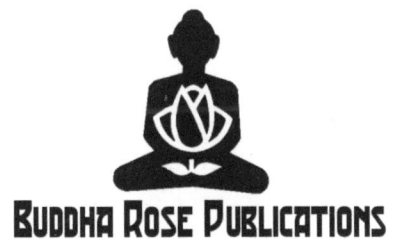

BUDDHA ROSE PUBLICATIONS

Bangkok: Beyond the Buddha
Copyright © 2012 by Scott Shaw

www.scottshaw.com

All Rights Reserved

No part of this book may be reproduced in any manner without the expressed written permission of the author or the publishing company.

ISBN: 1-877792-64-0
ISBN 13: 978-1-877792-64-9

BANGKOK
BEYOND THE BUDDHA

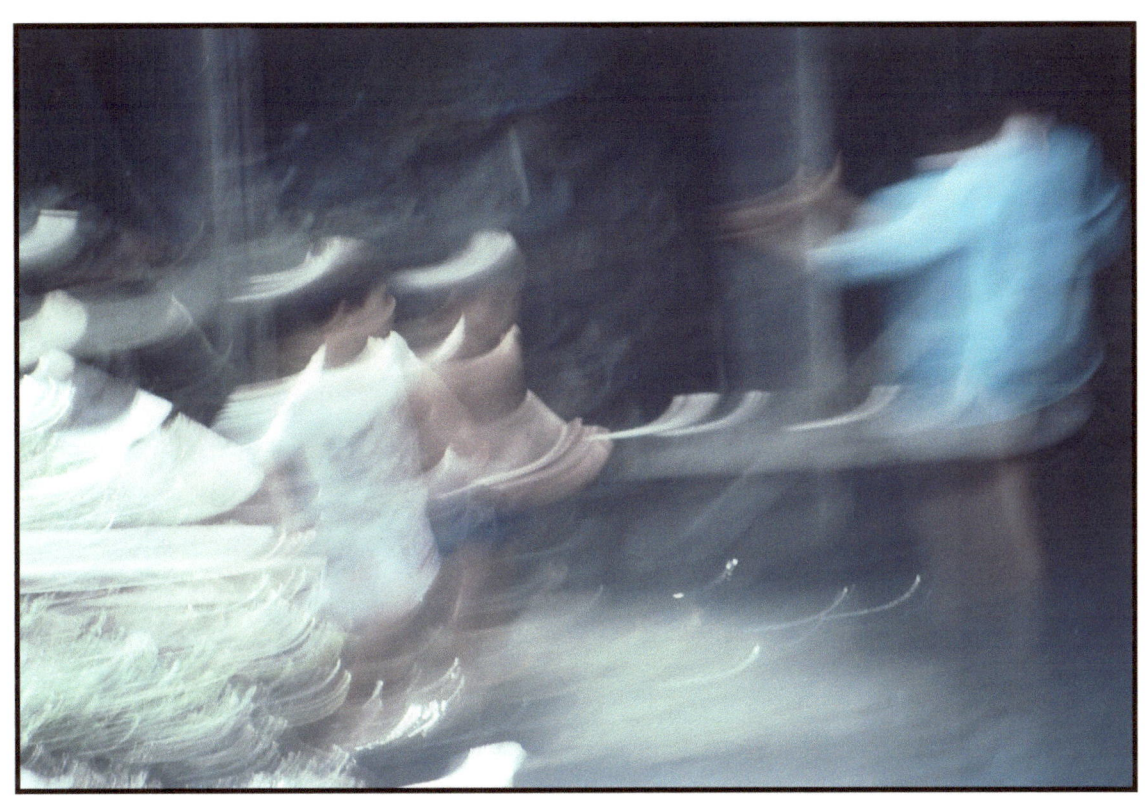

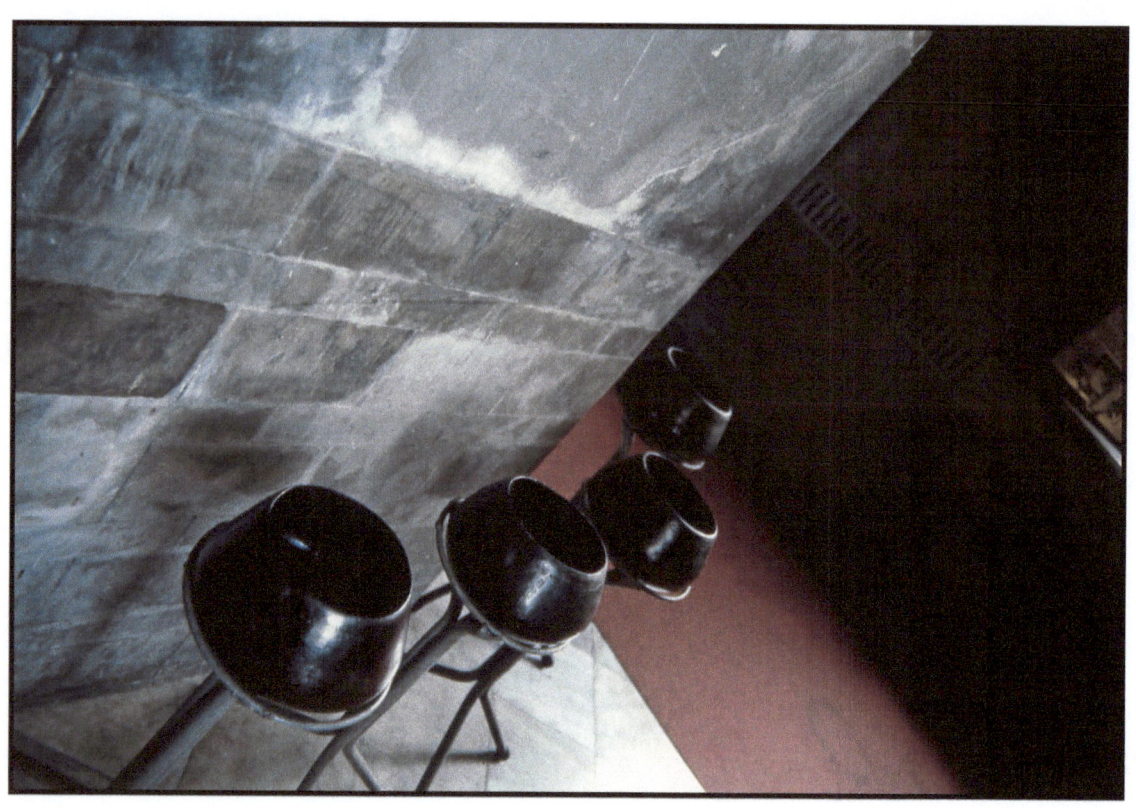

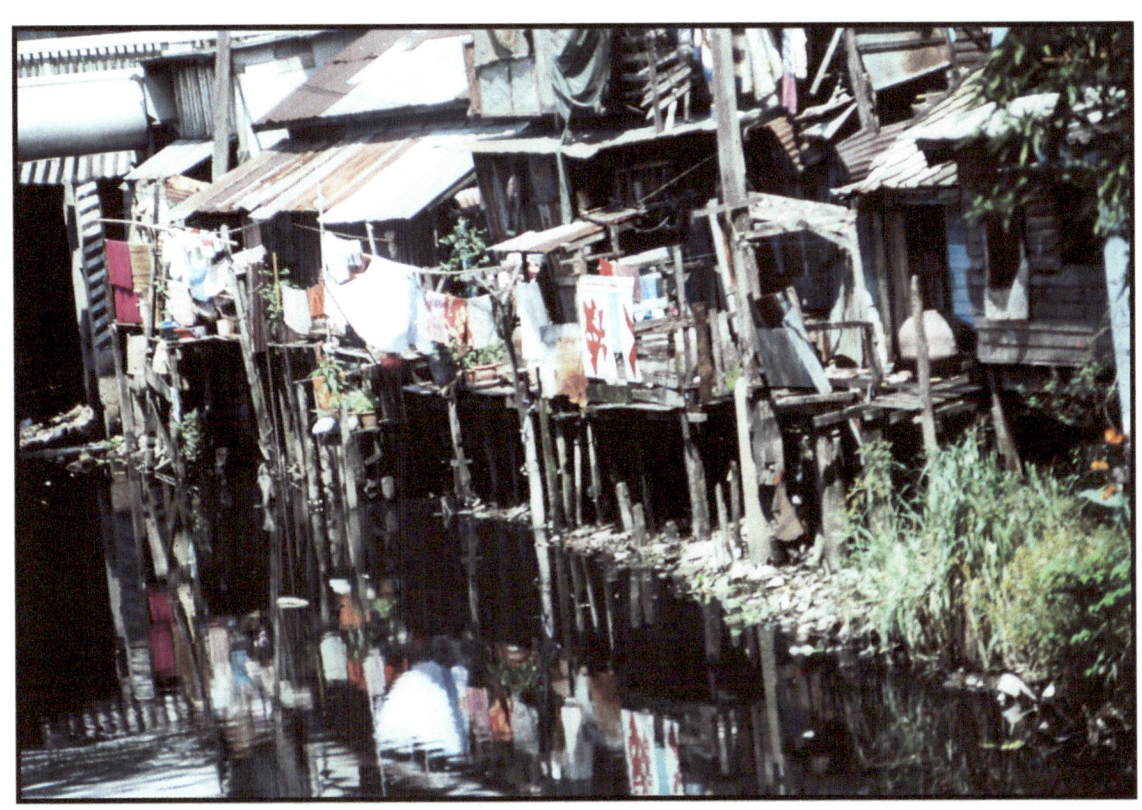

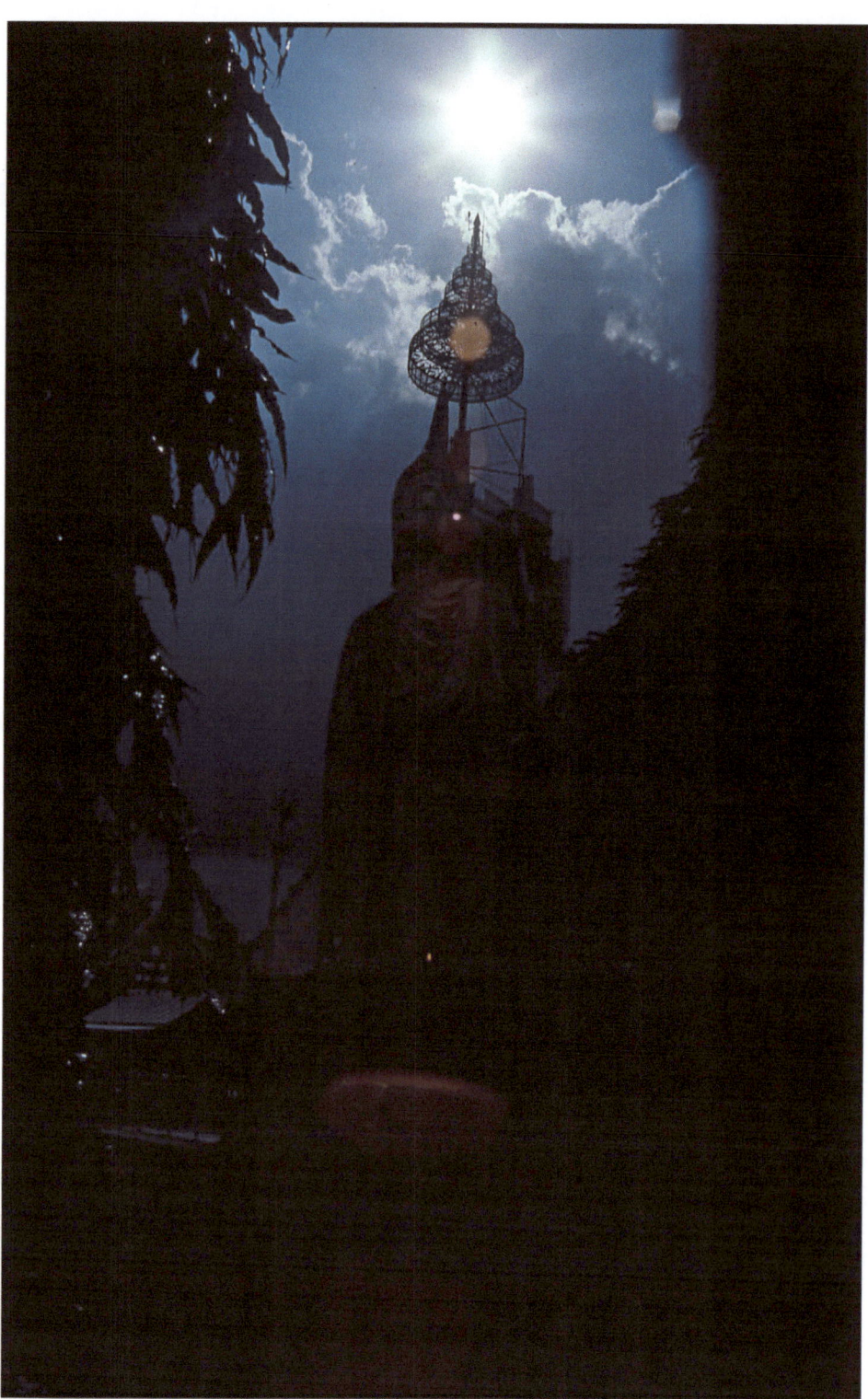

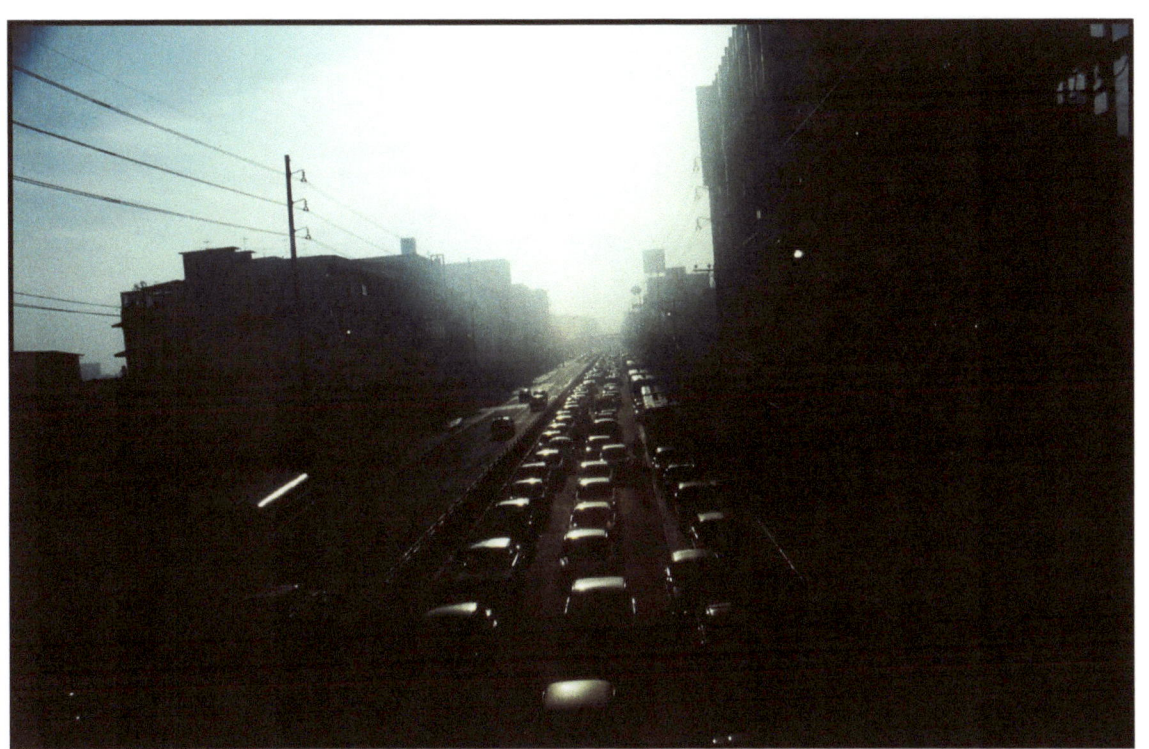

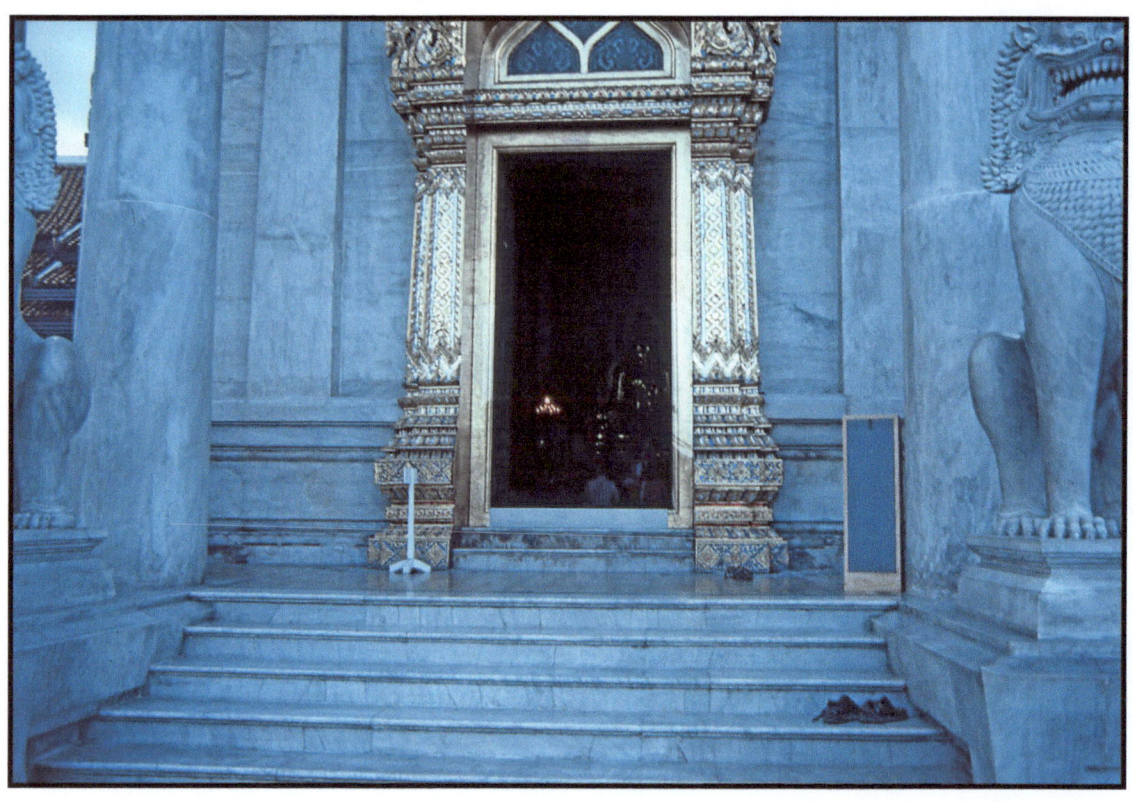

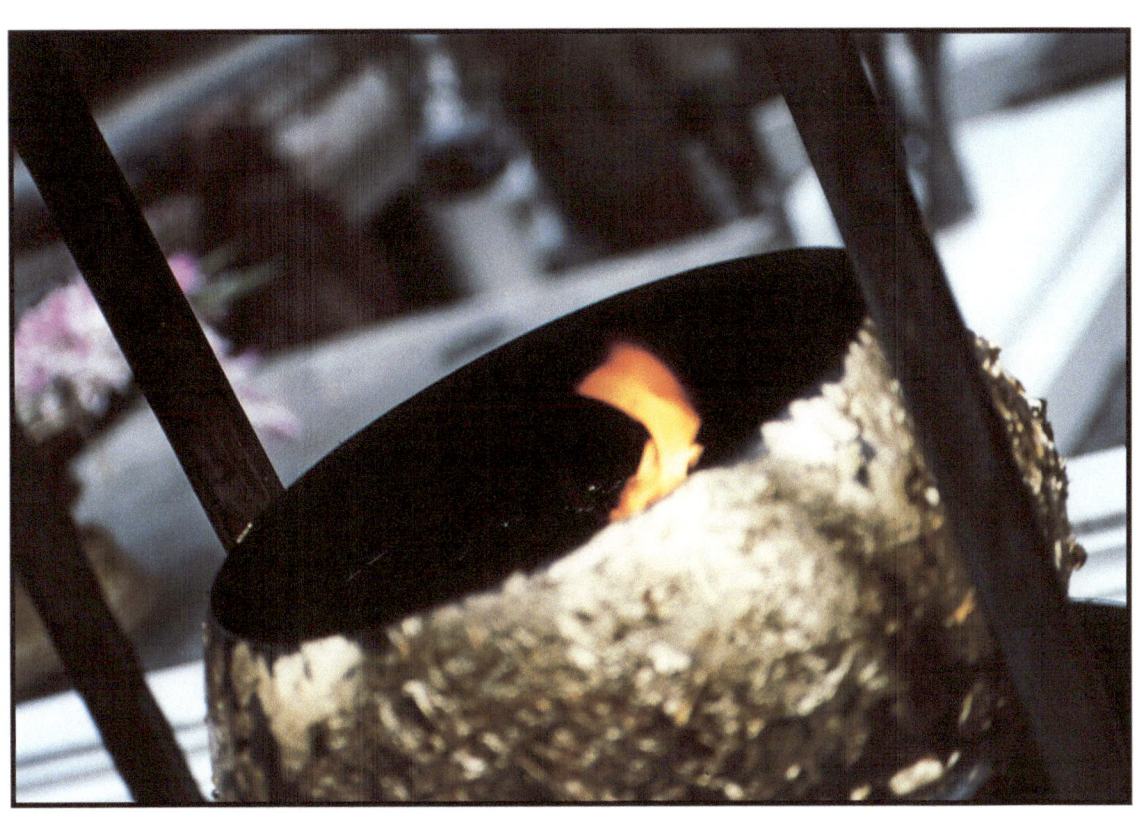

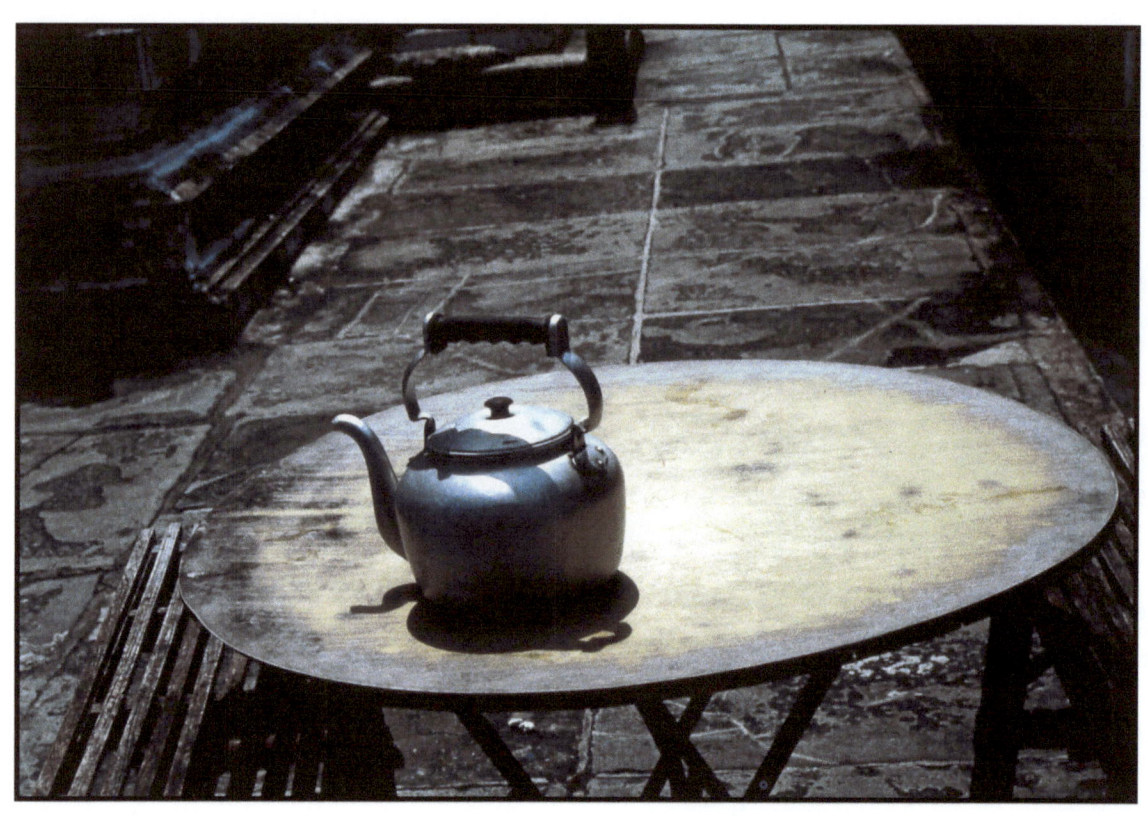

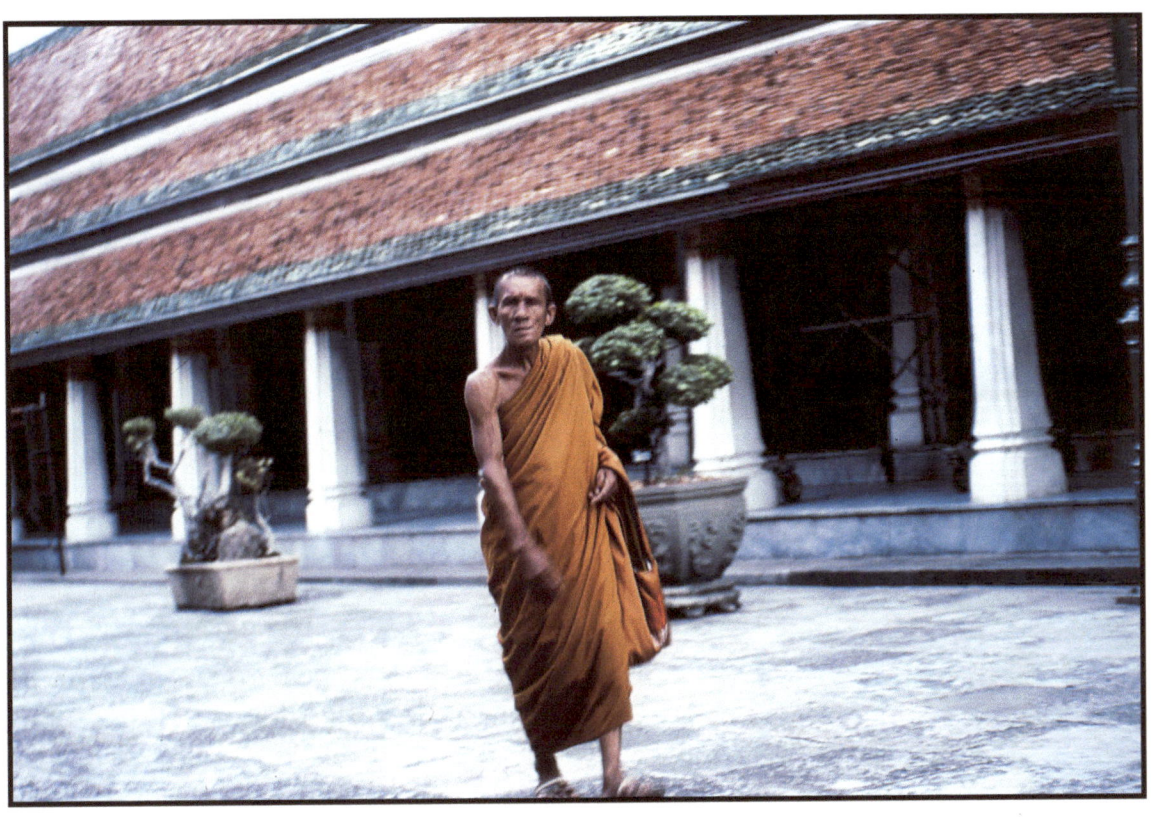

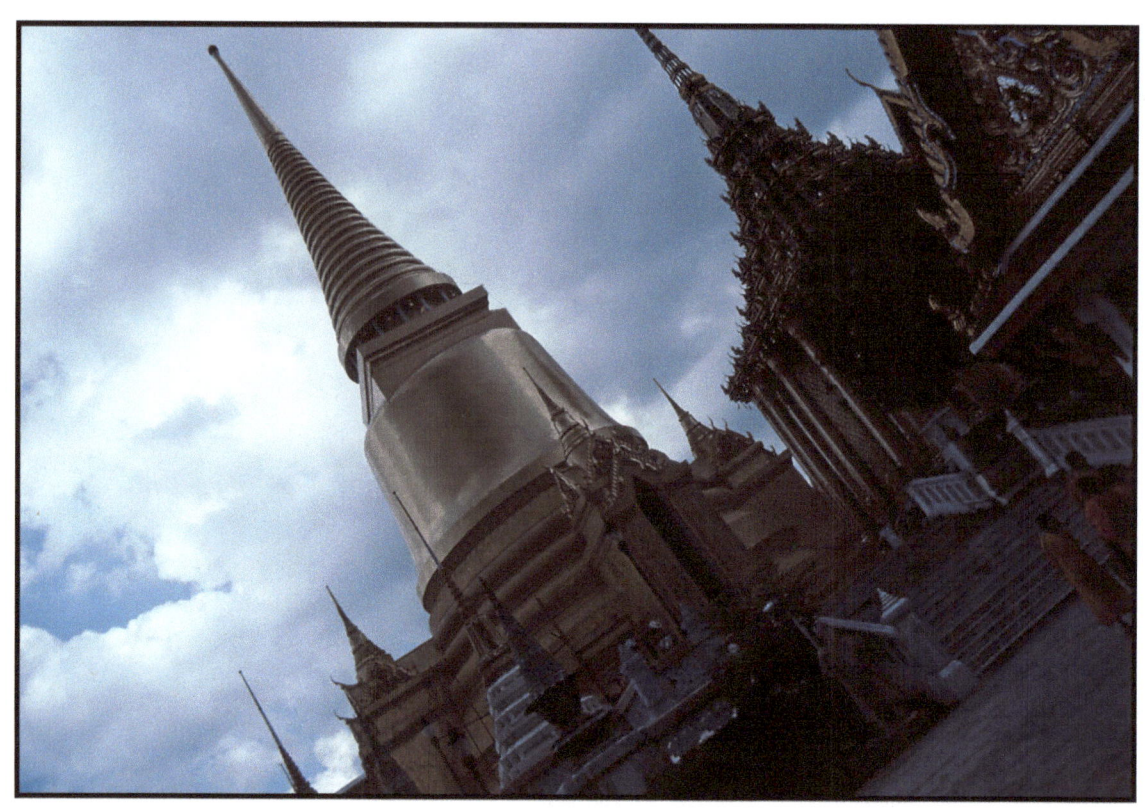

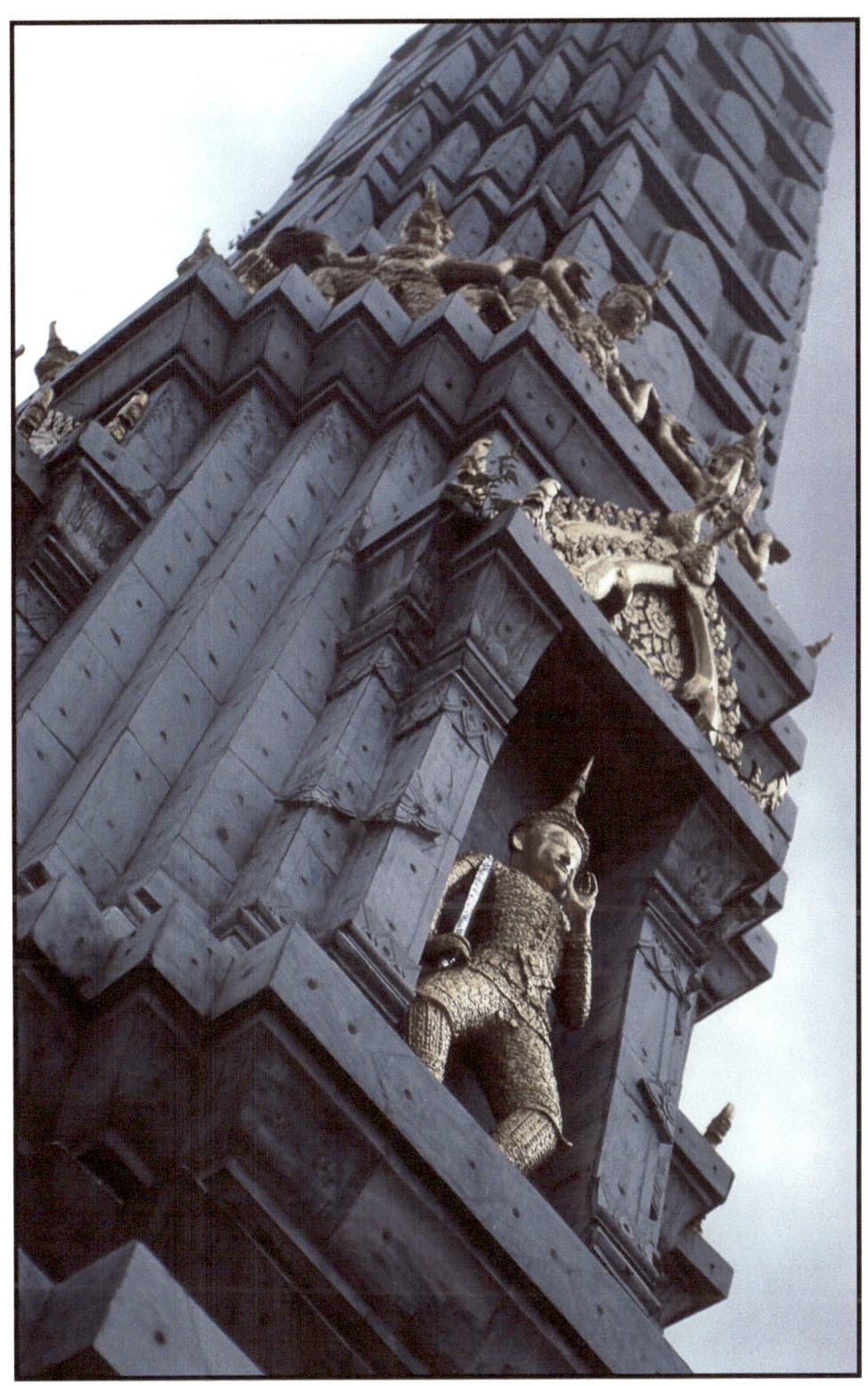

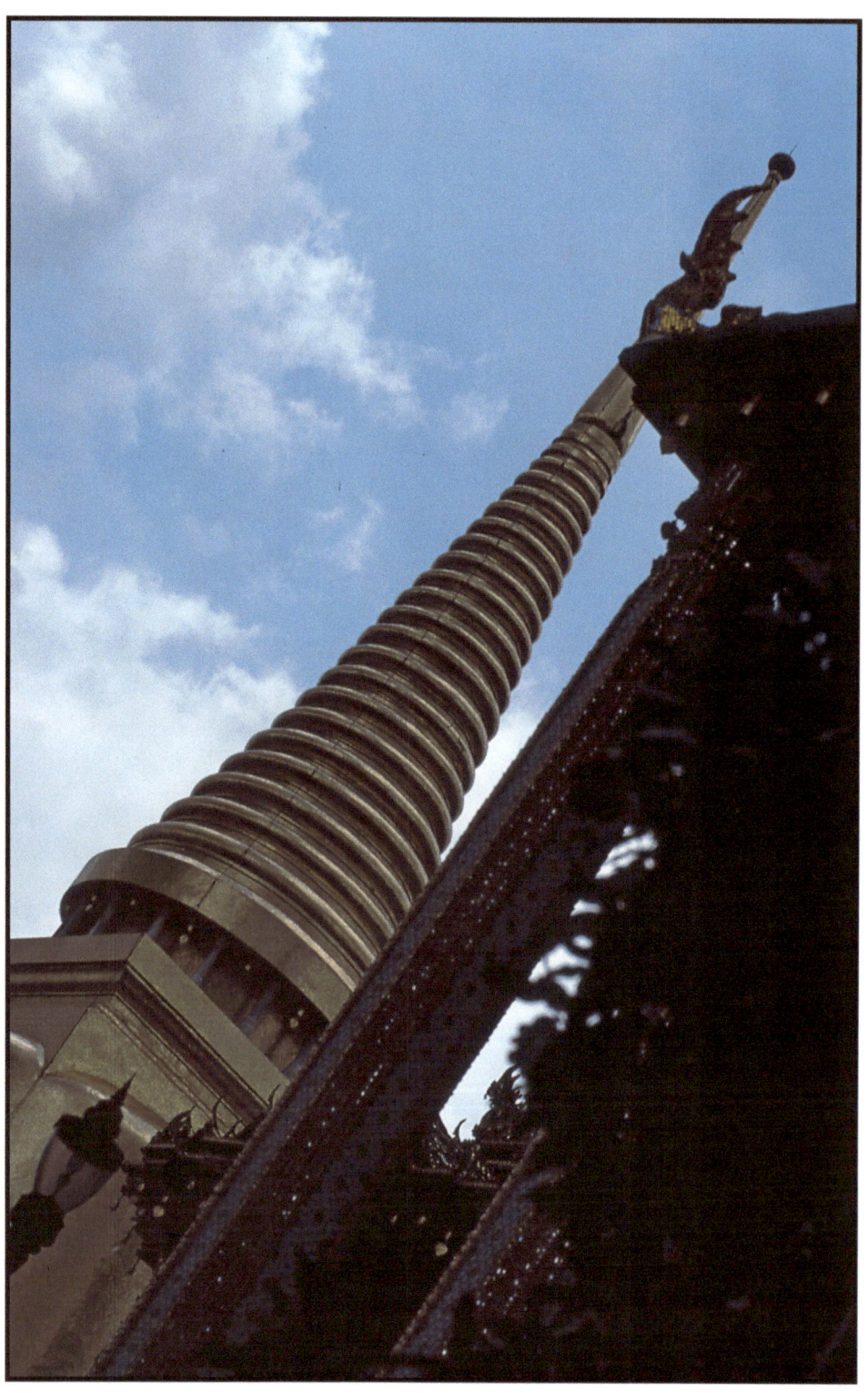

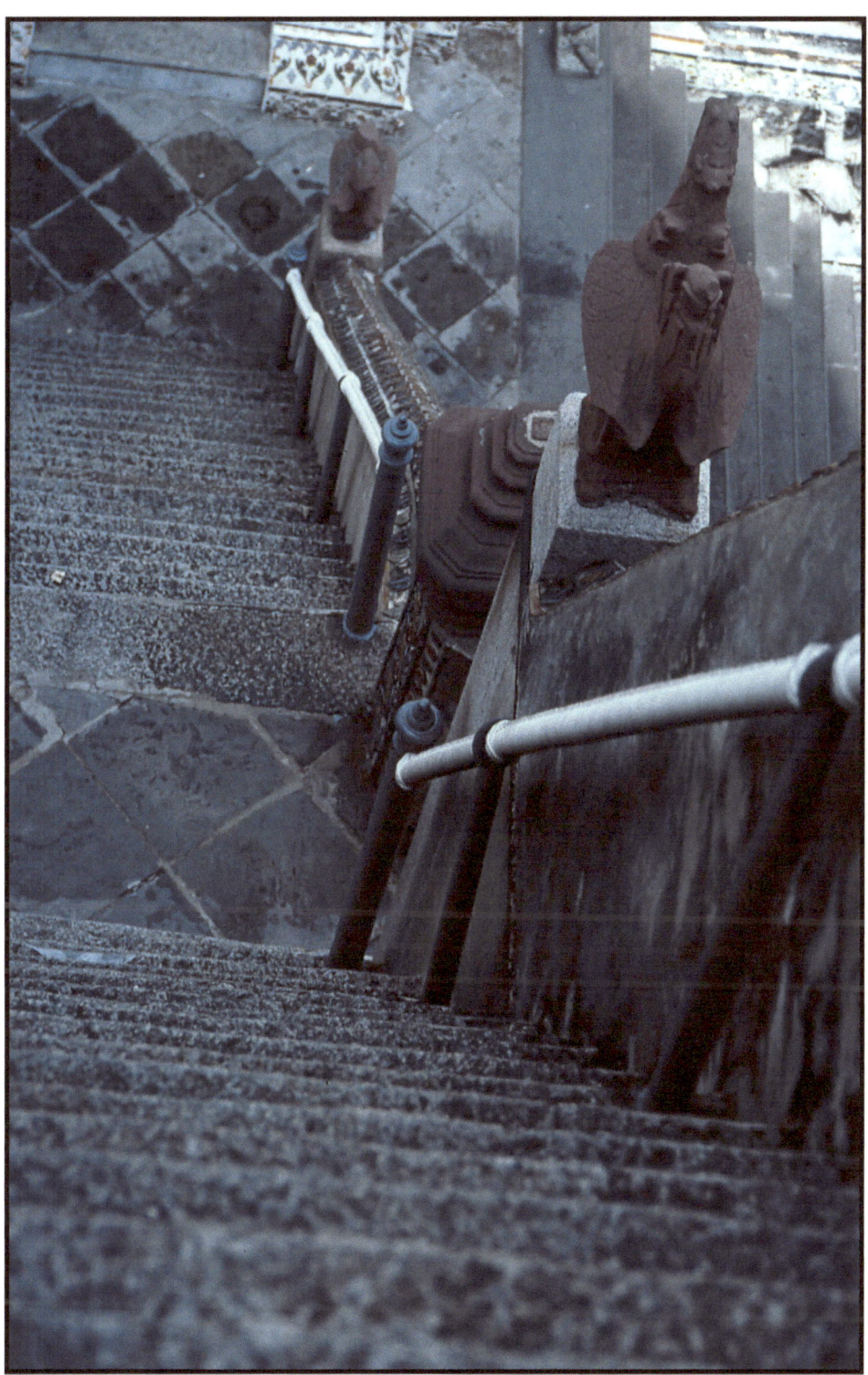

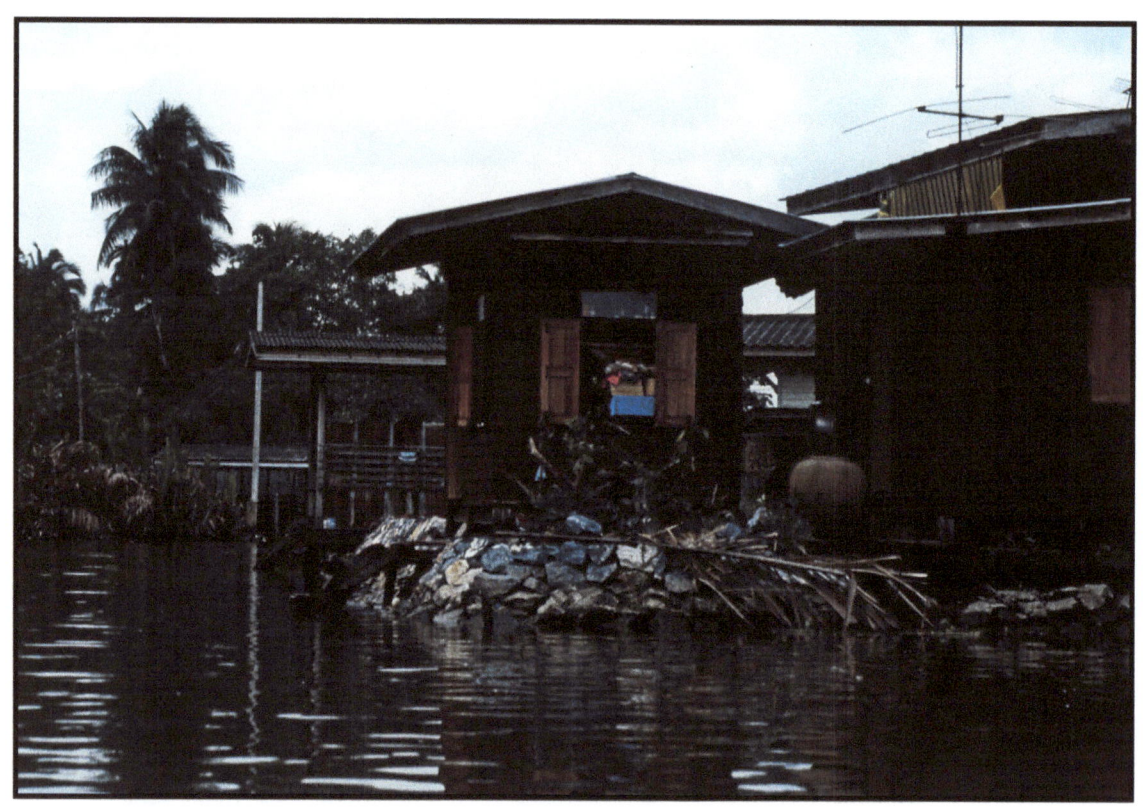

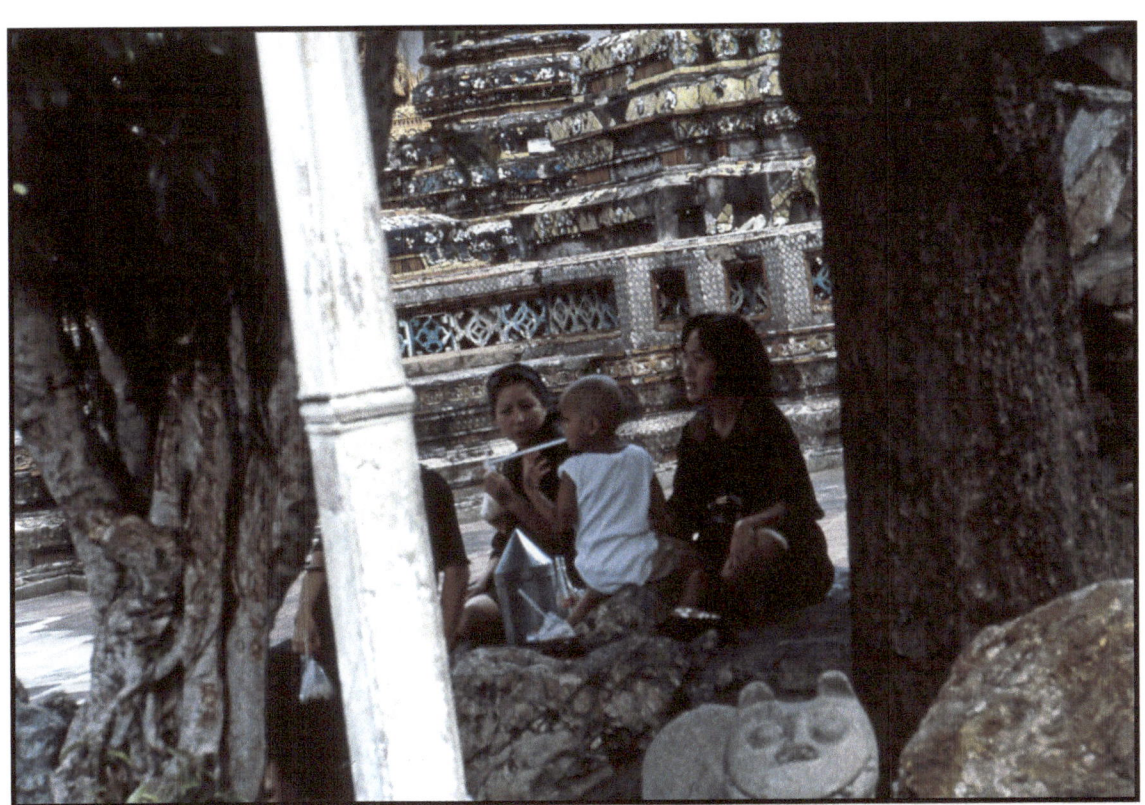

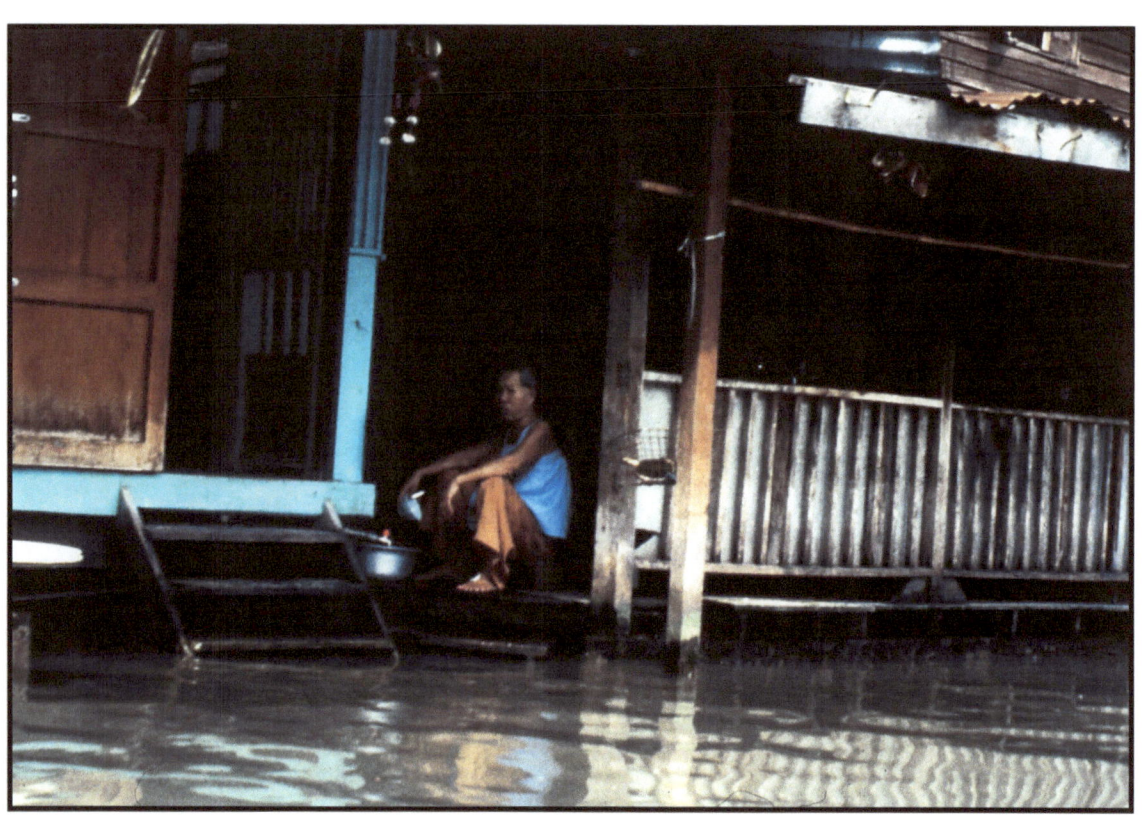

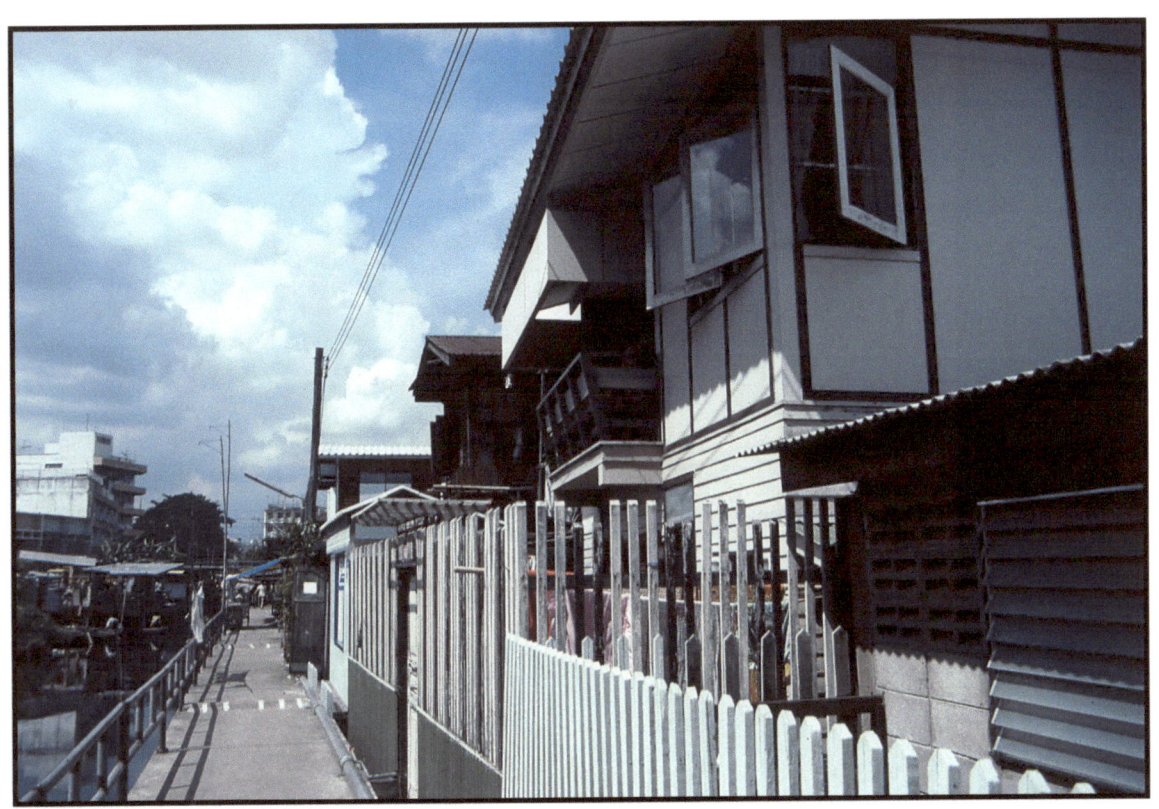

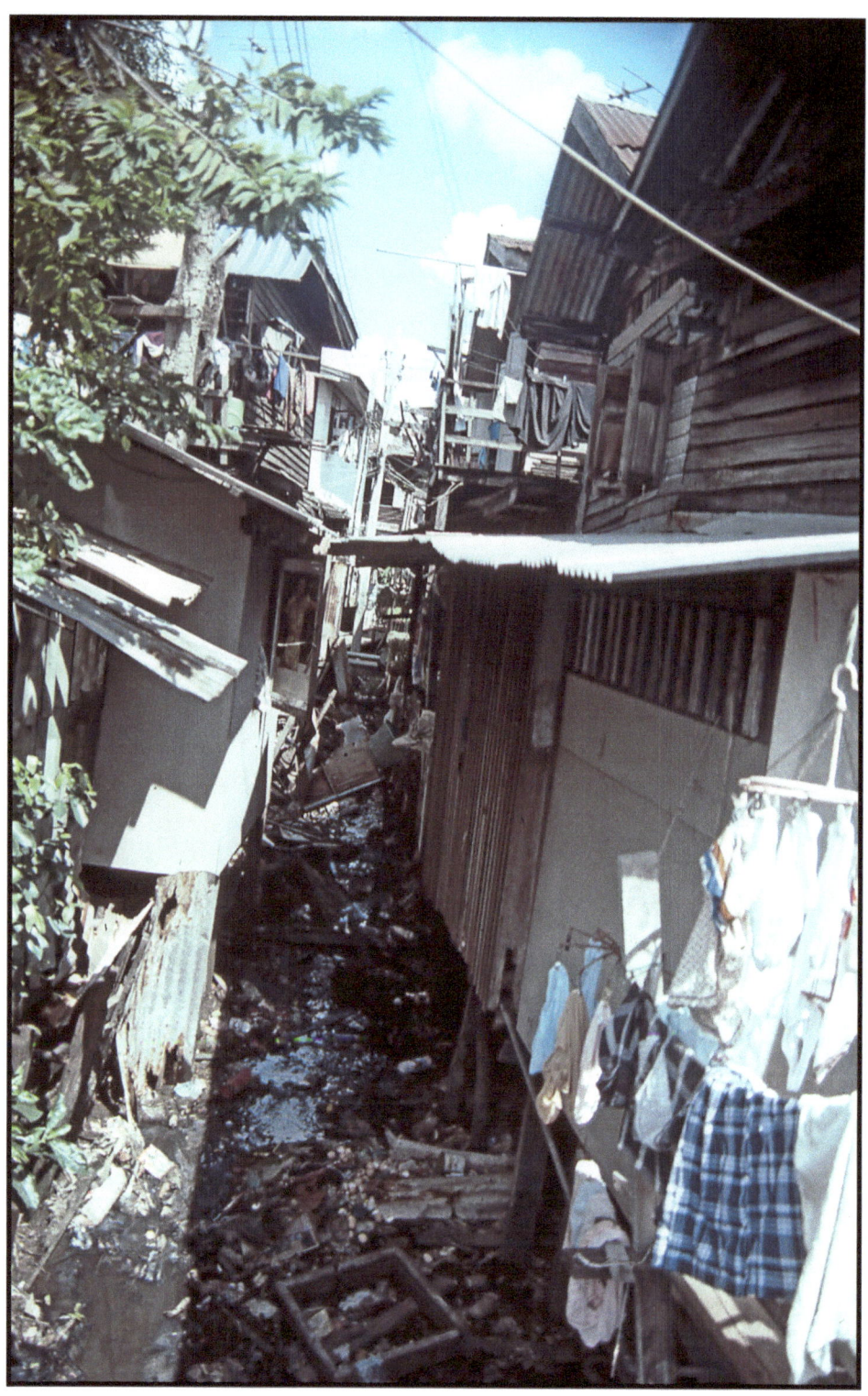

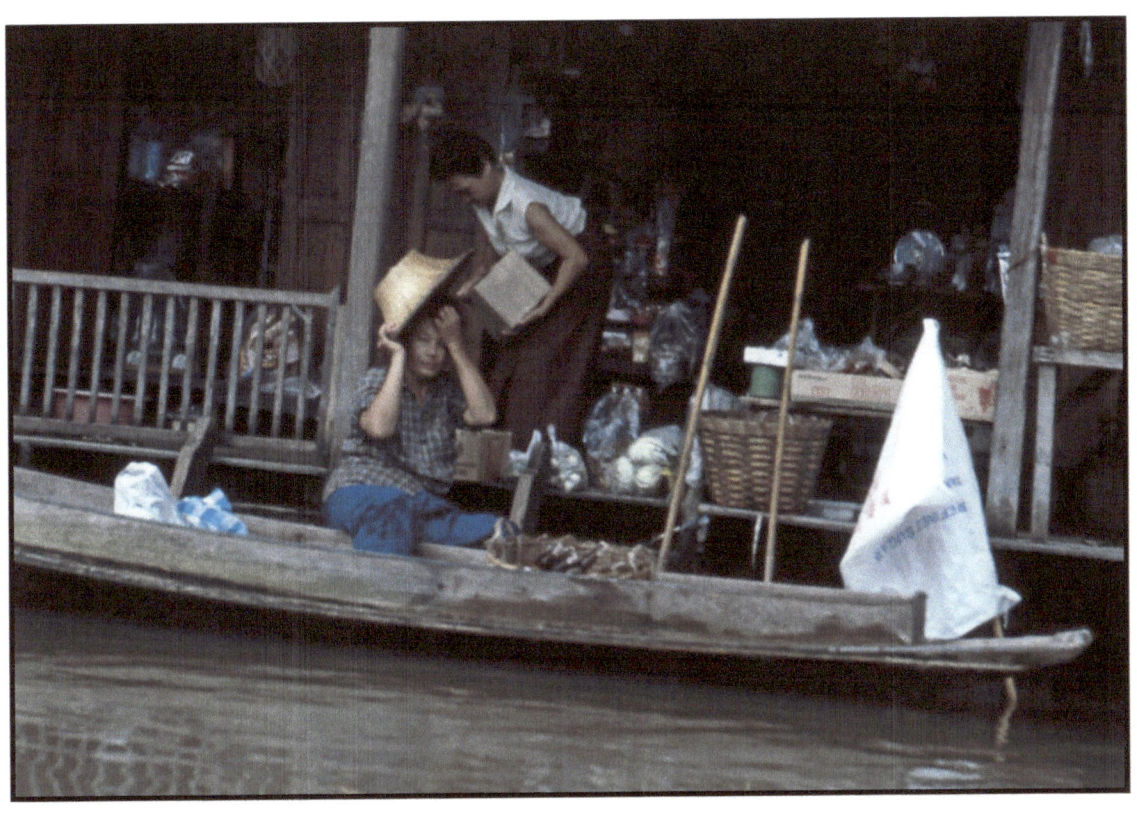

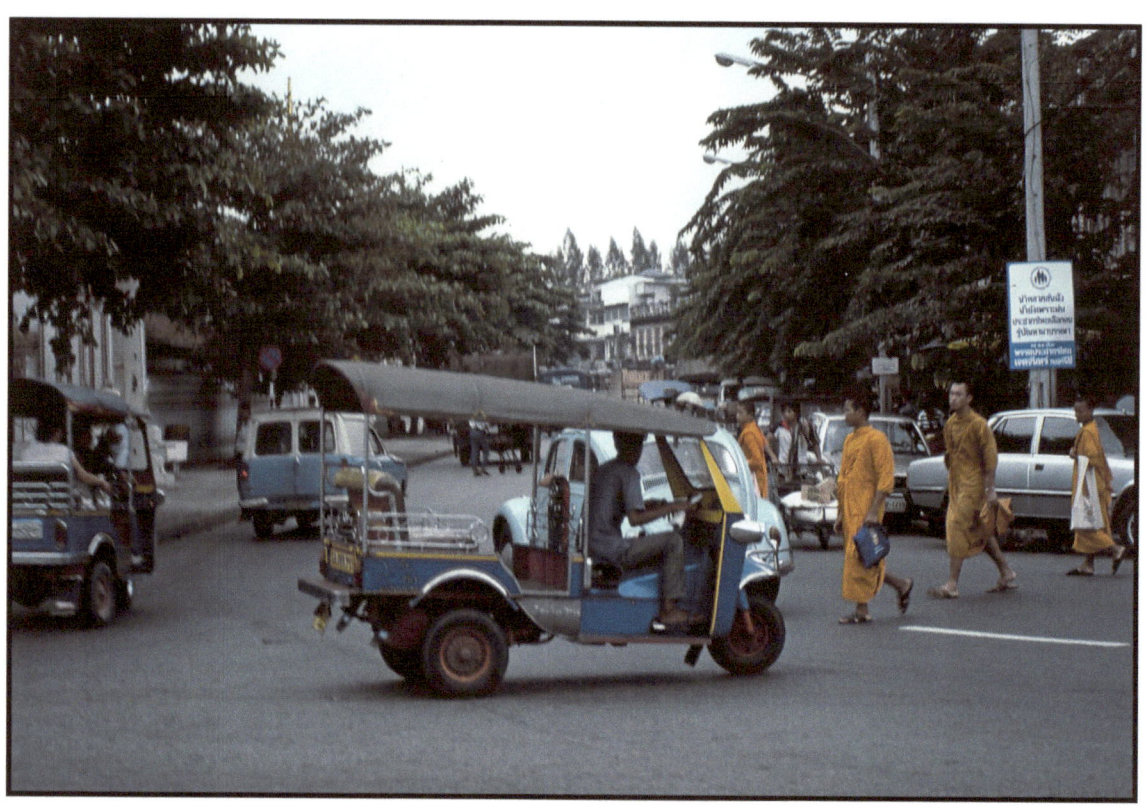

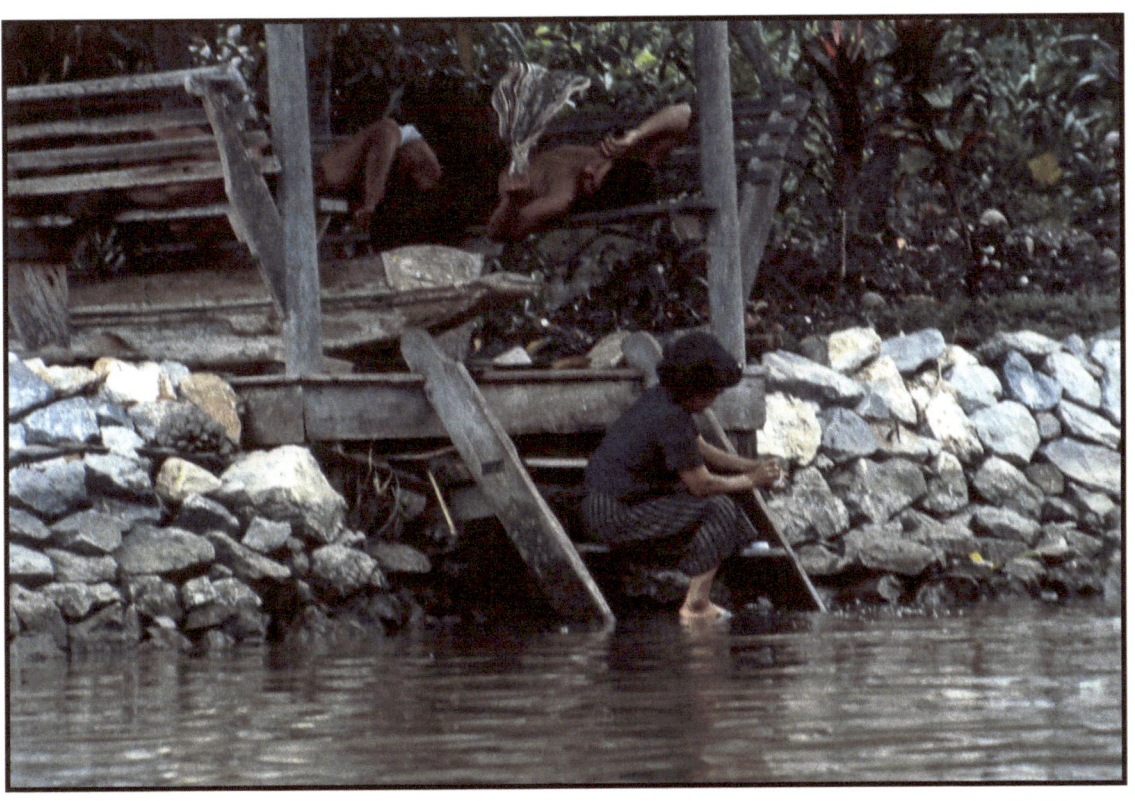

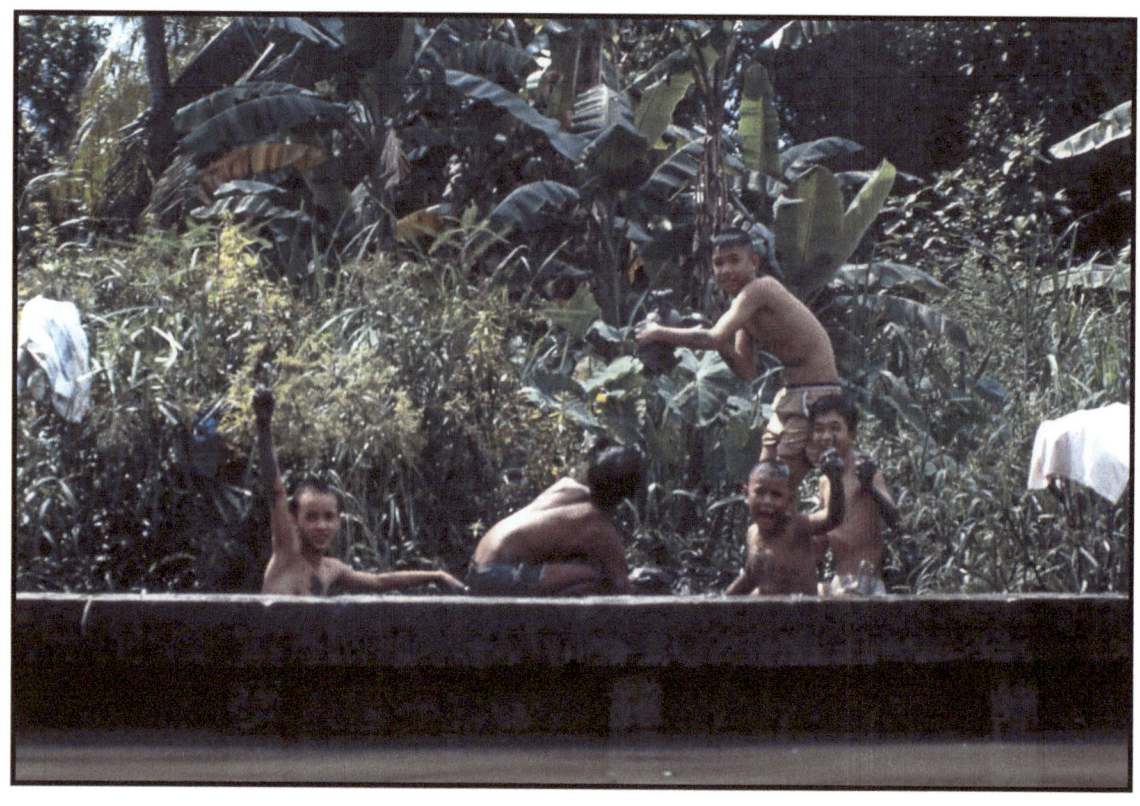

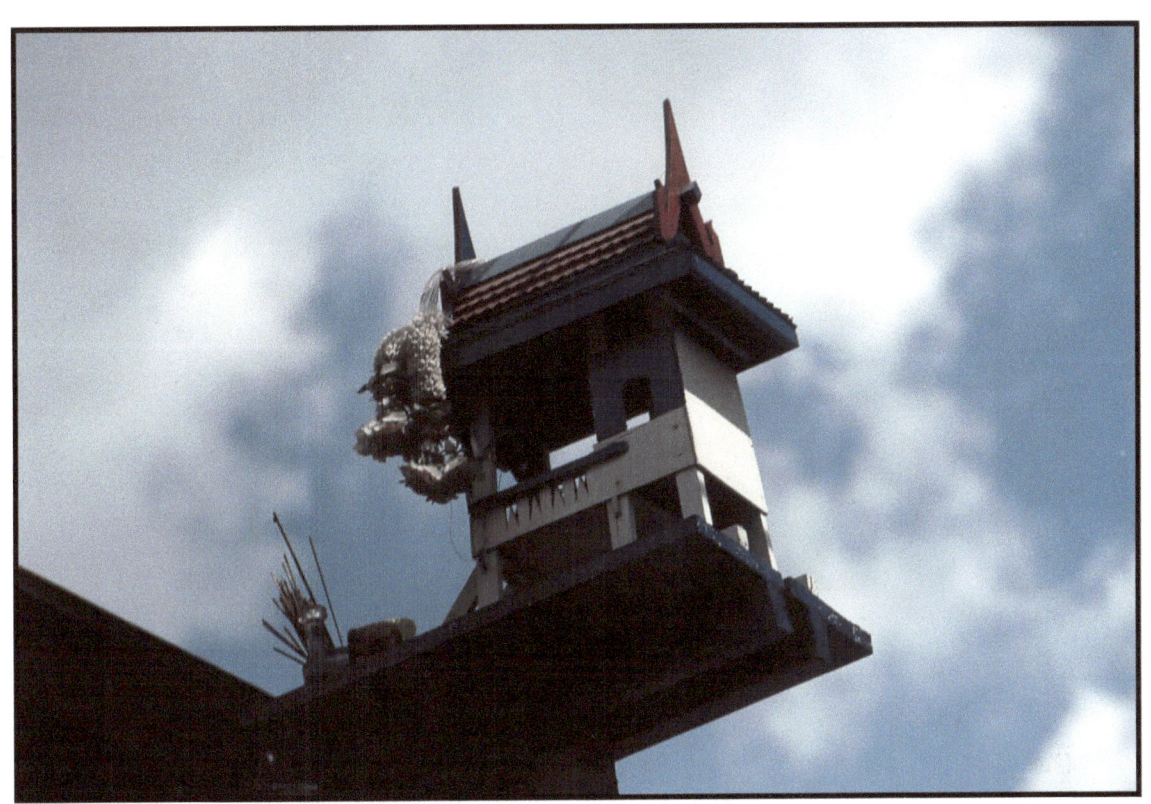

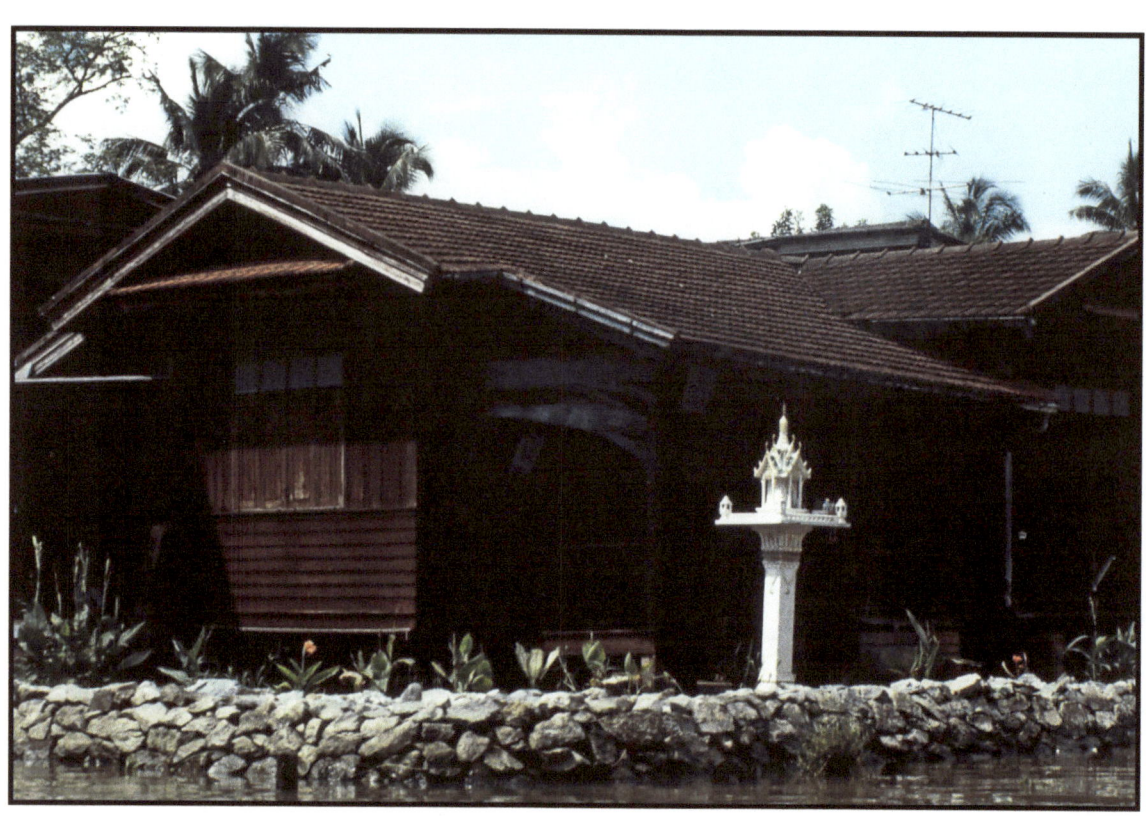

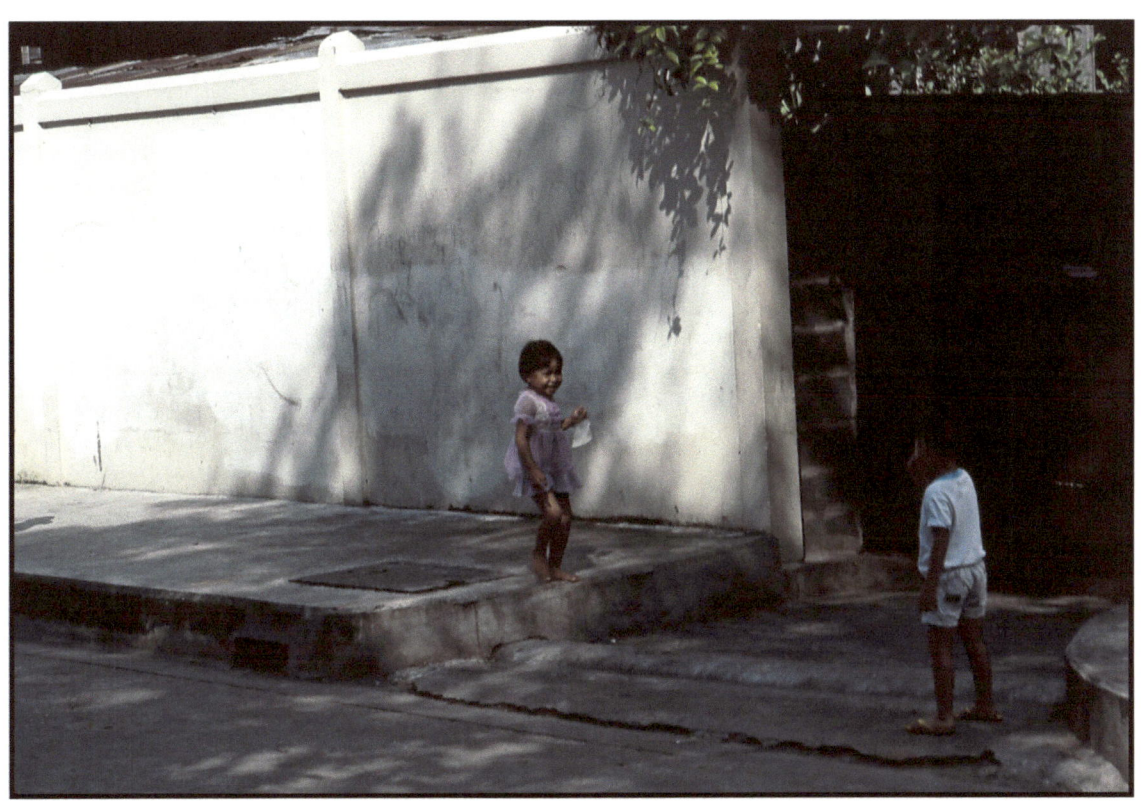

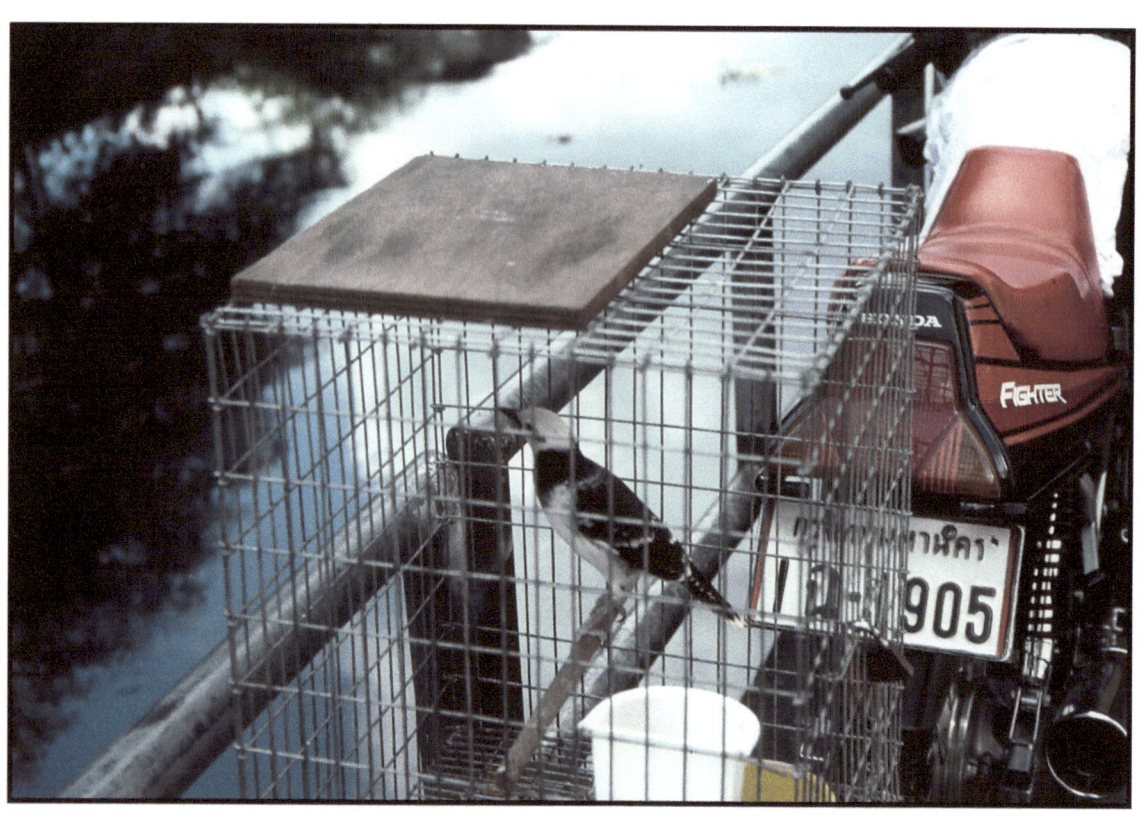

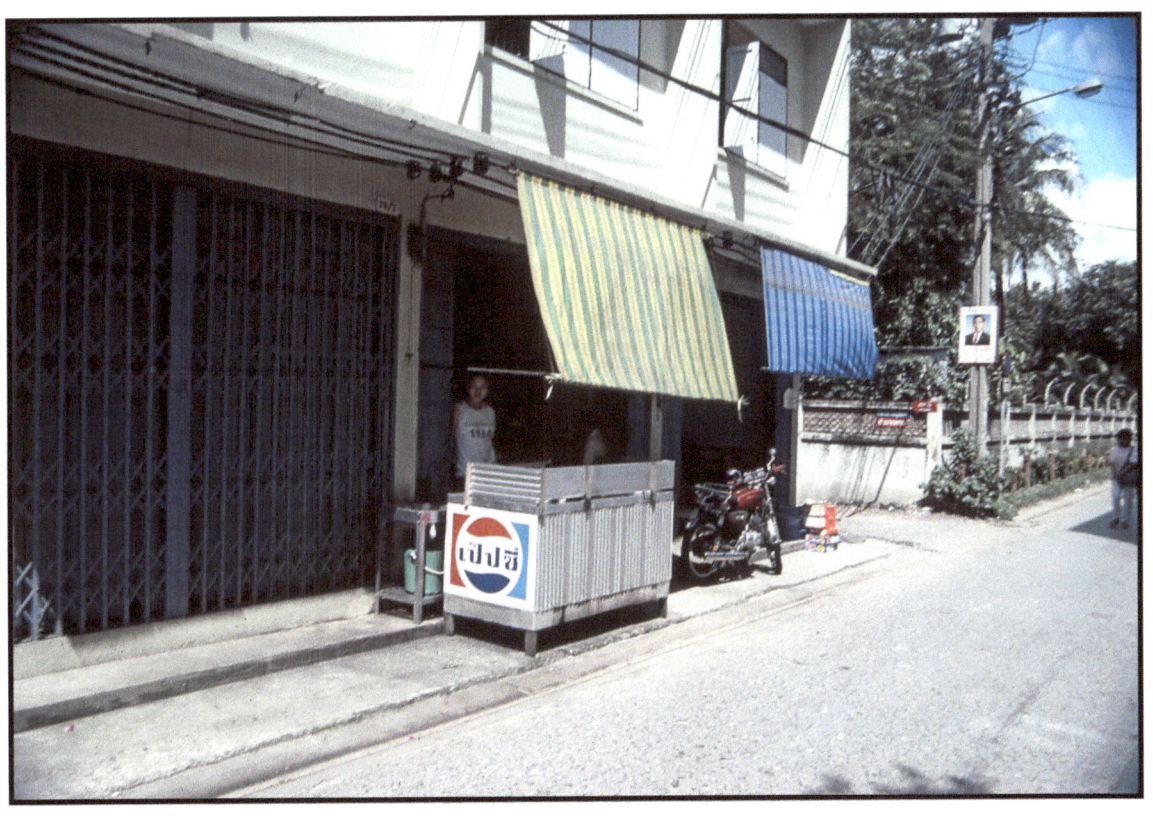

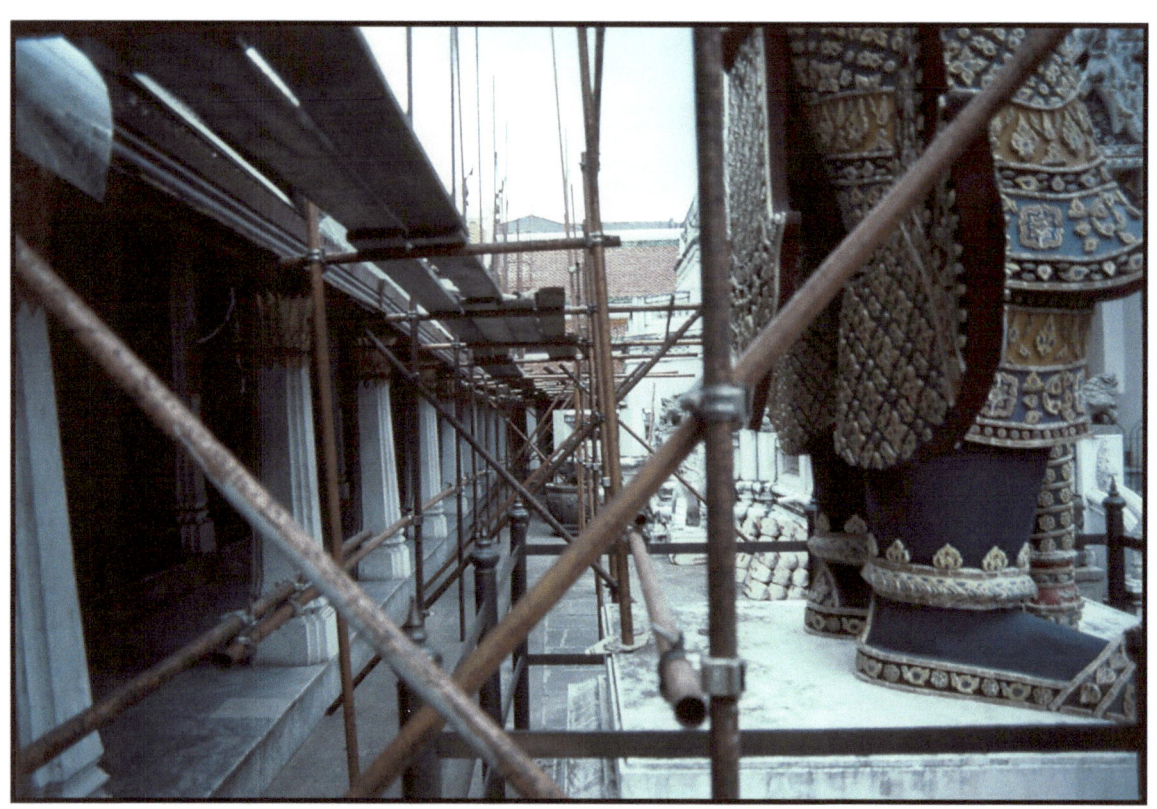

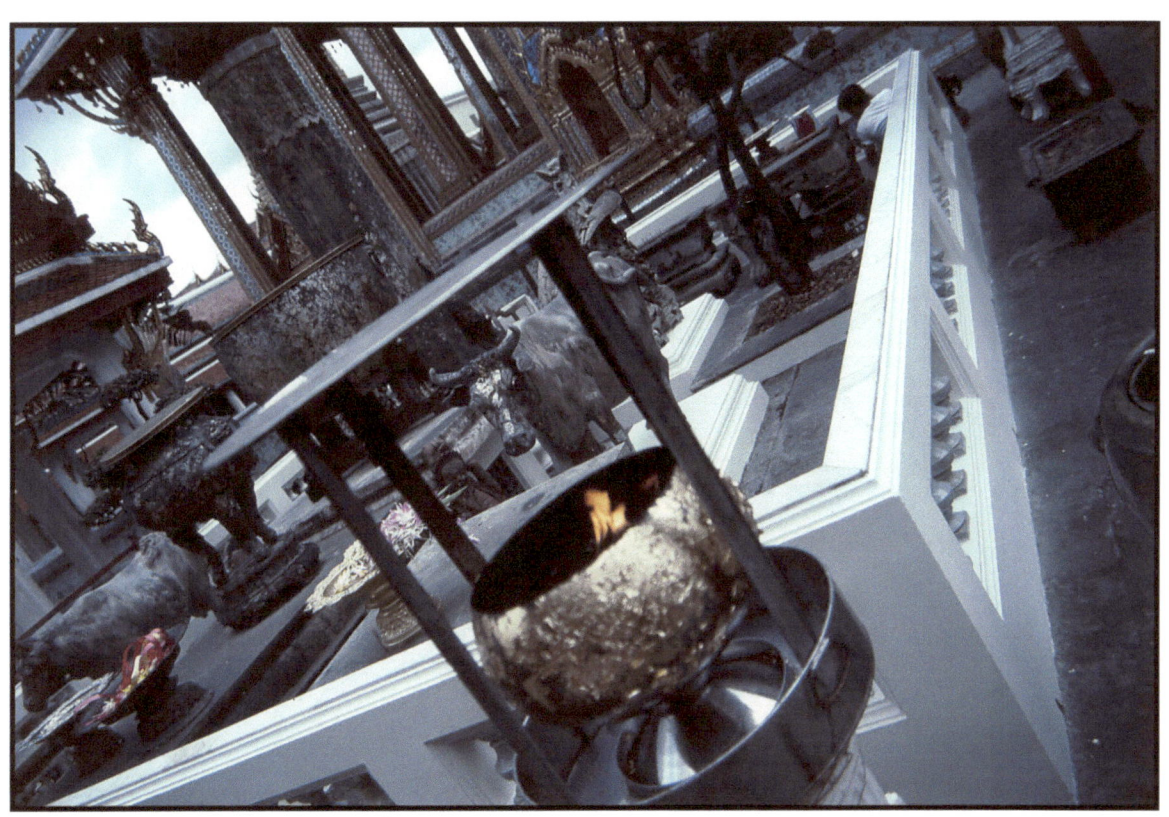

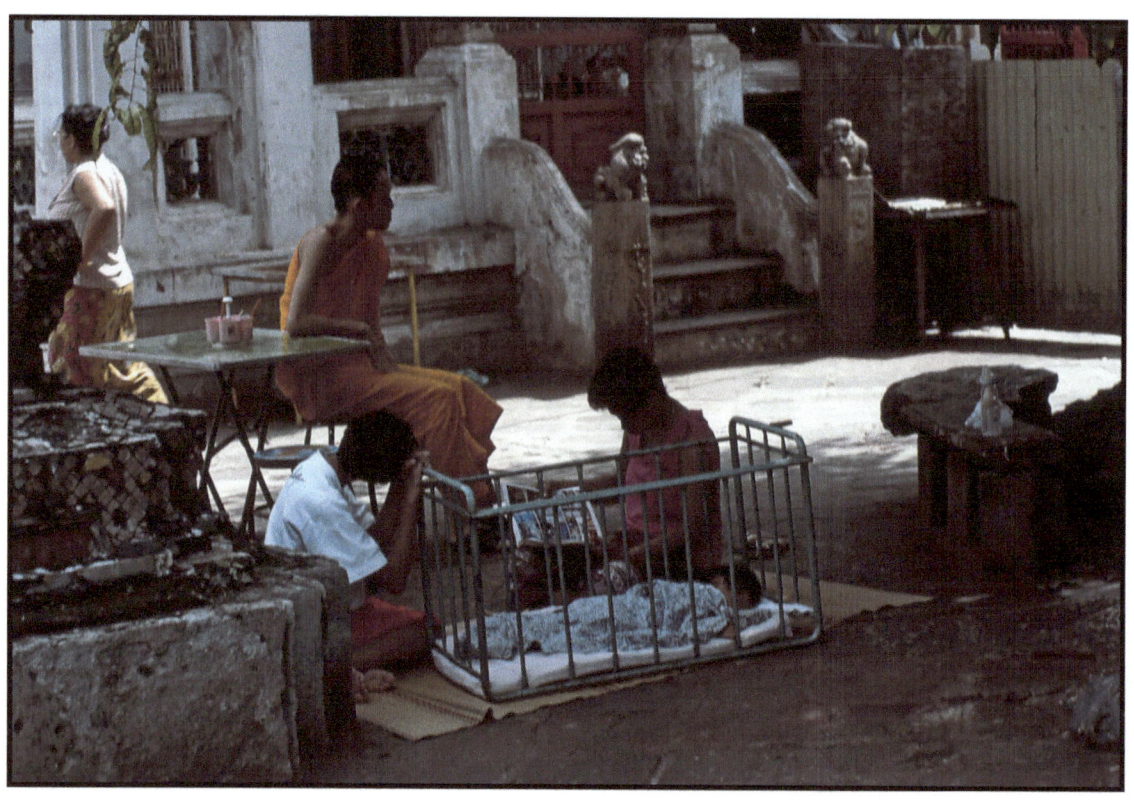

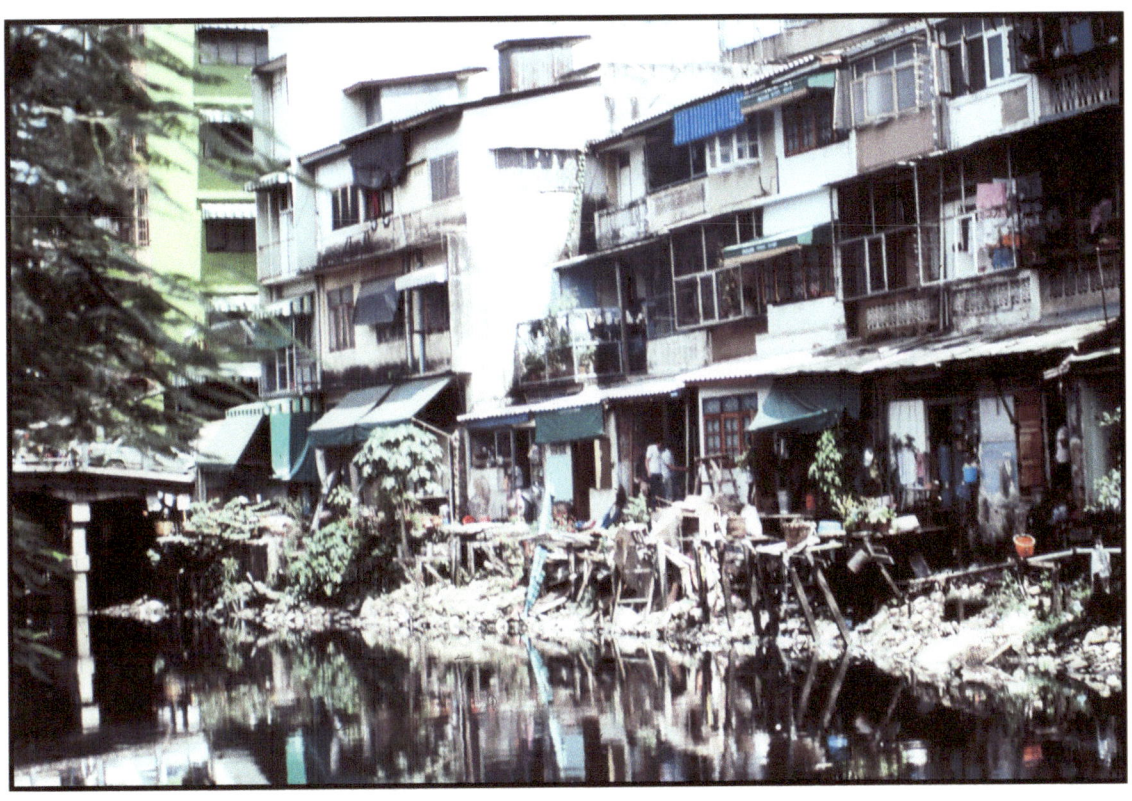

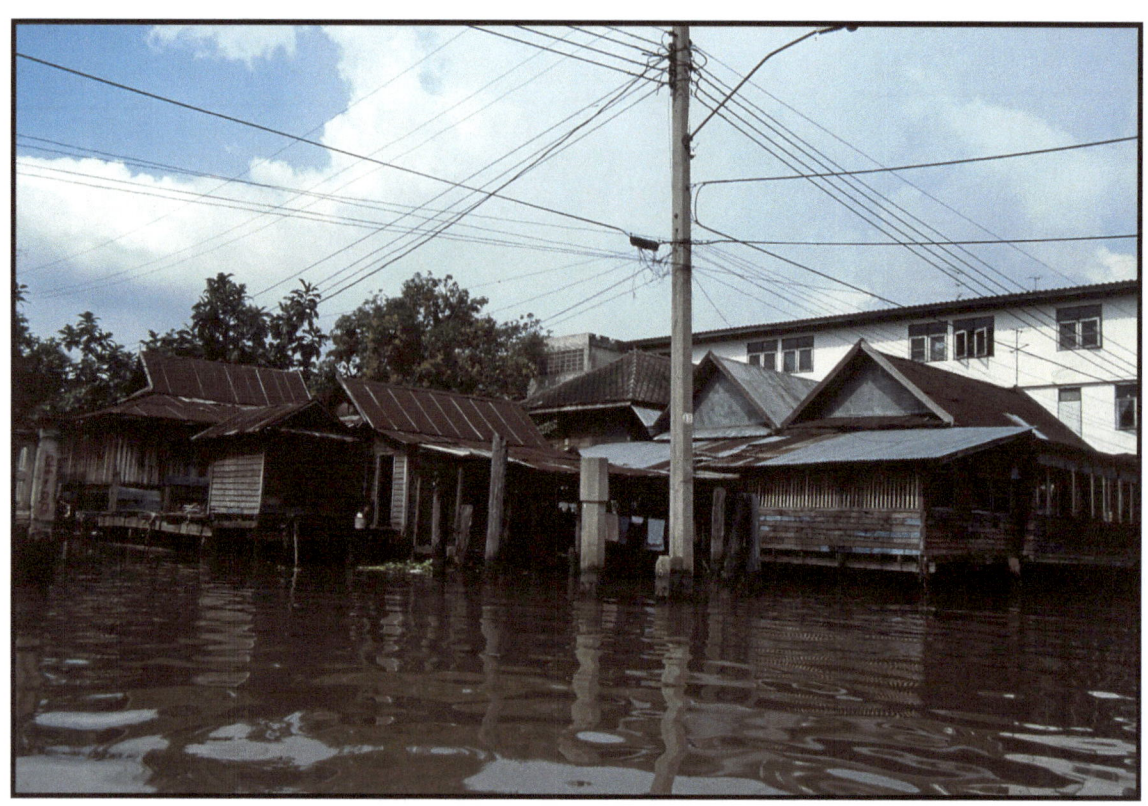

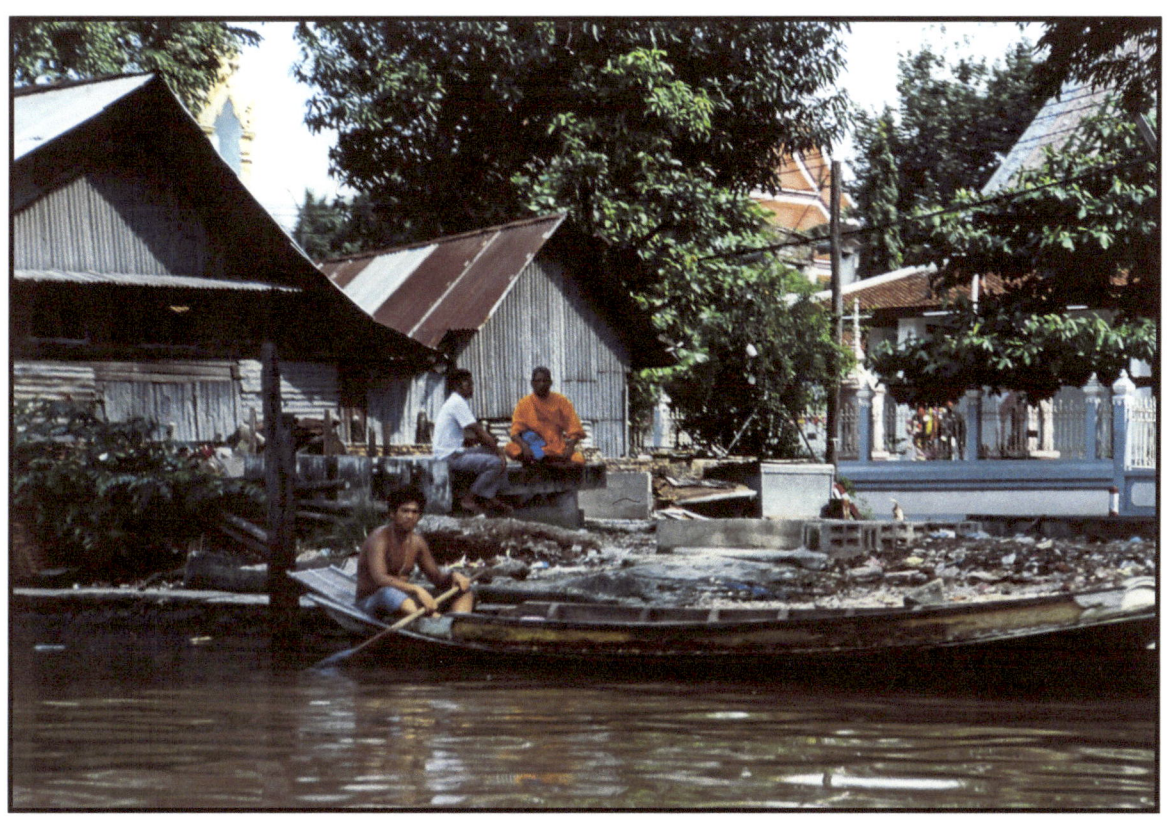

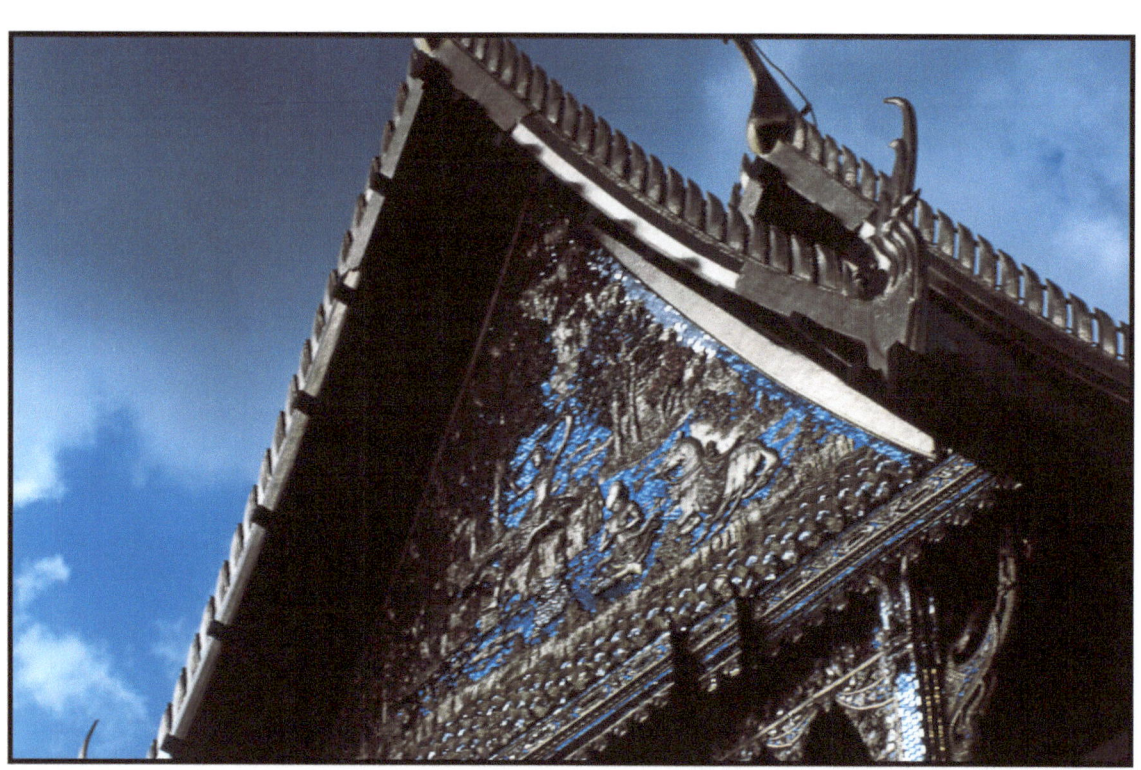

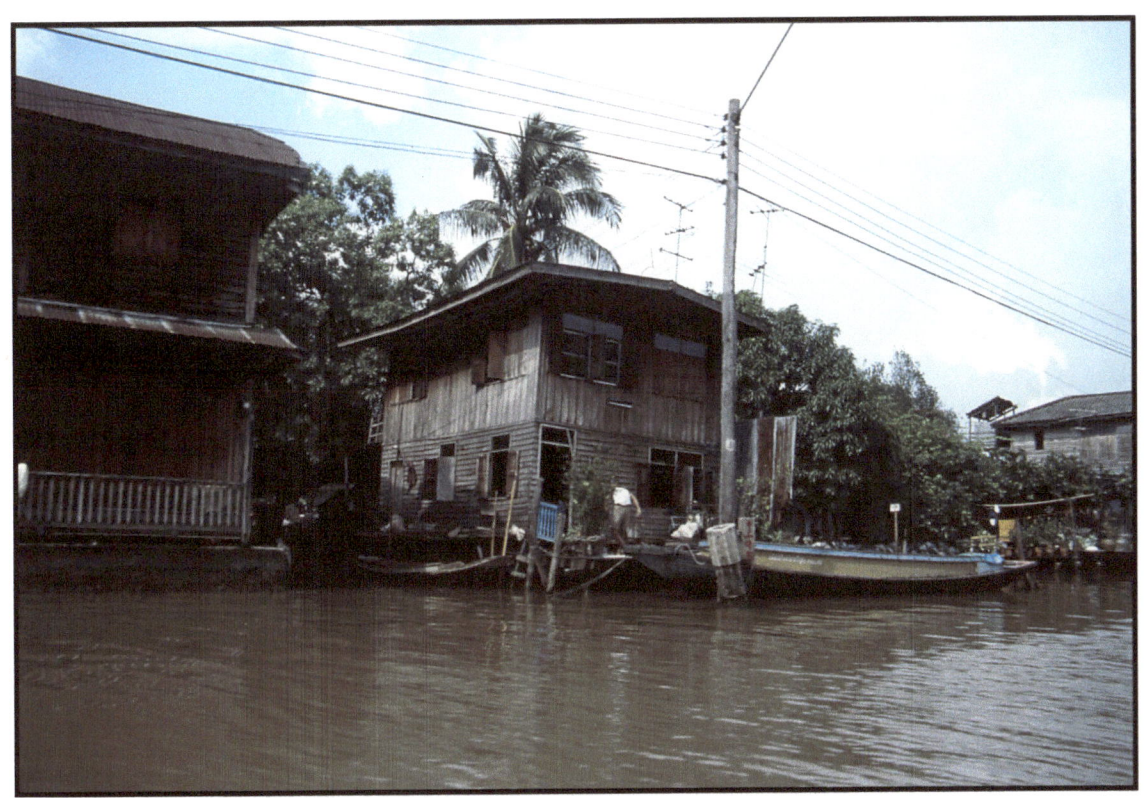

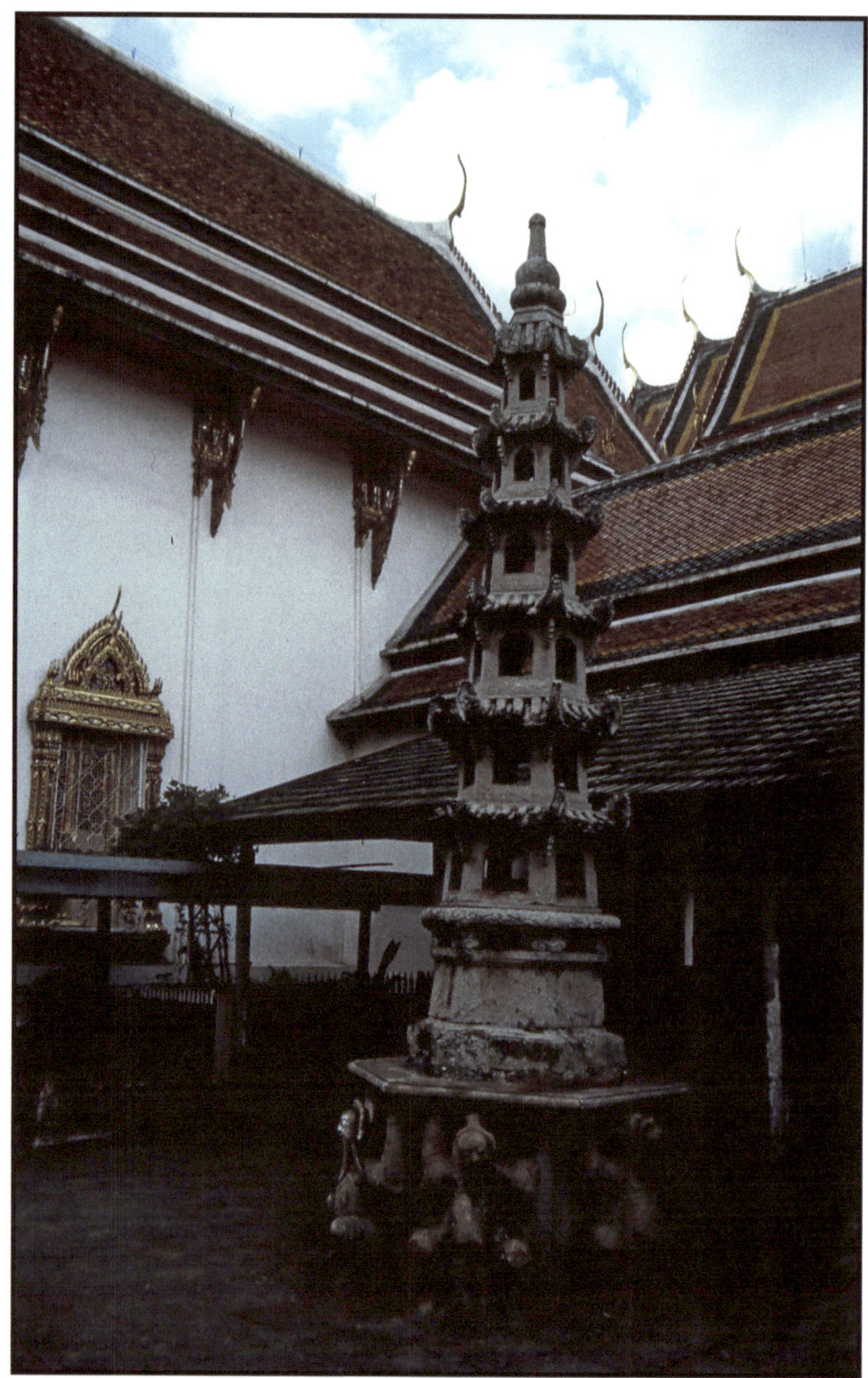

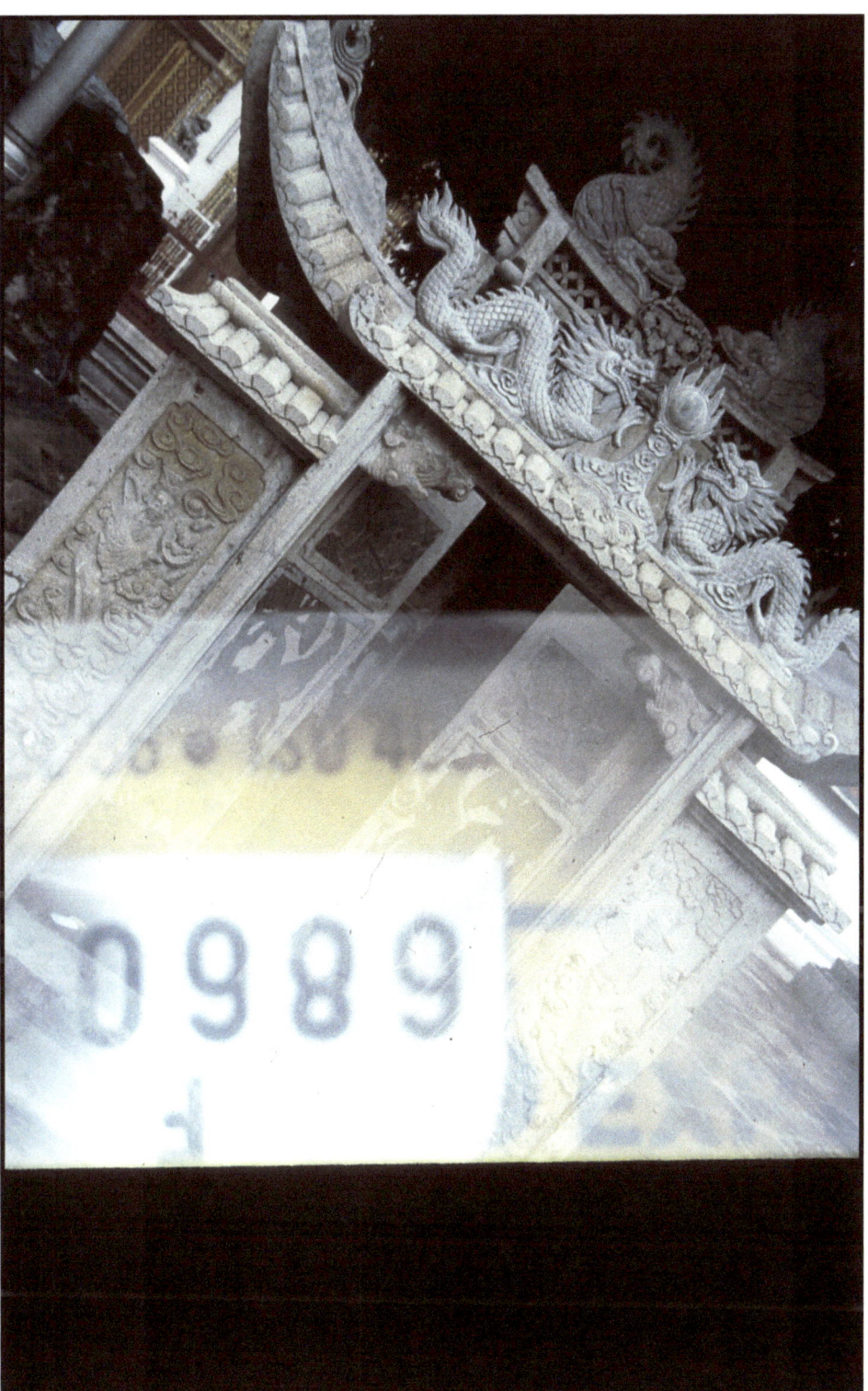

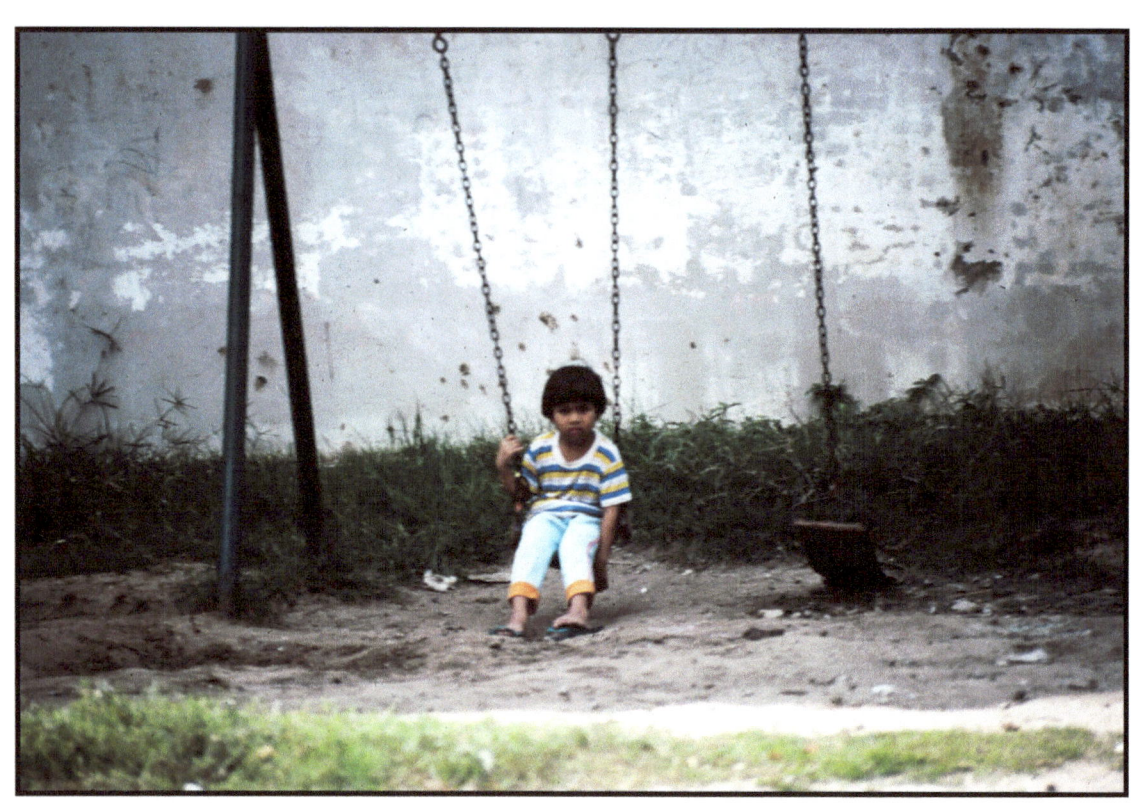

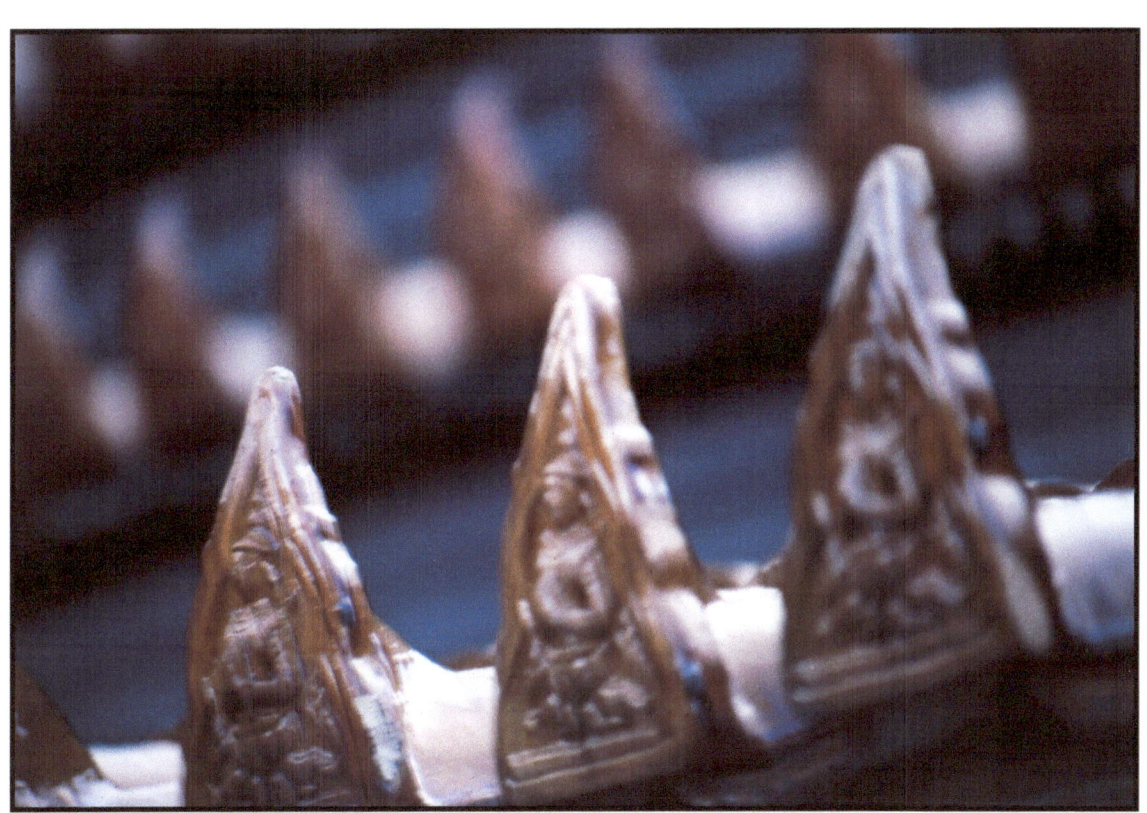

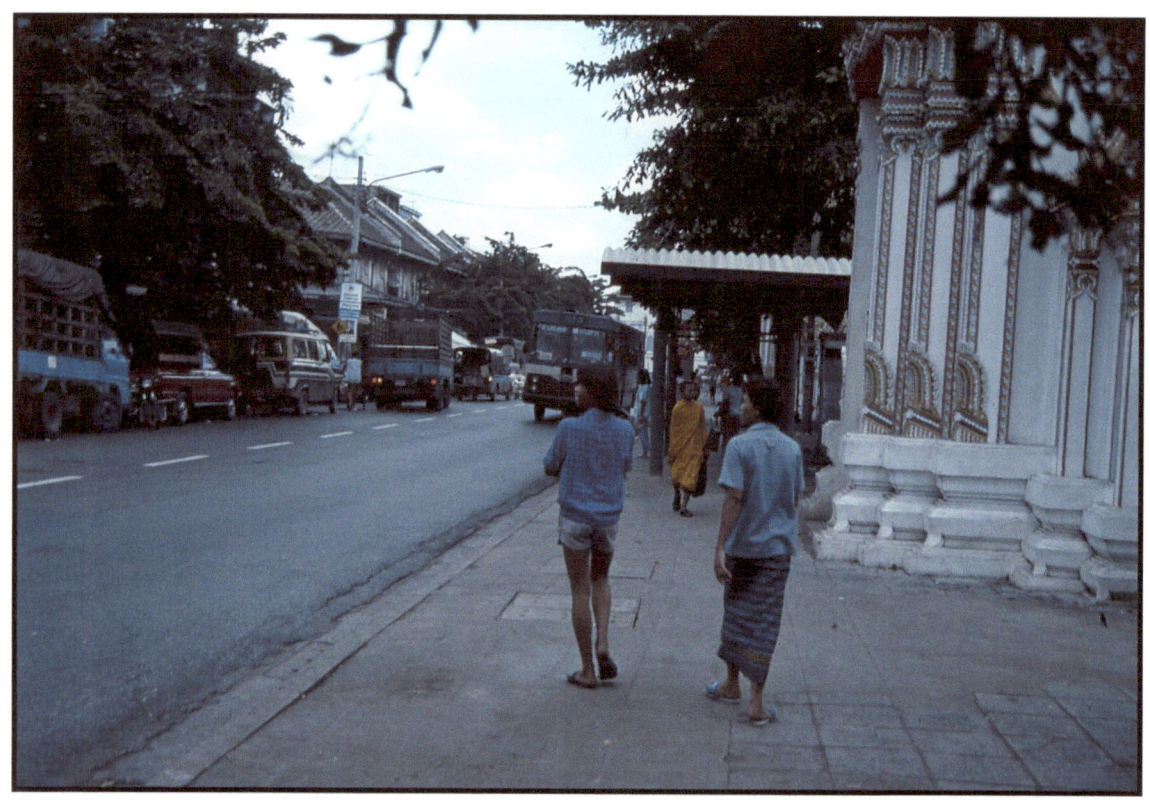

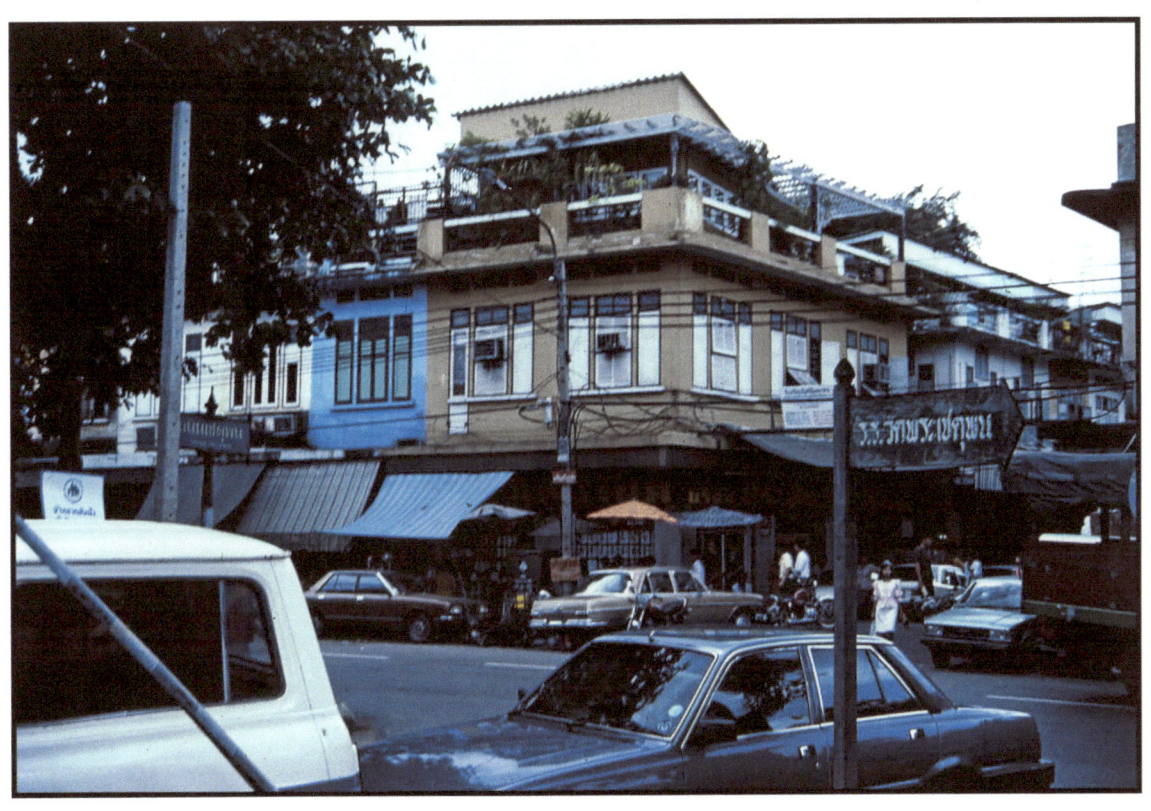

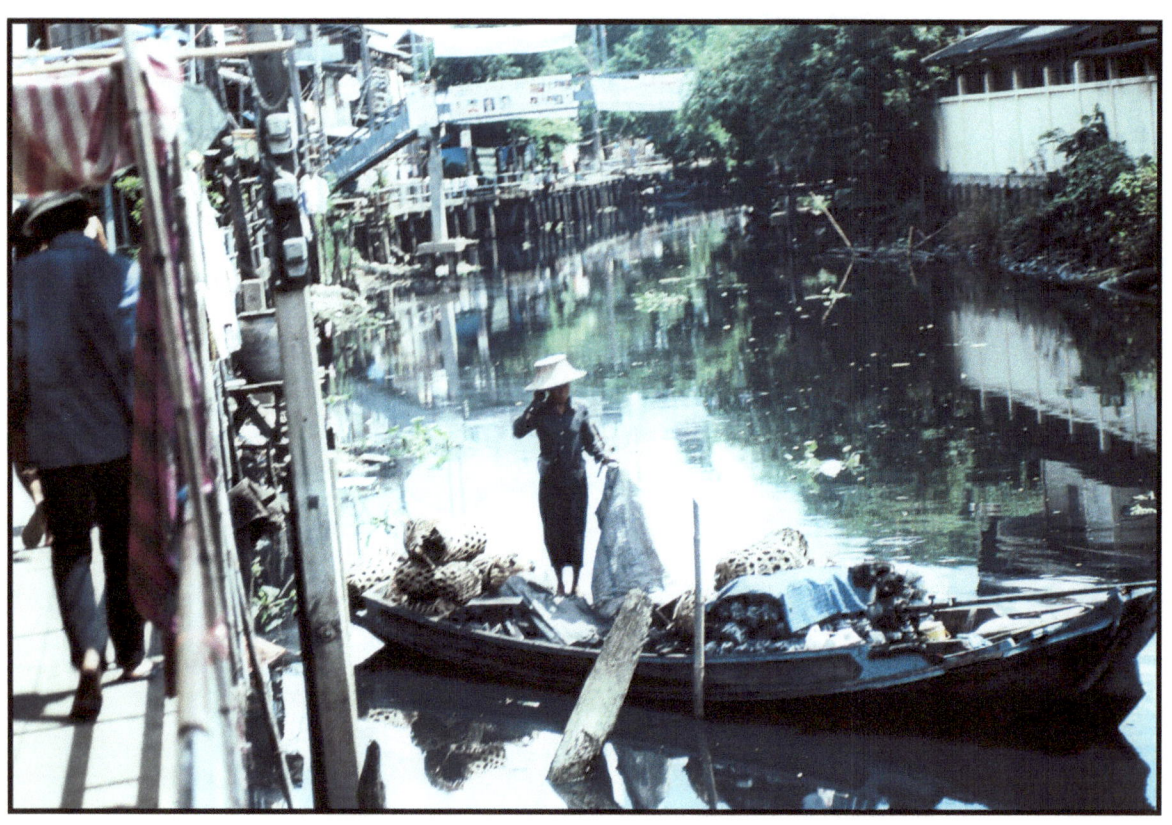

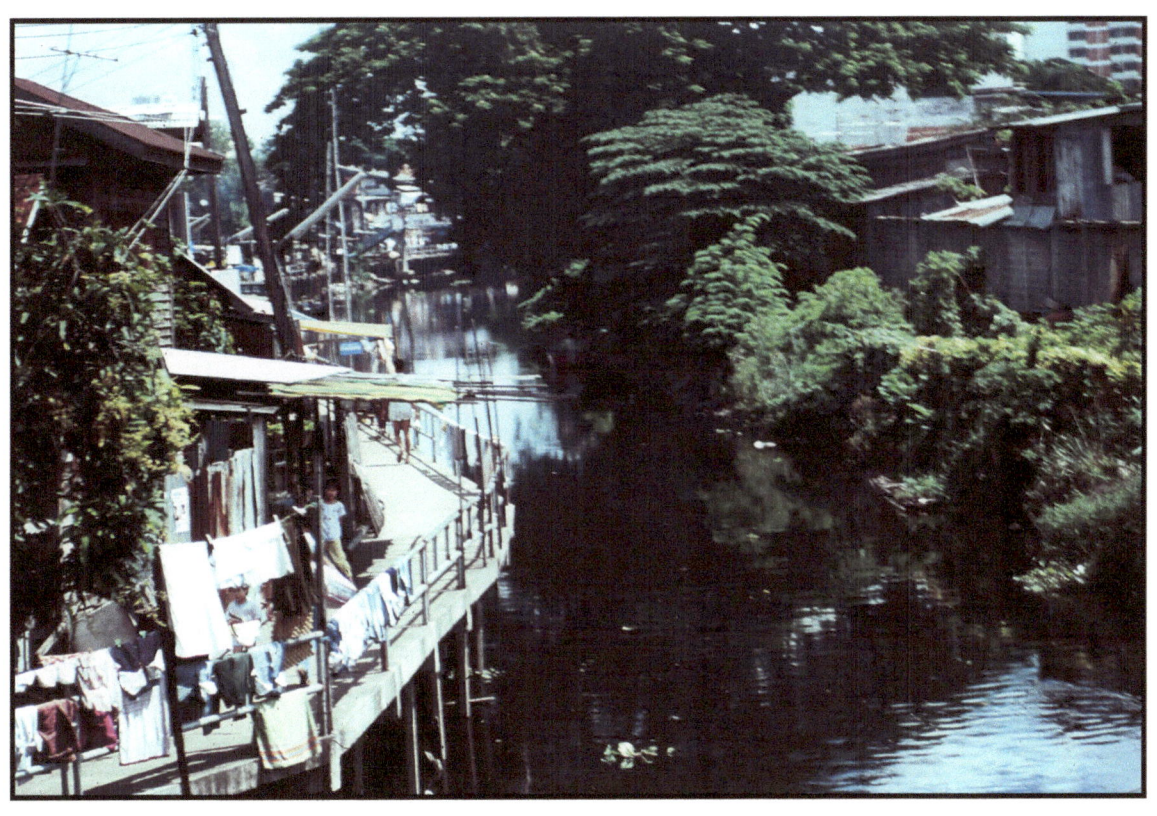

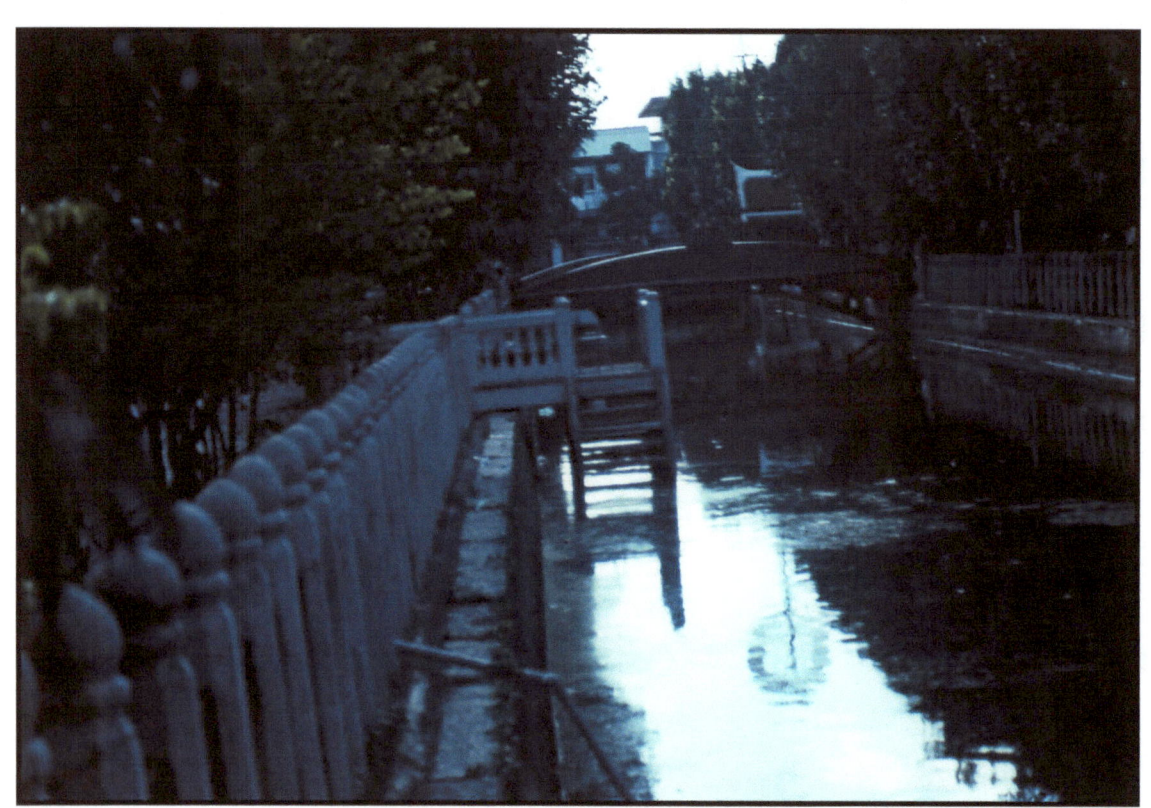

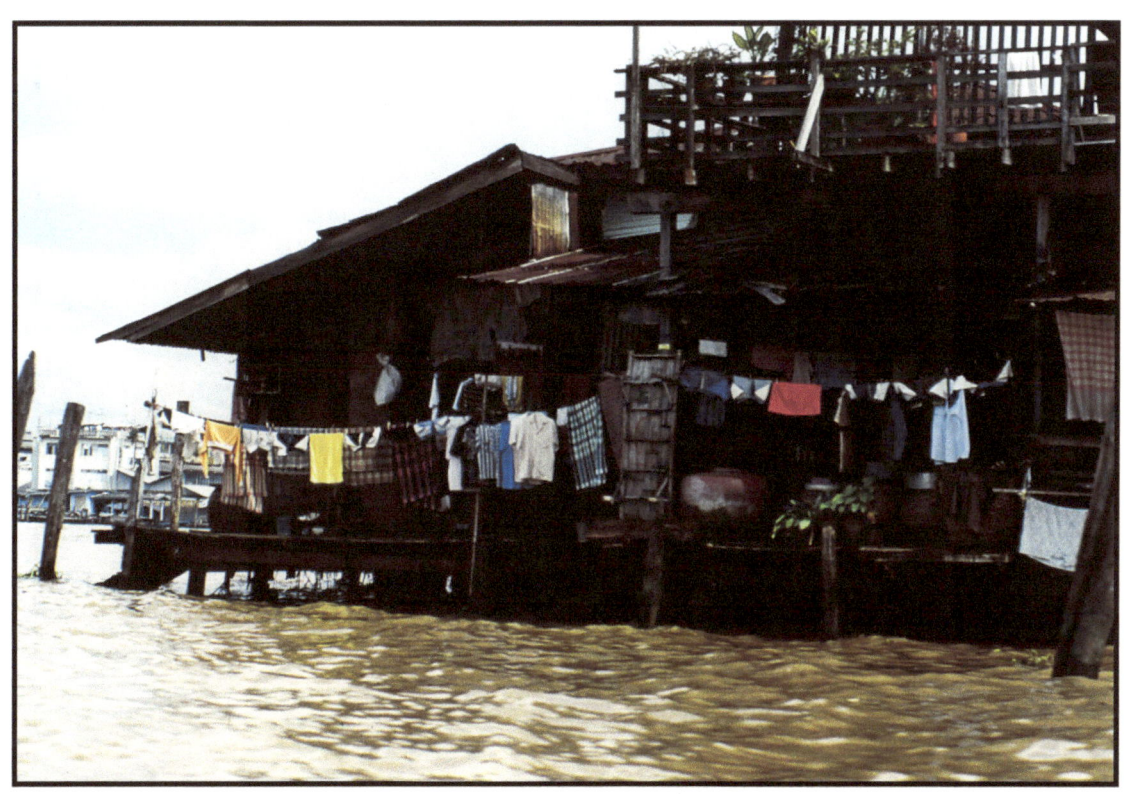

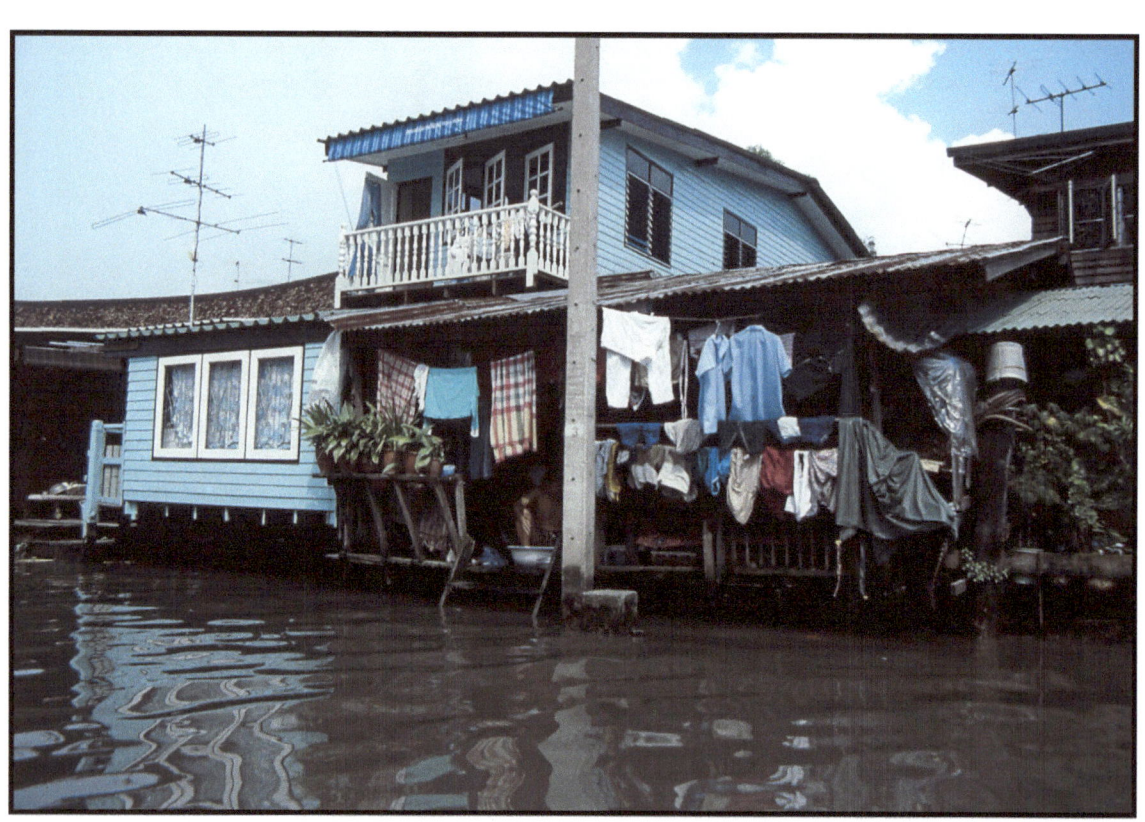

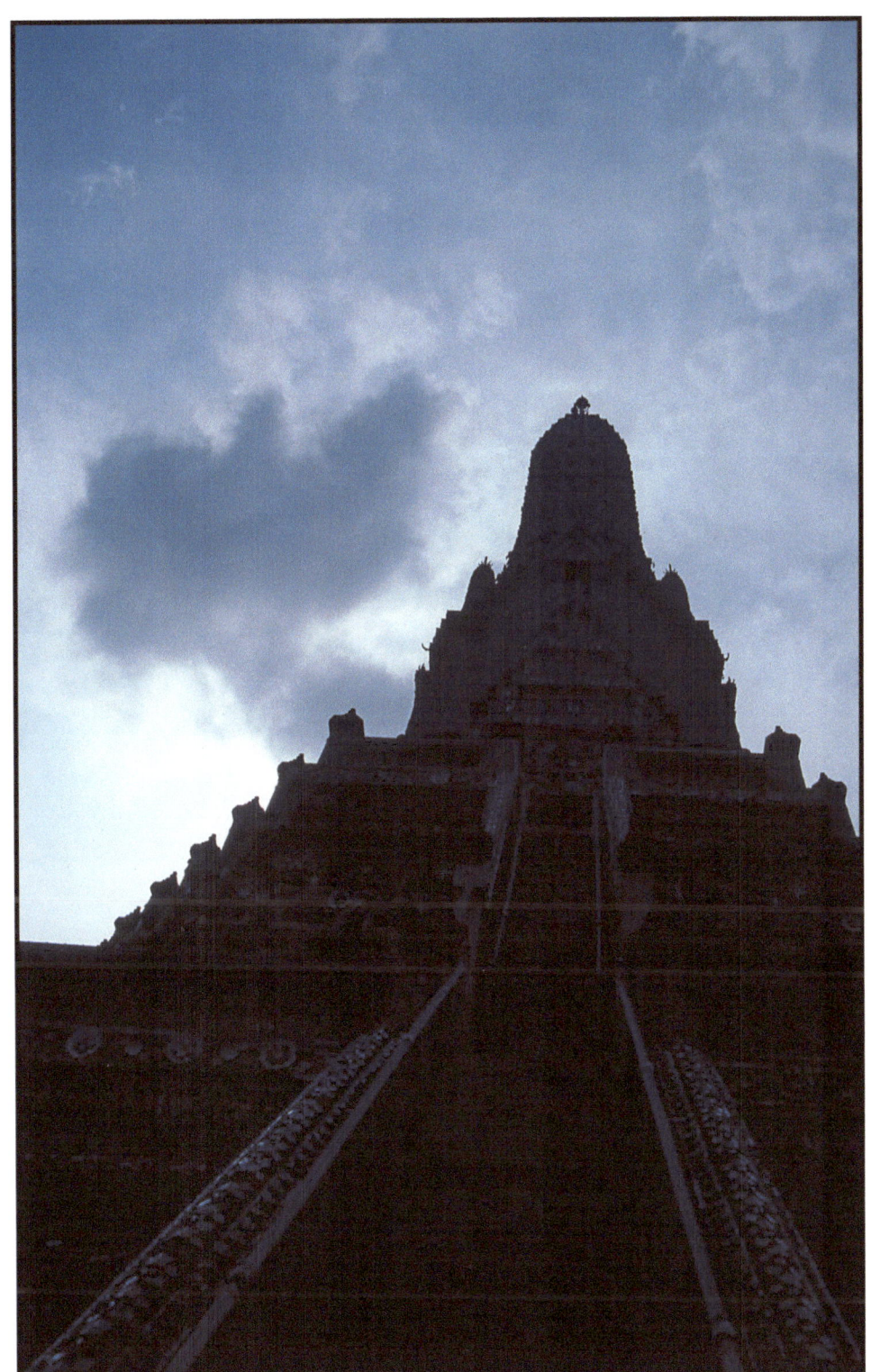

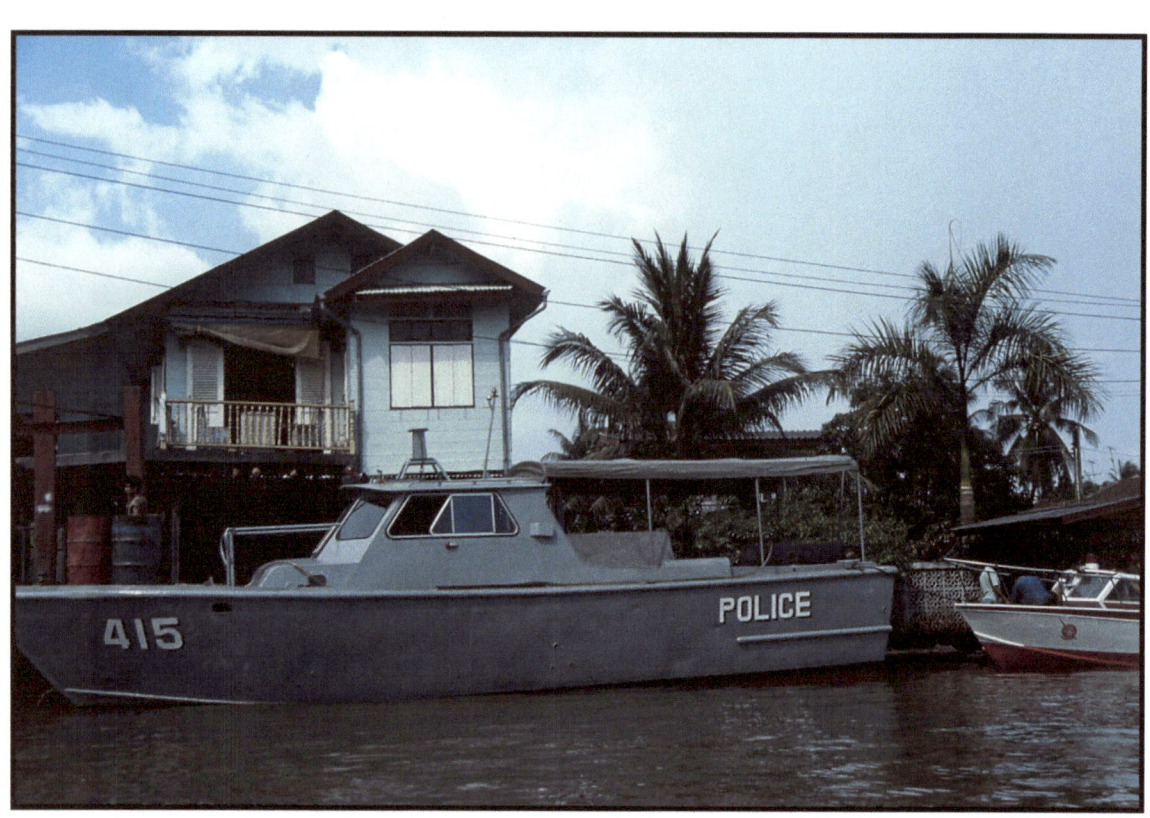

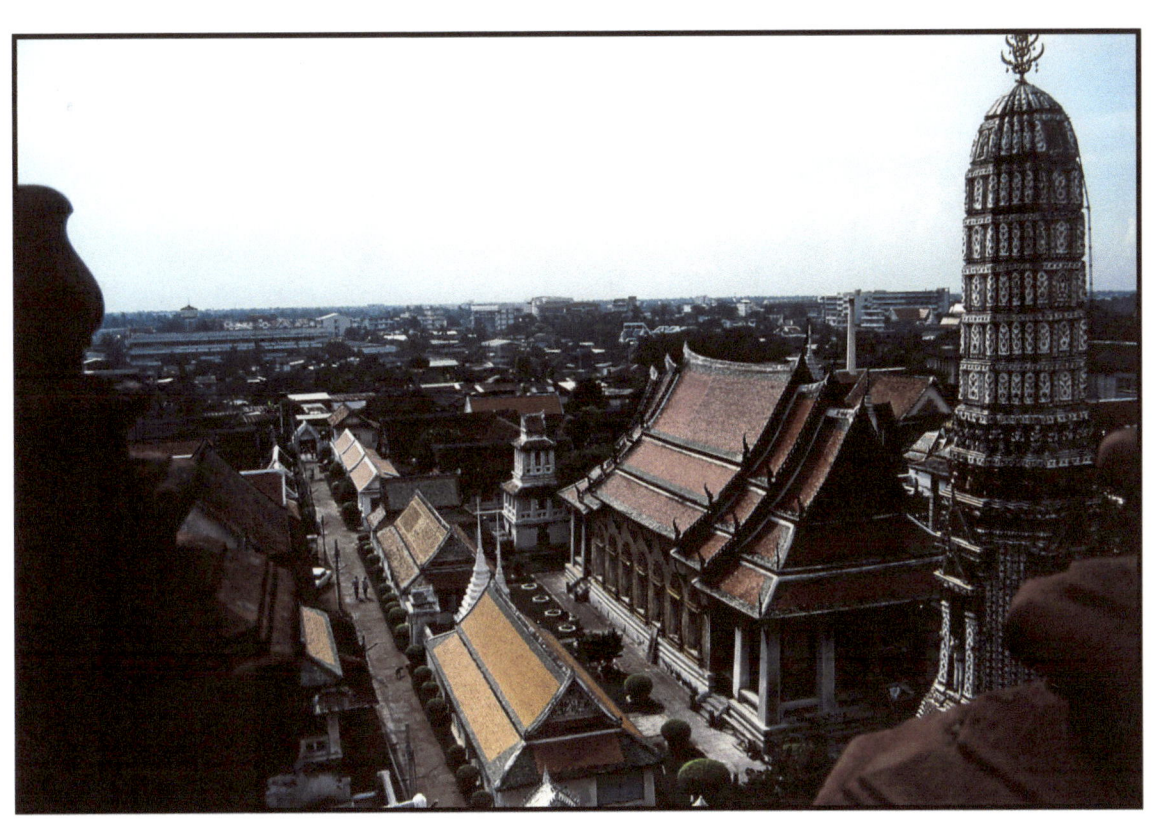

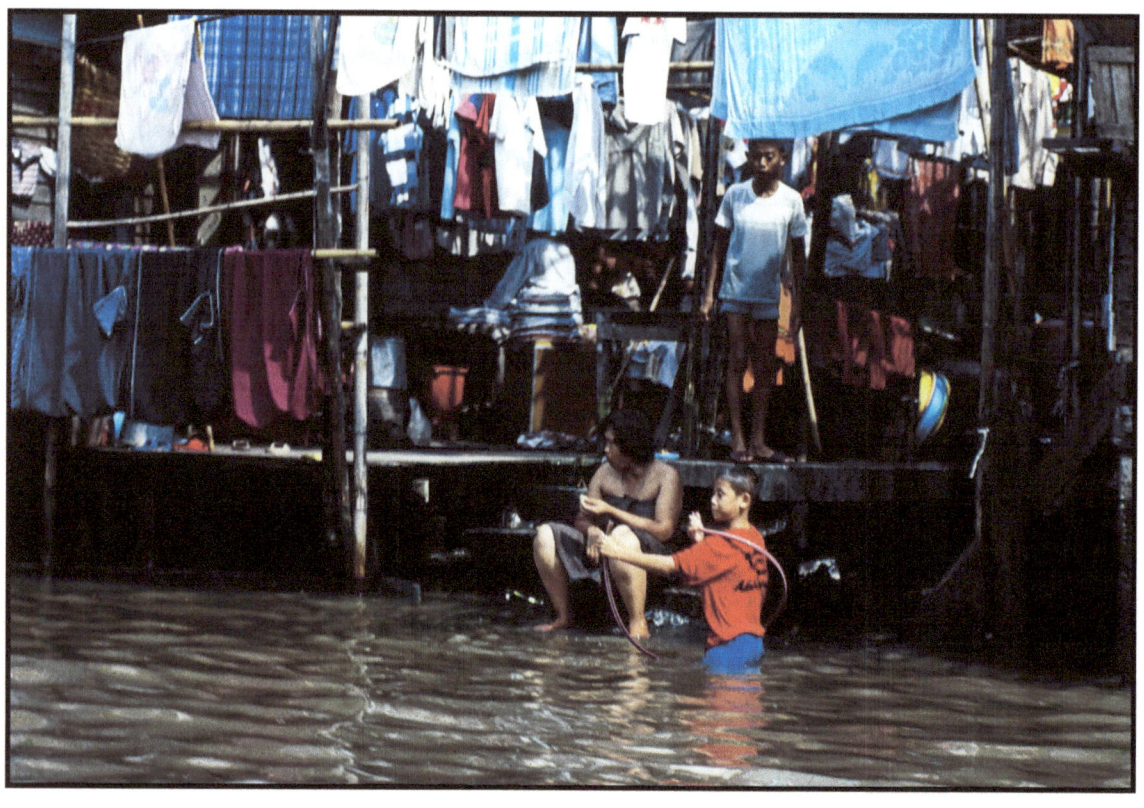

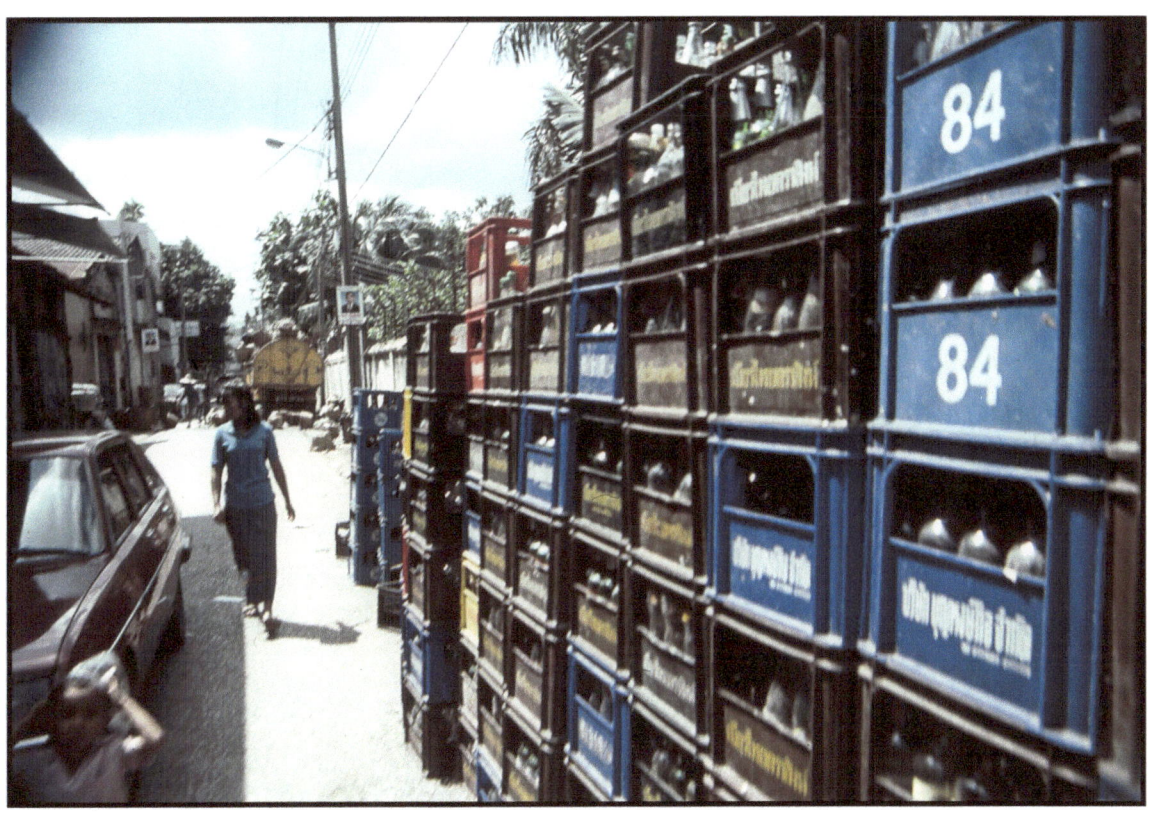

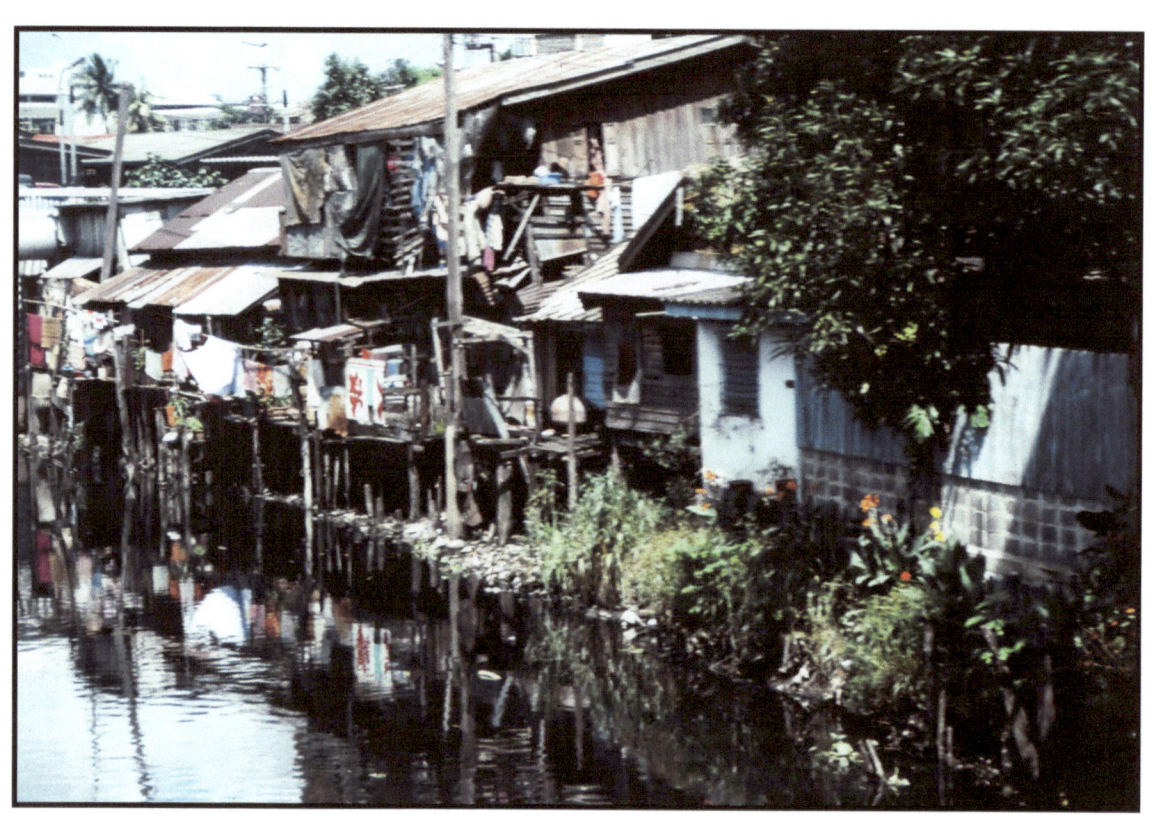

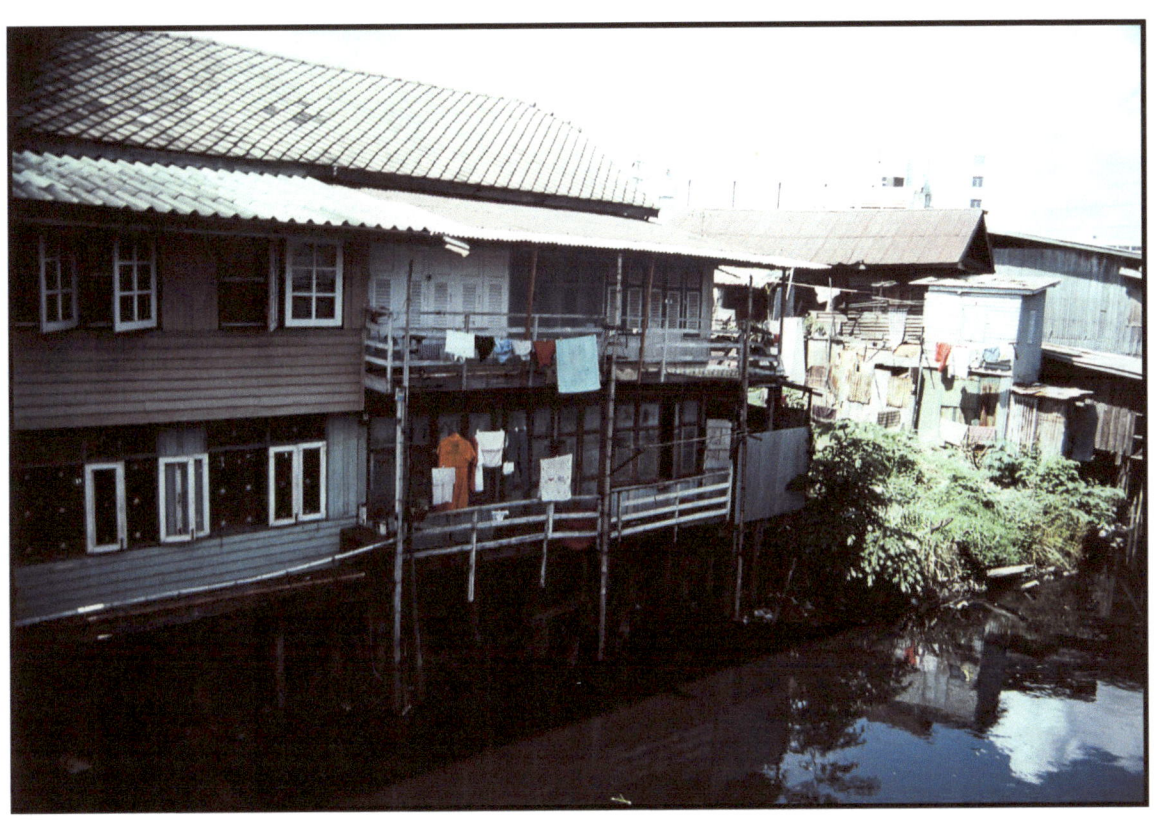

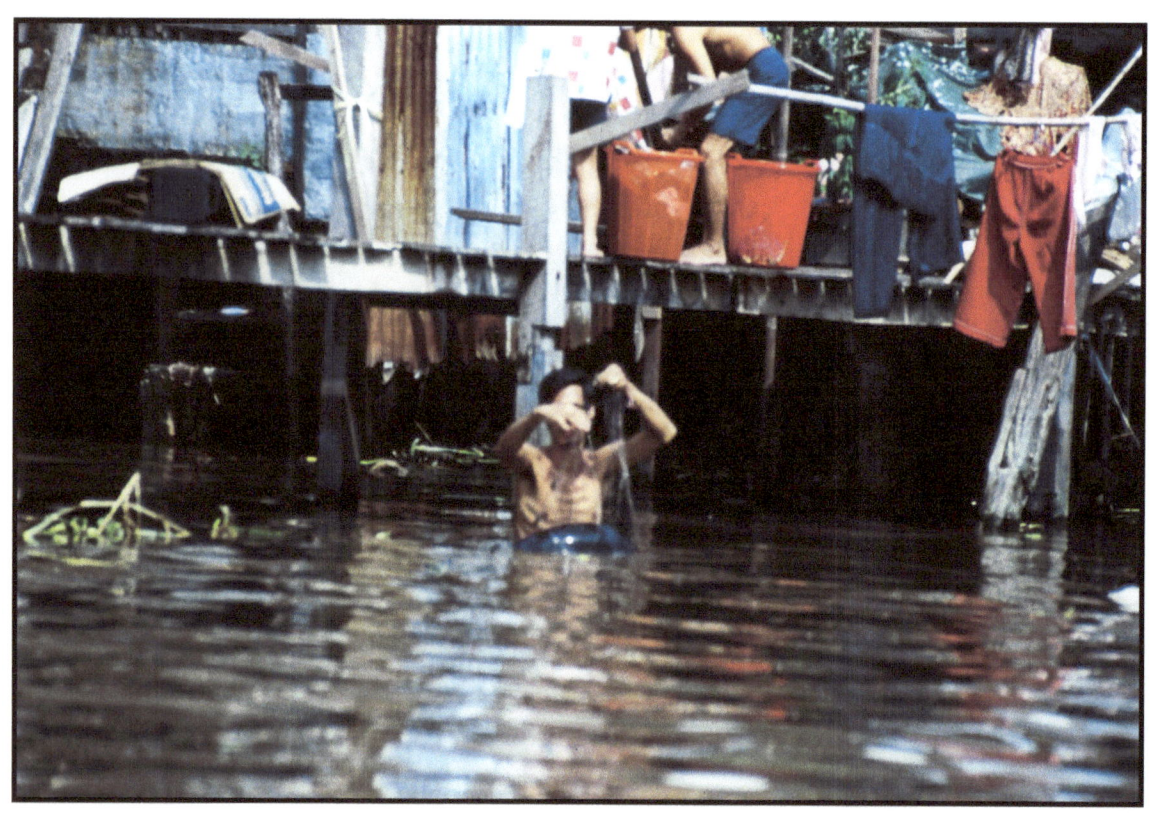

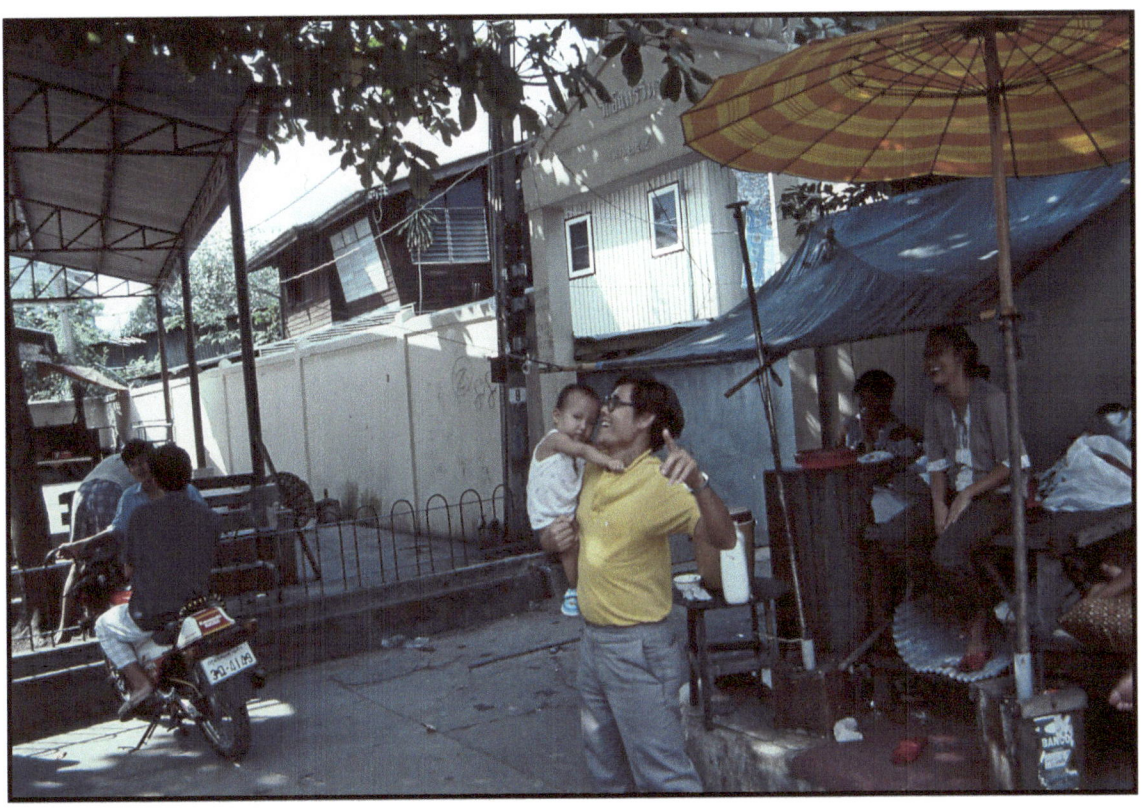

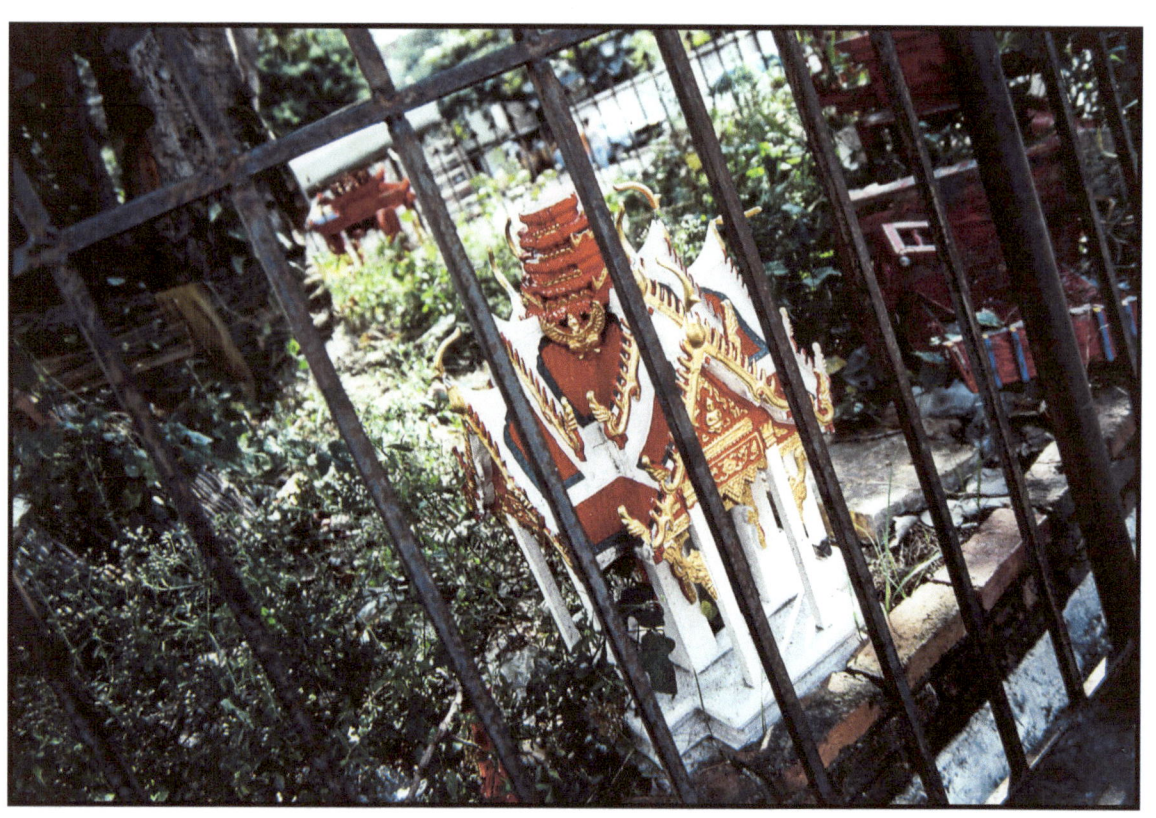

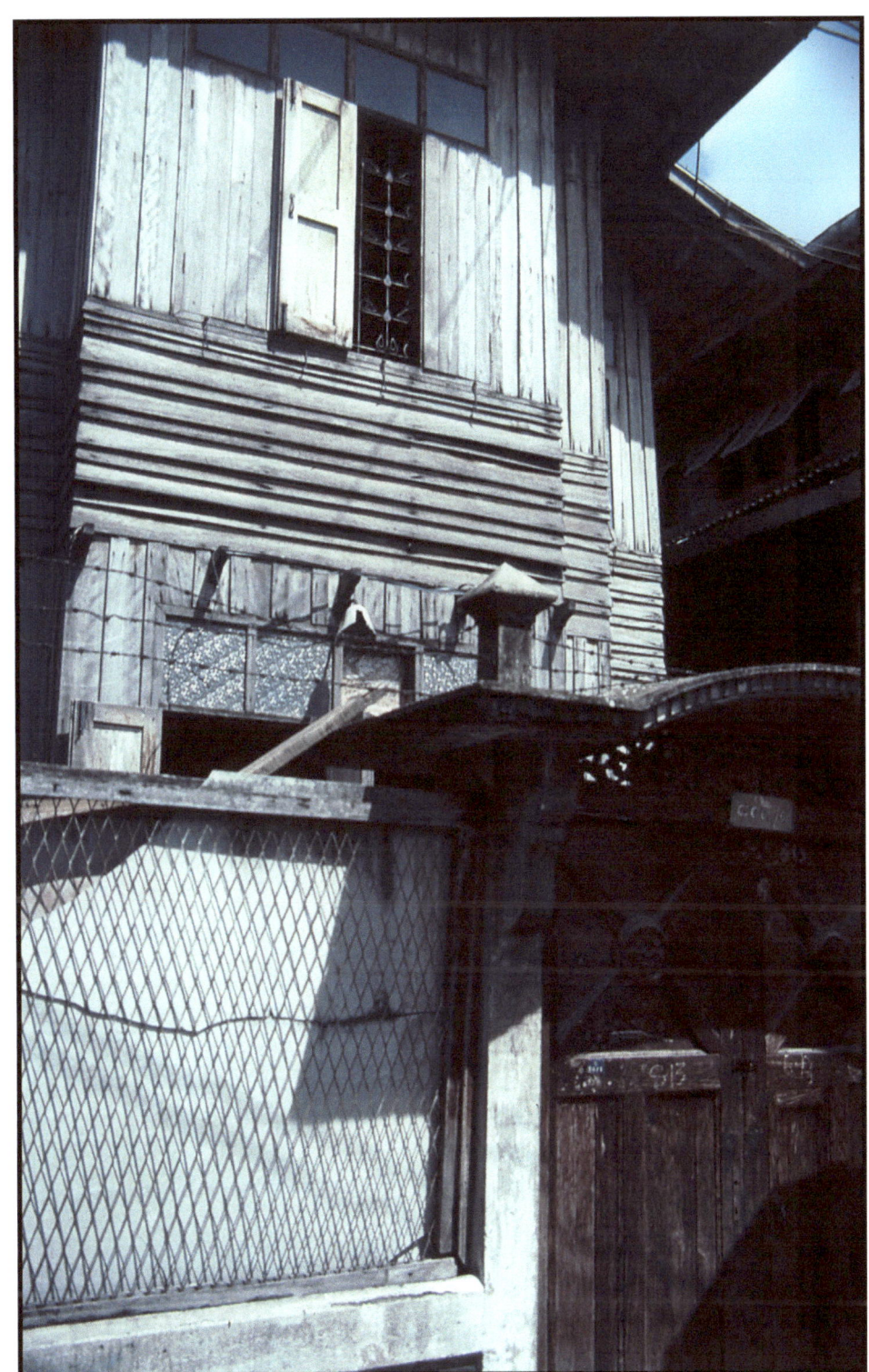

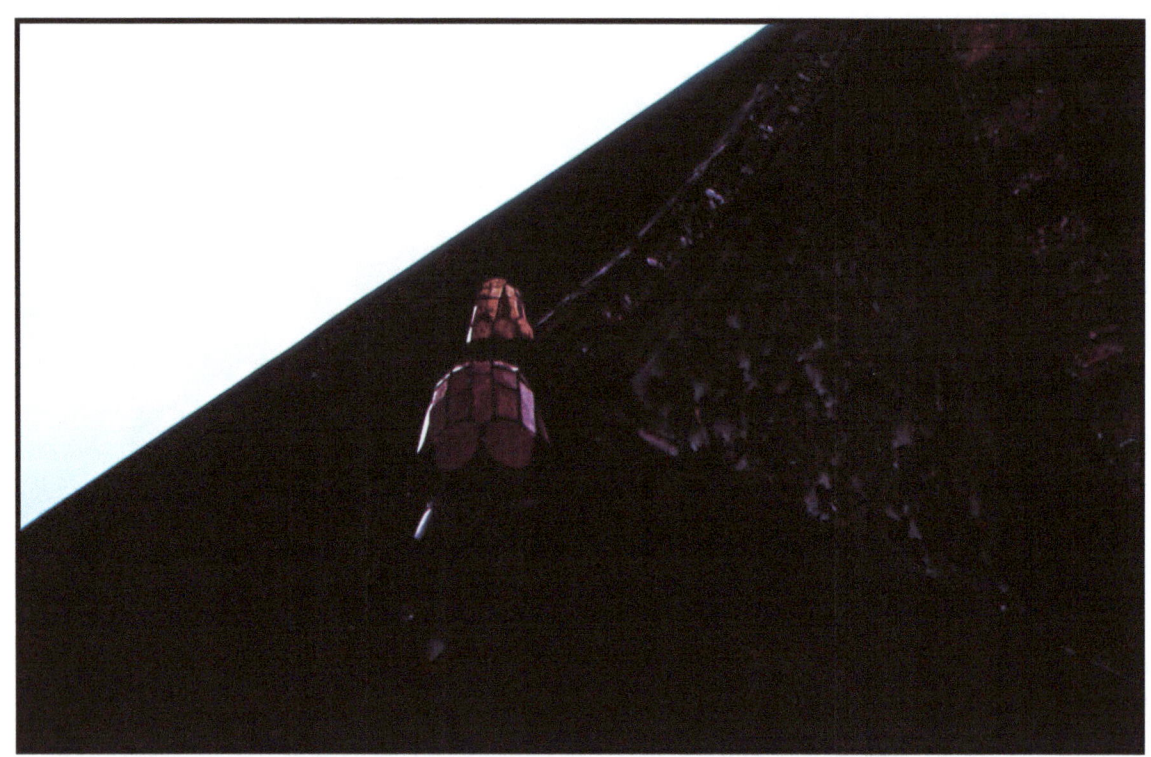

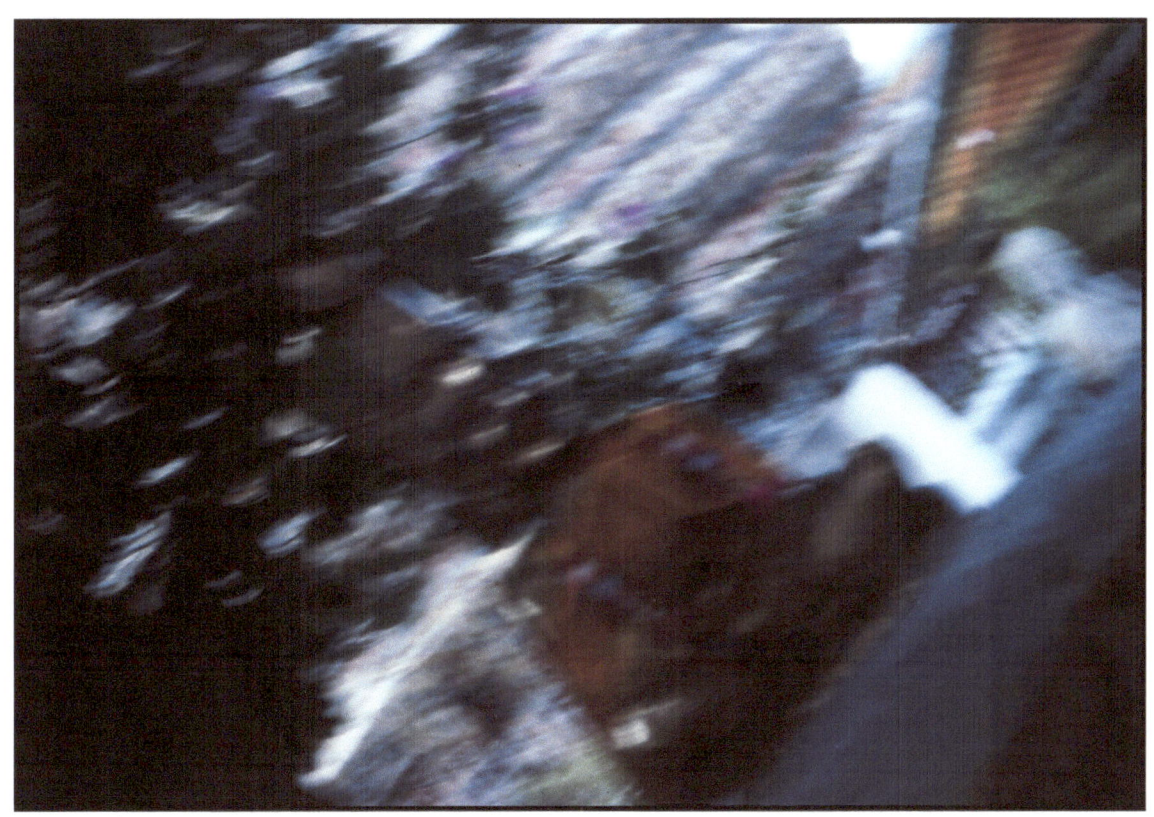

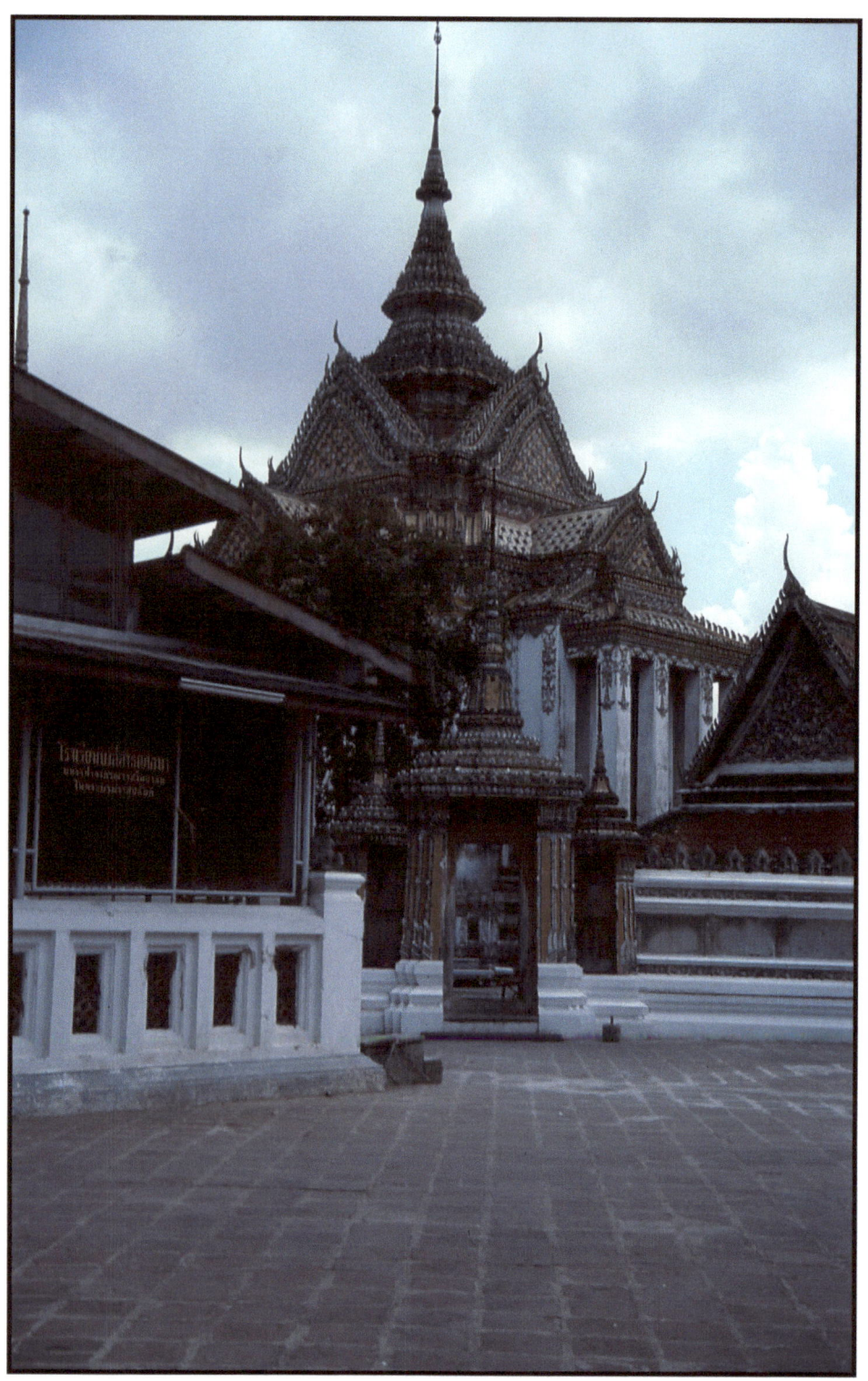

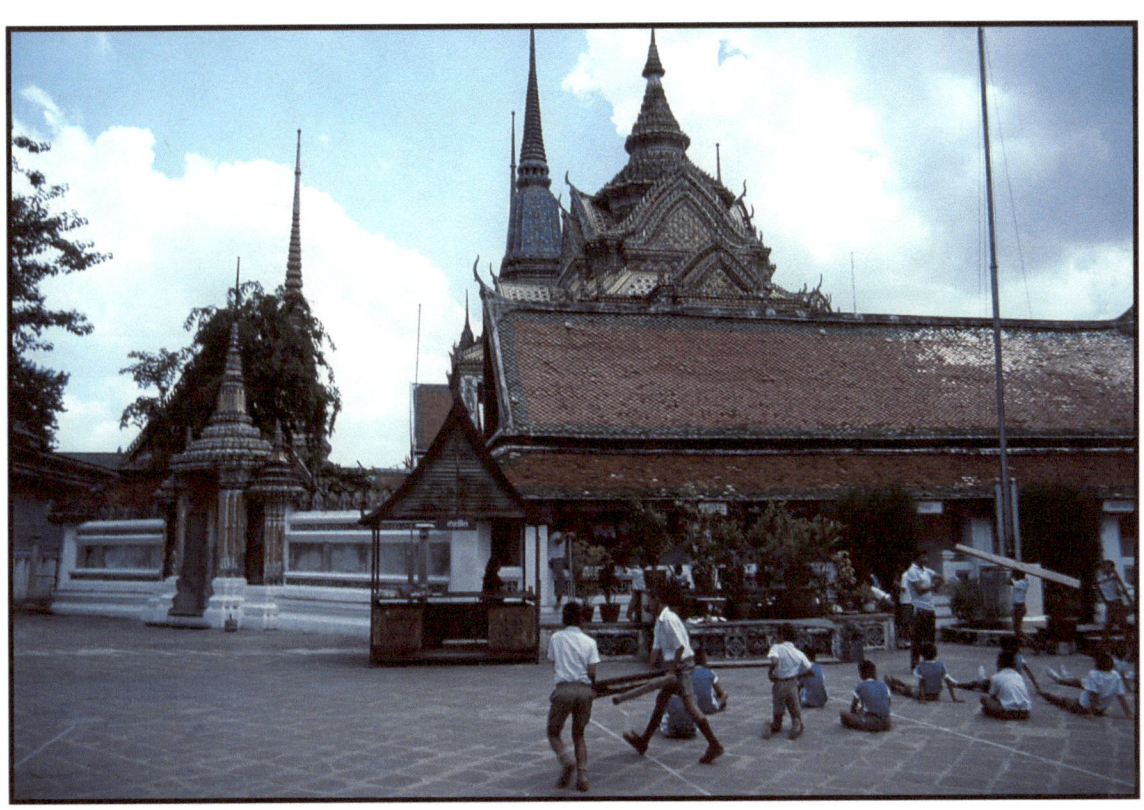

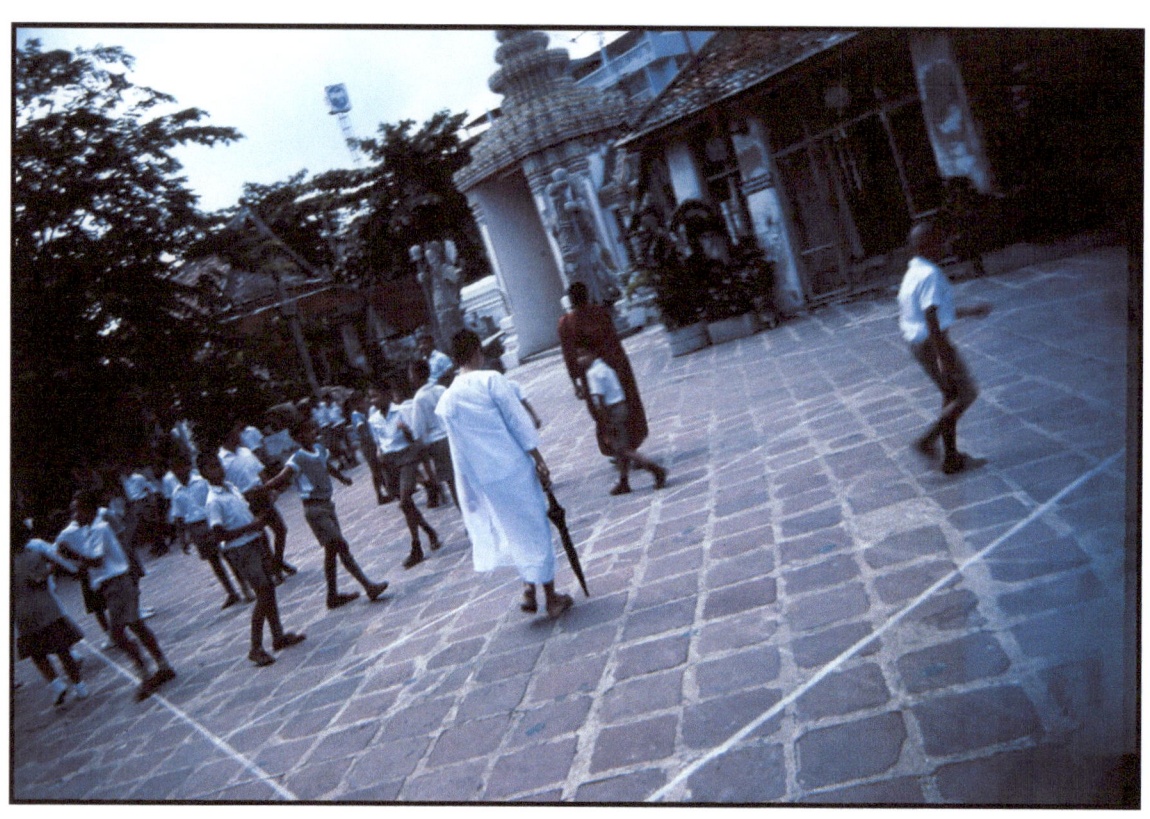

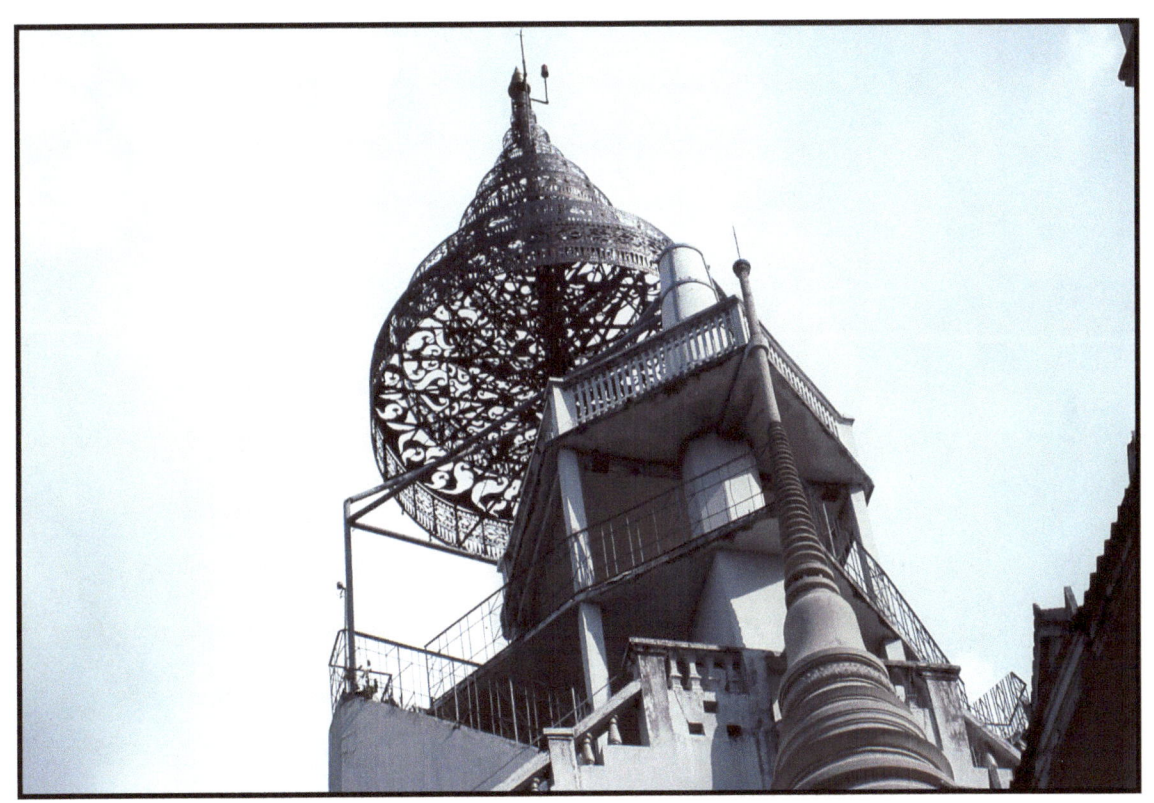

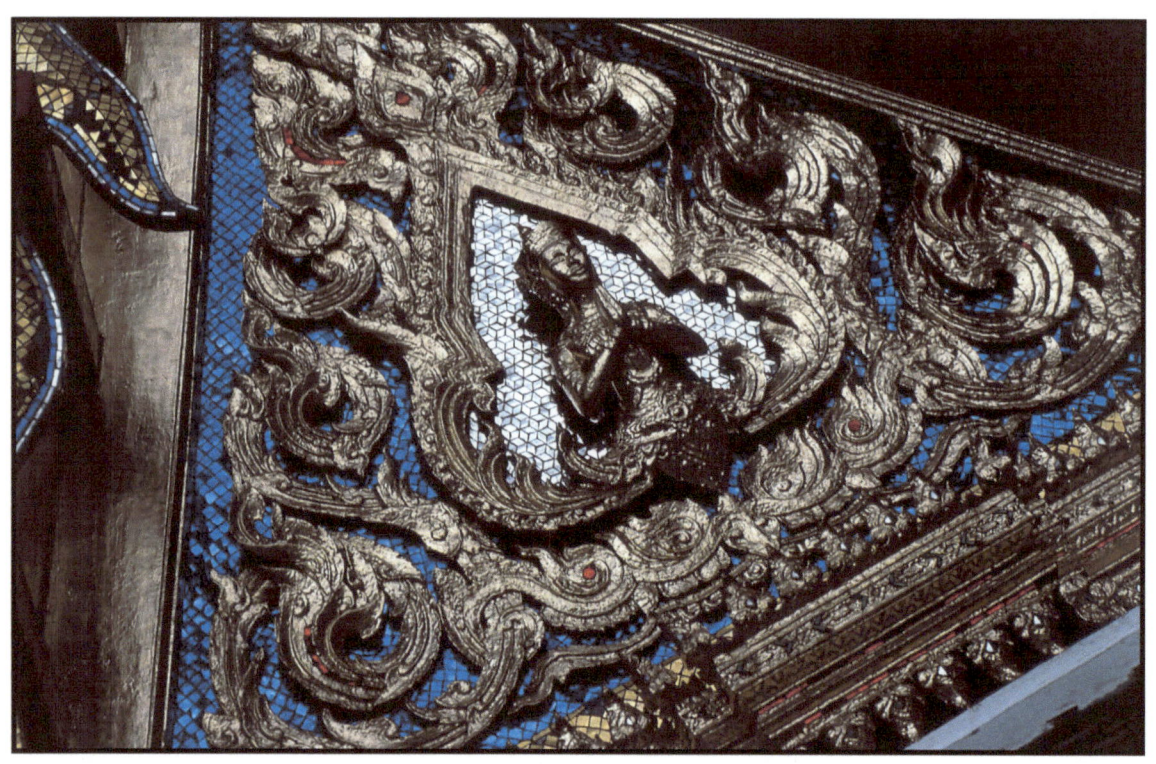

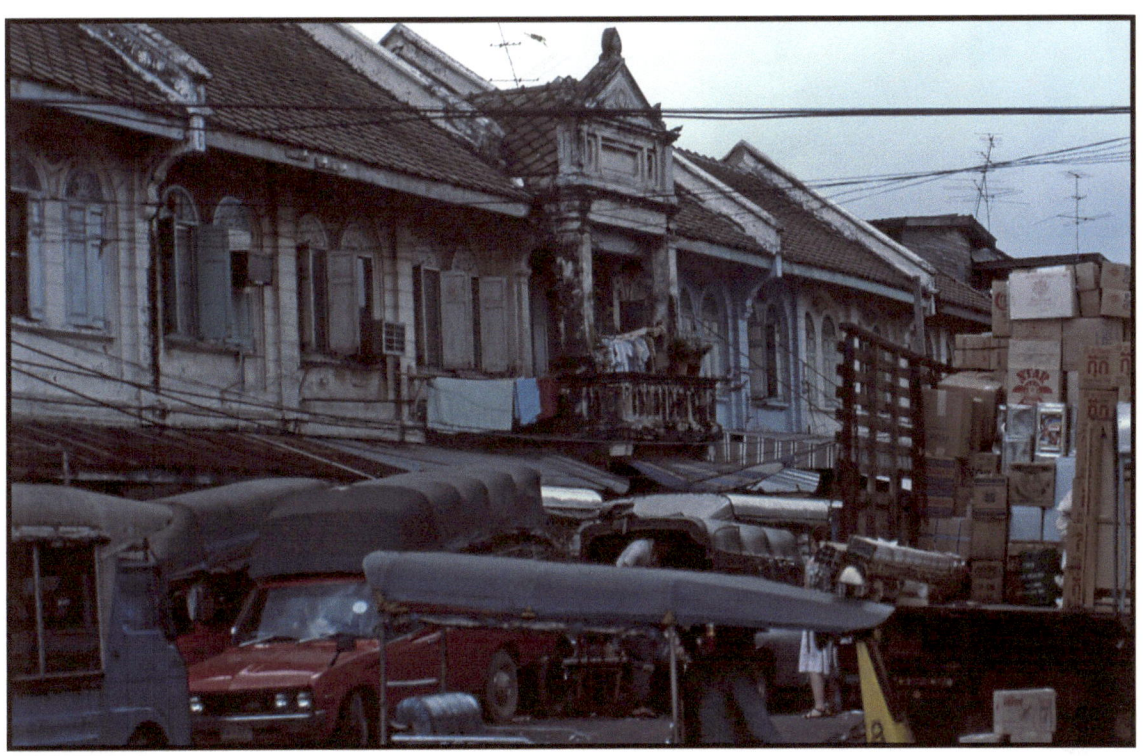

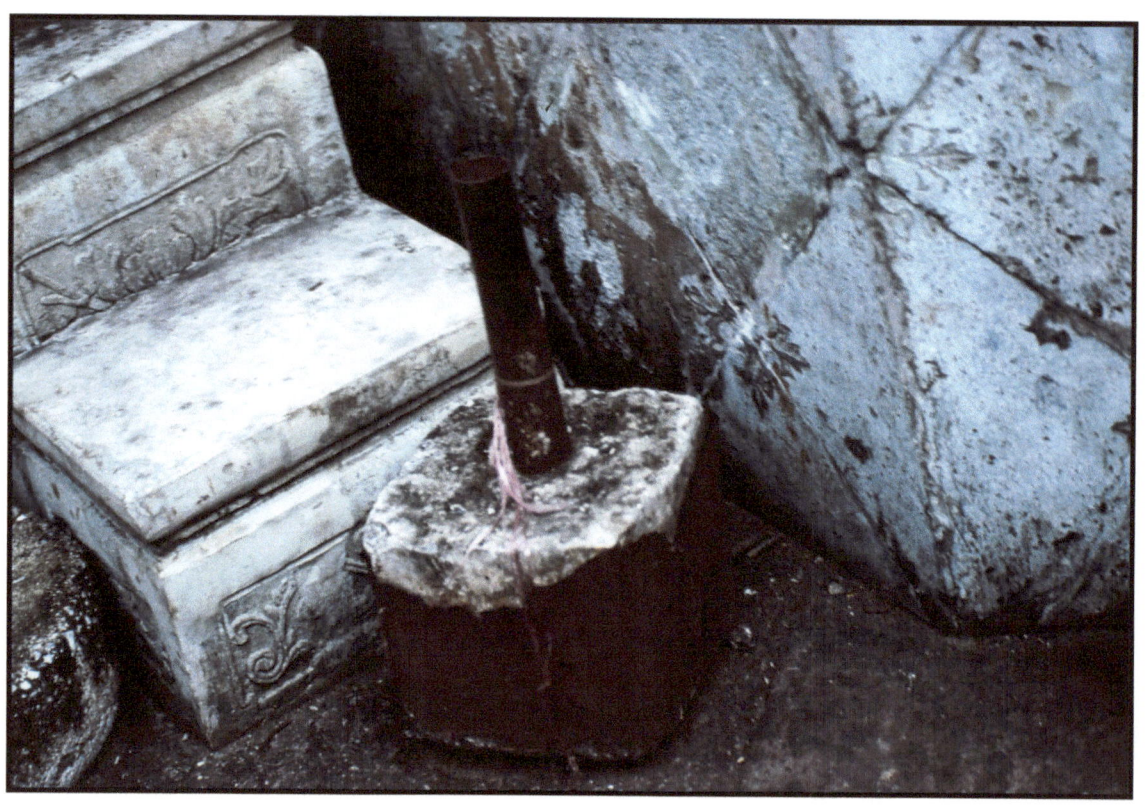

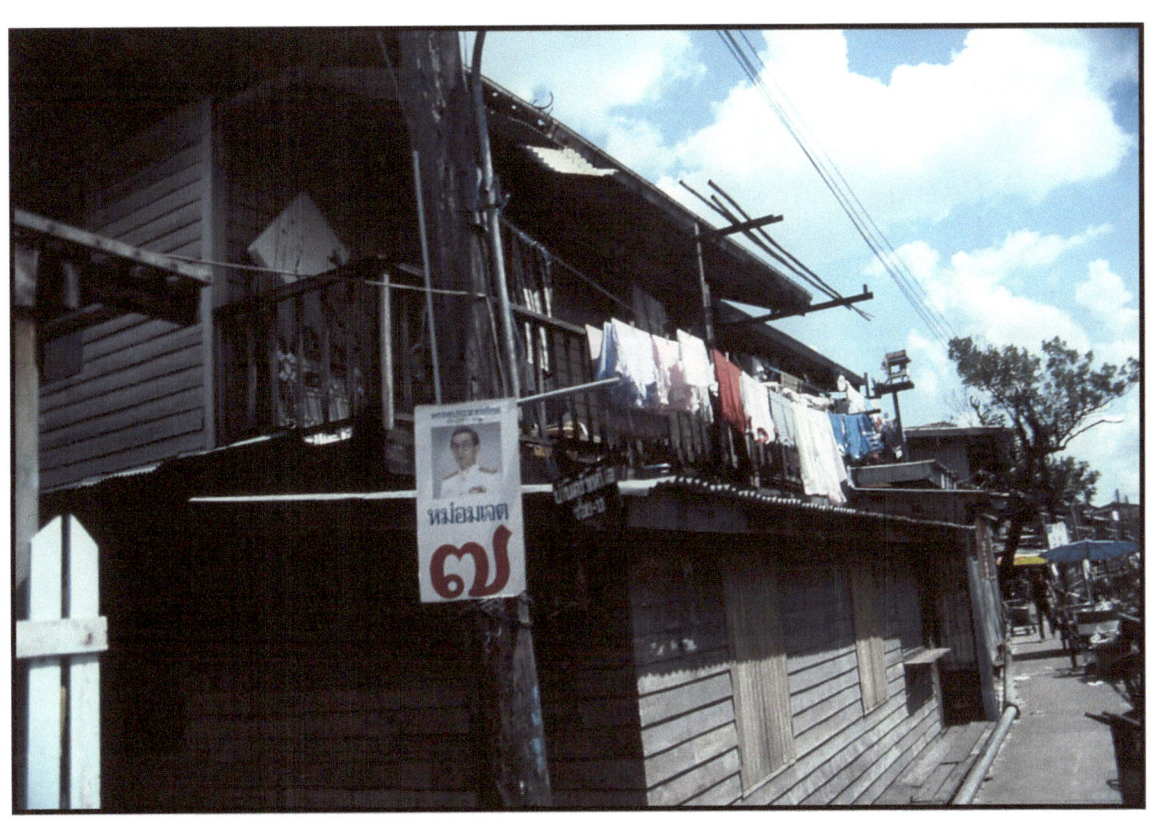

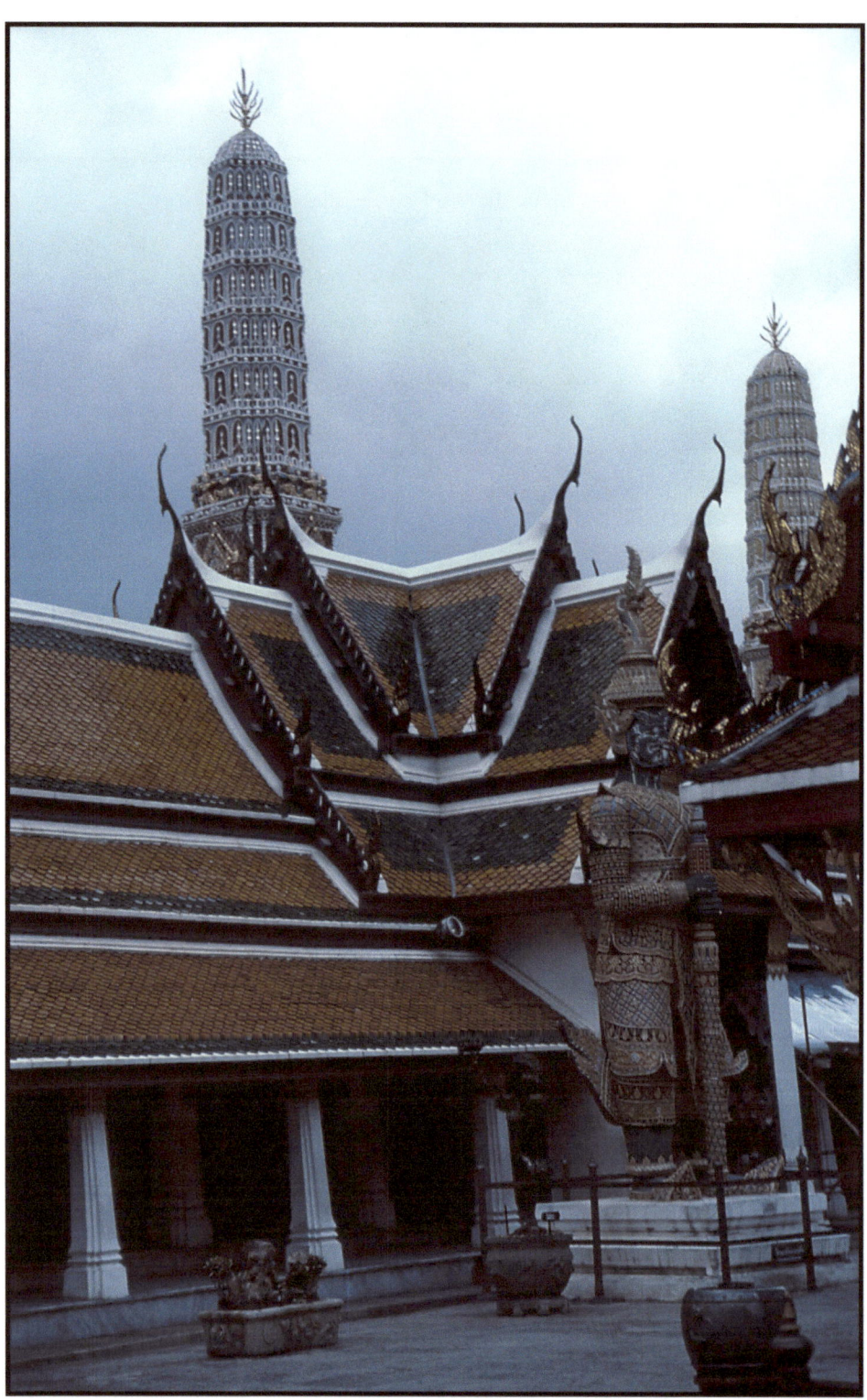

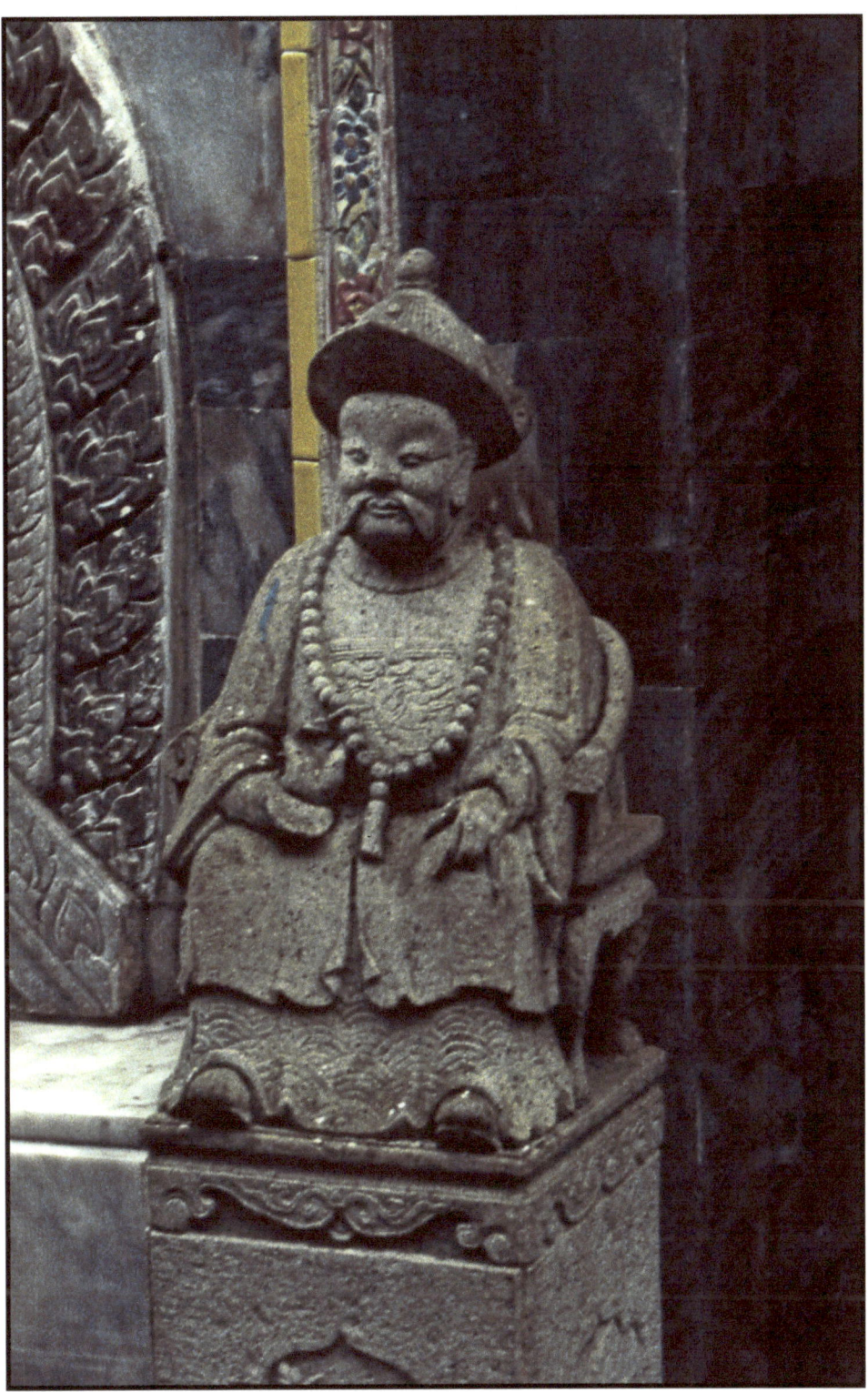

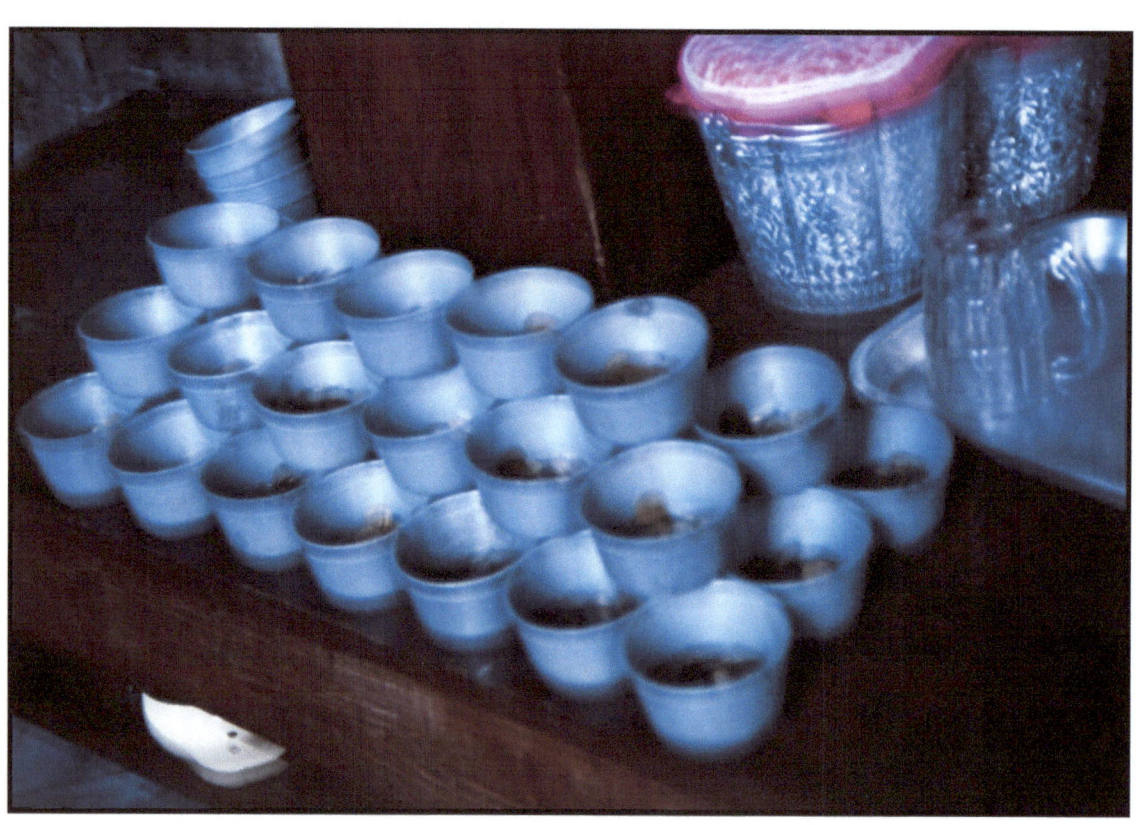

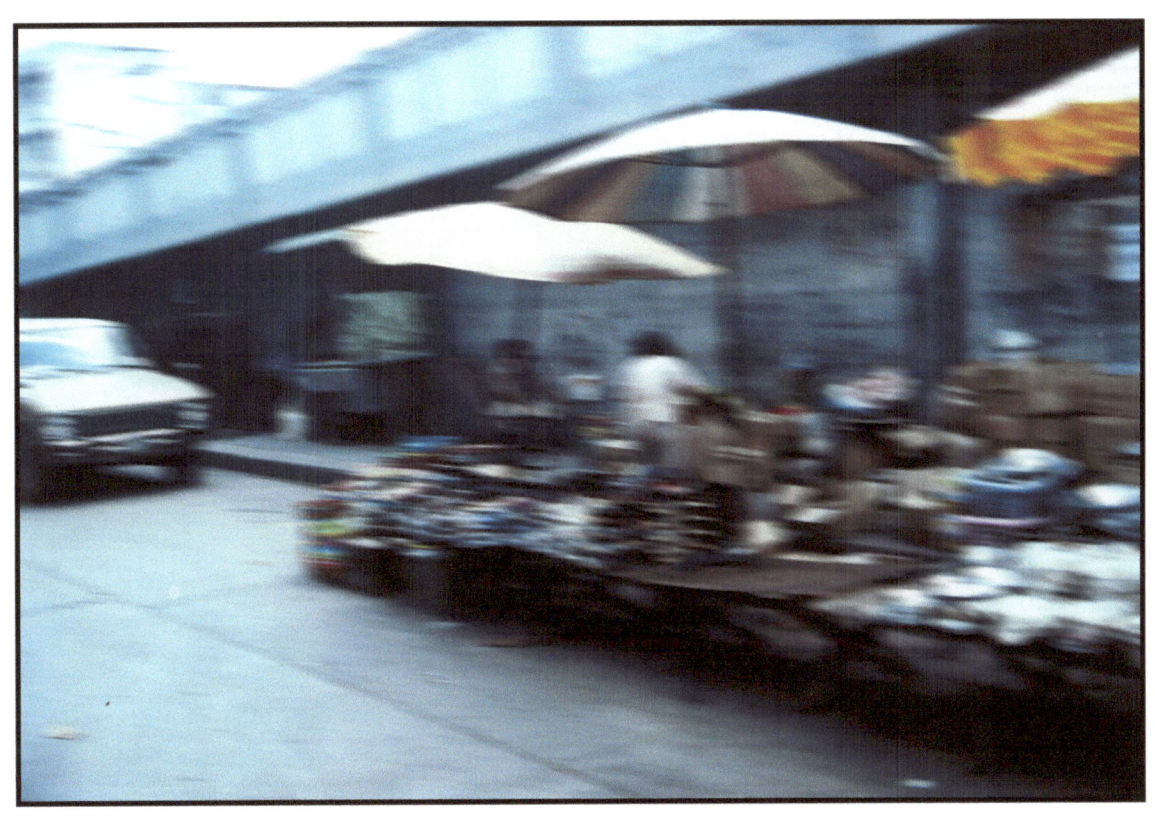

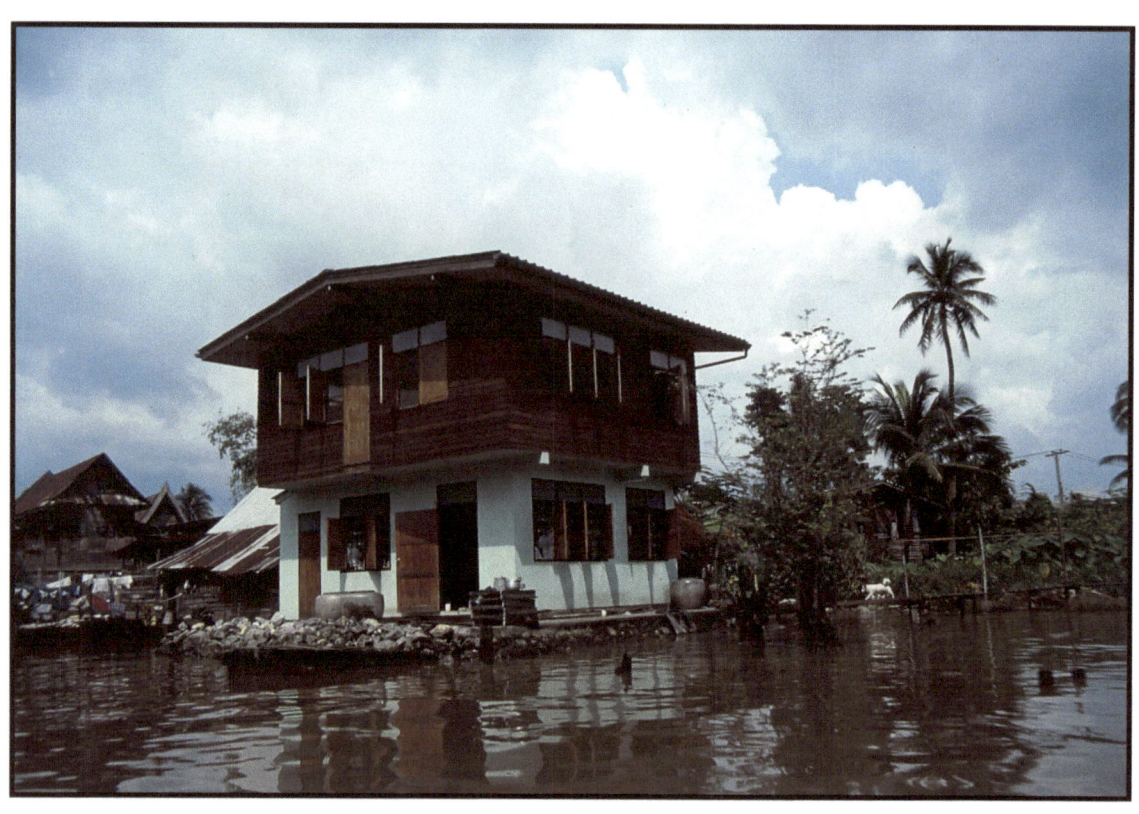

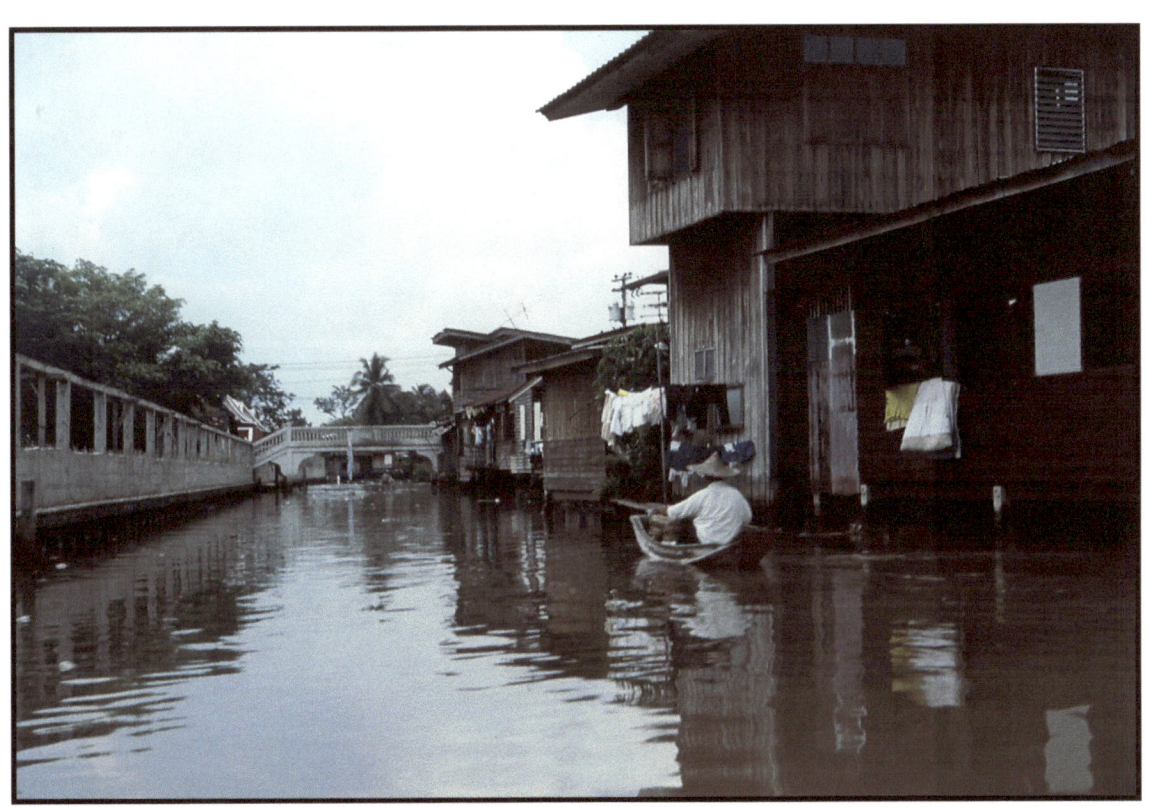

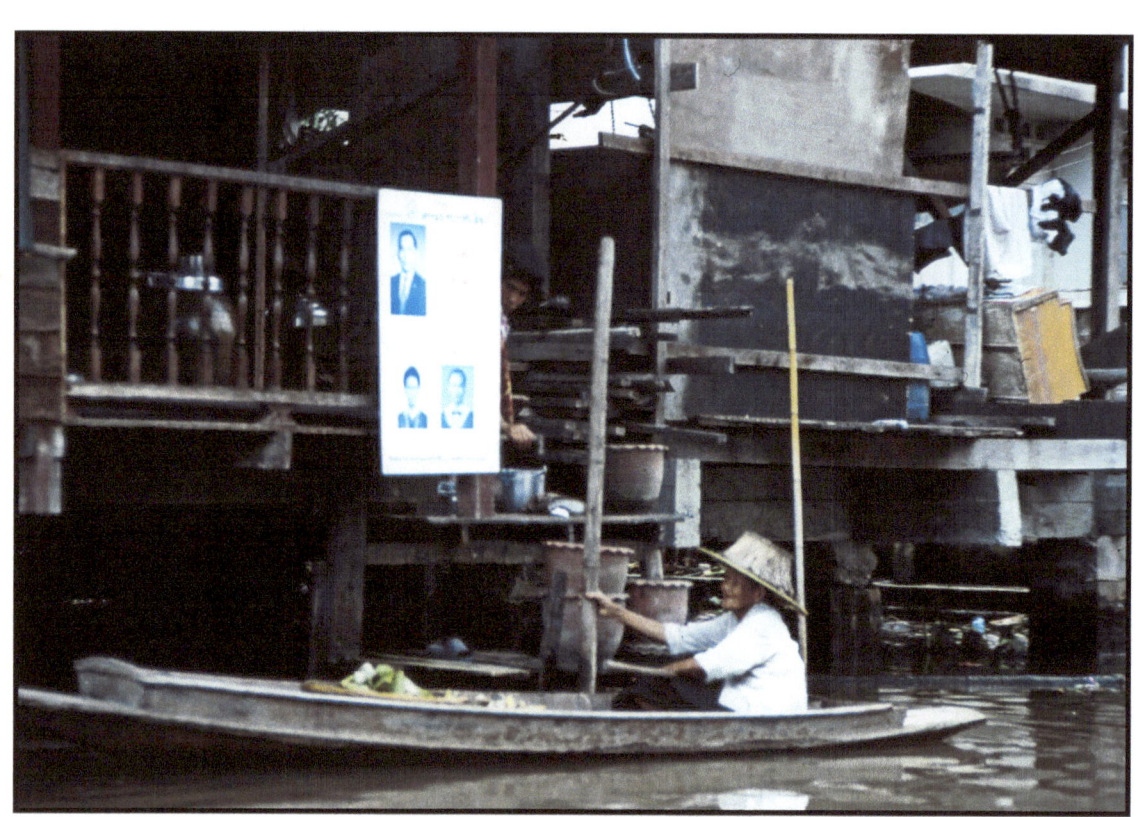

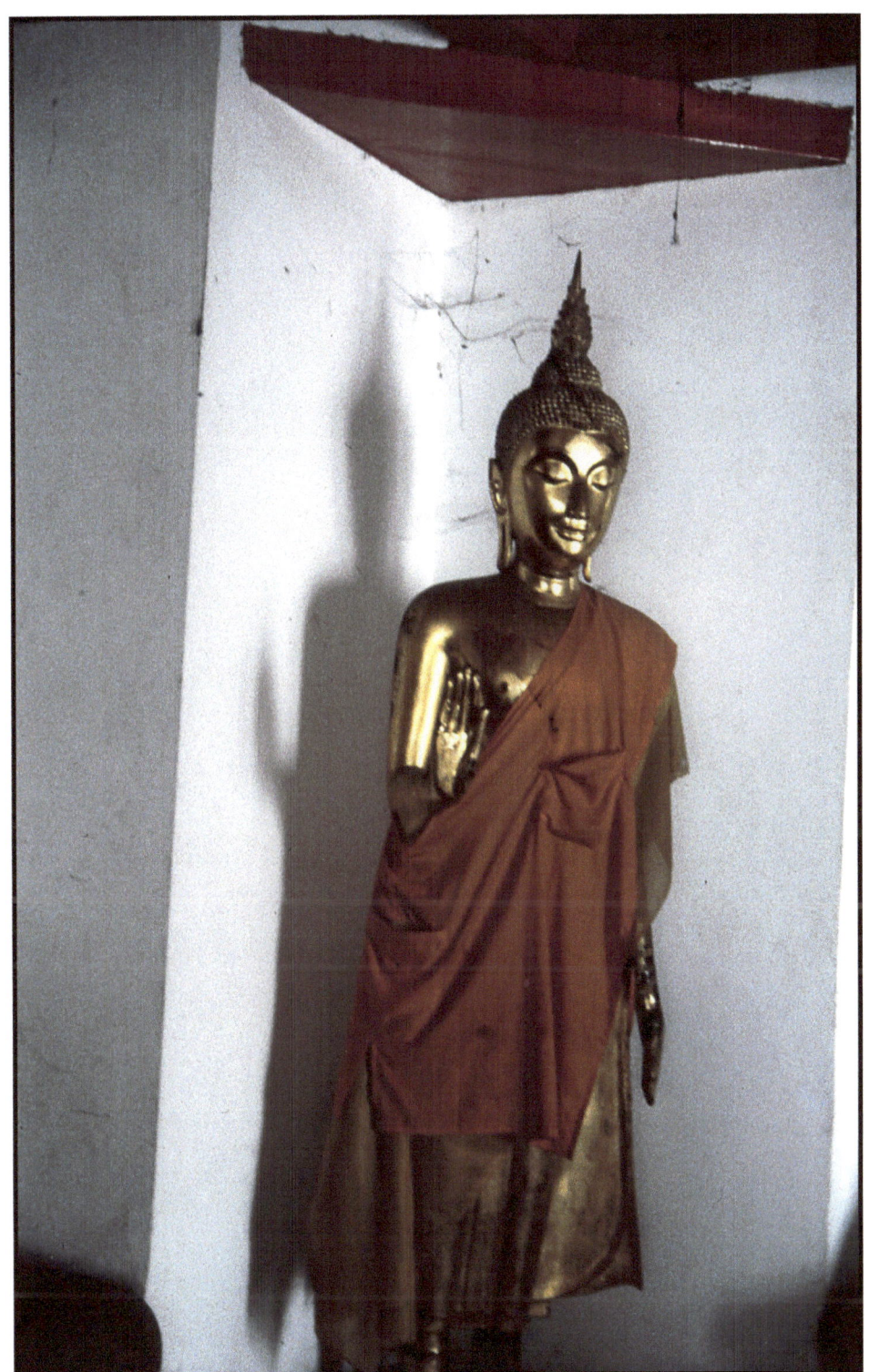

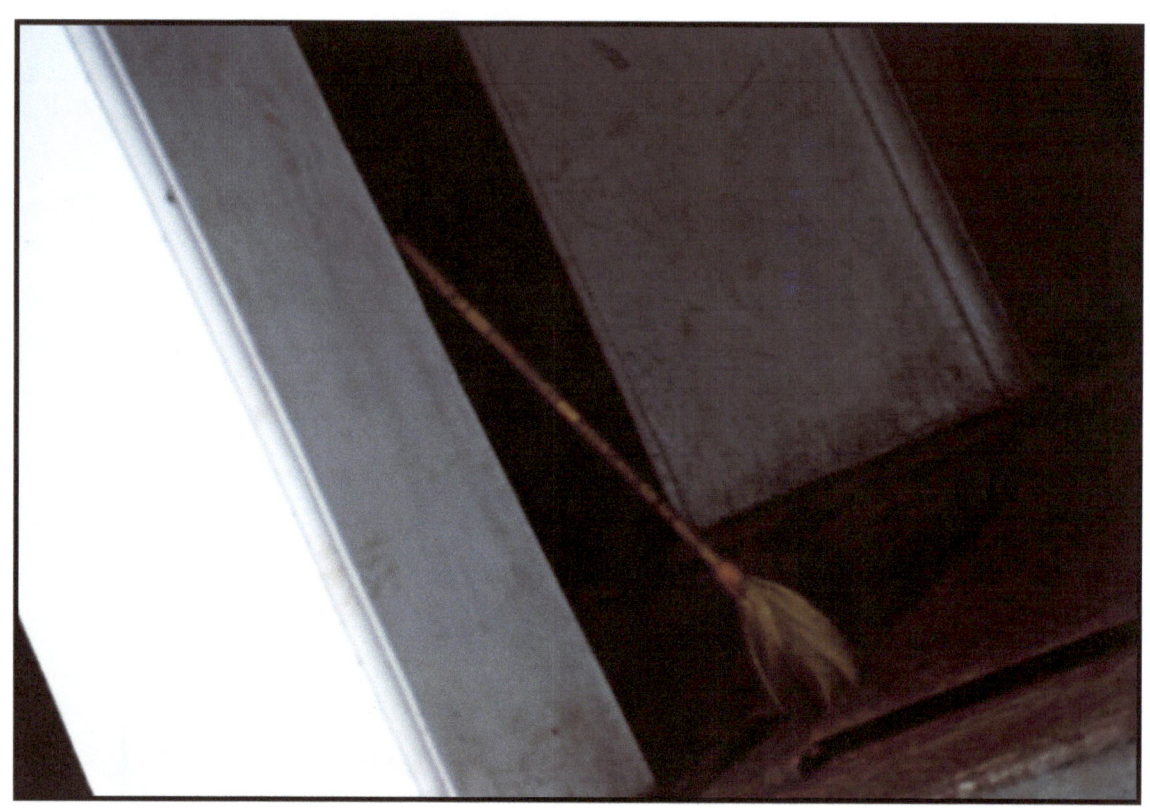

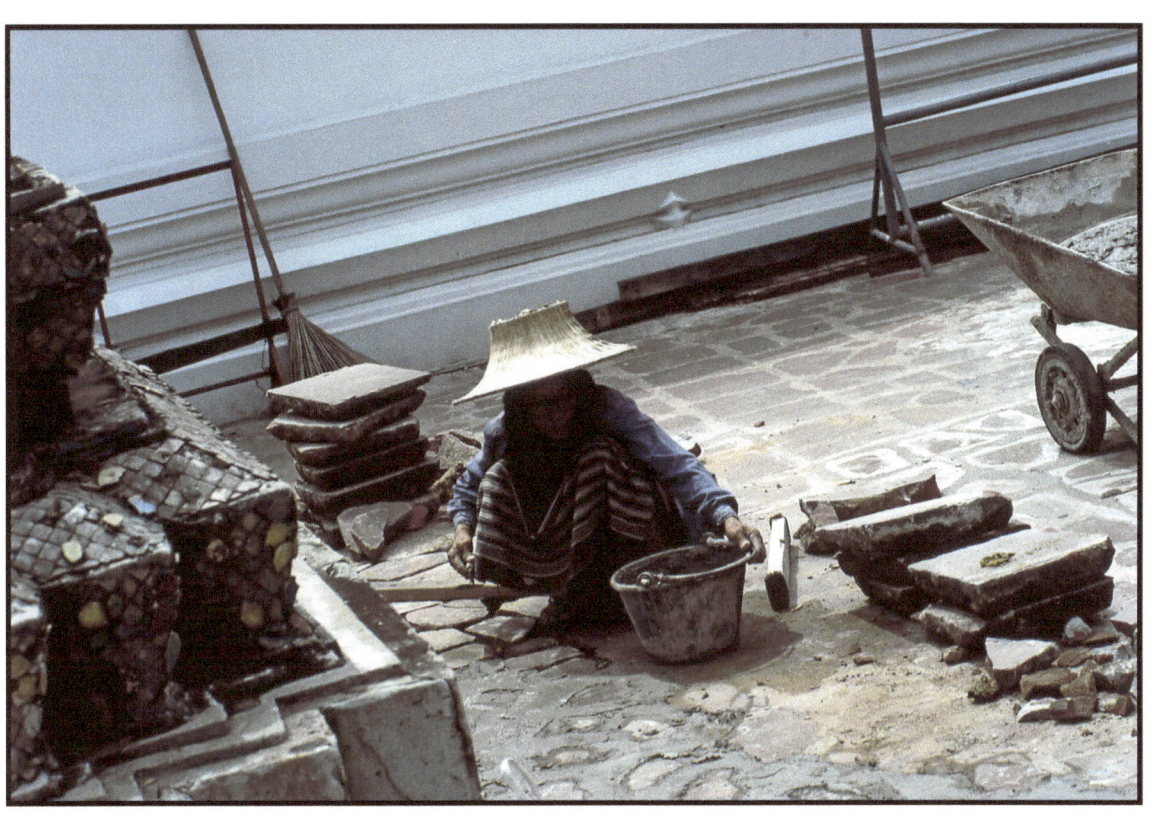

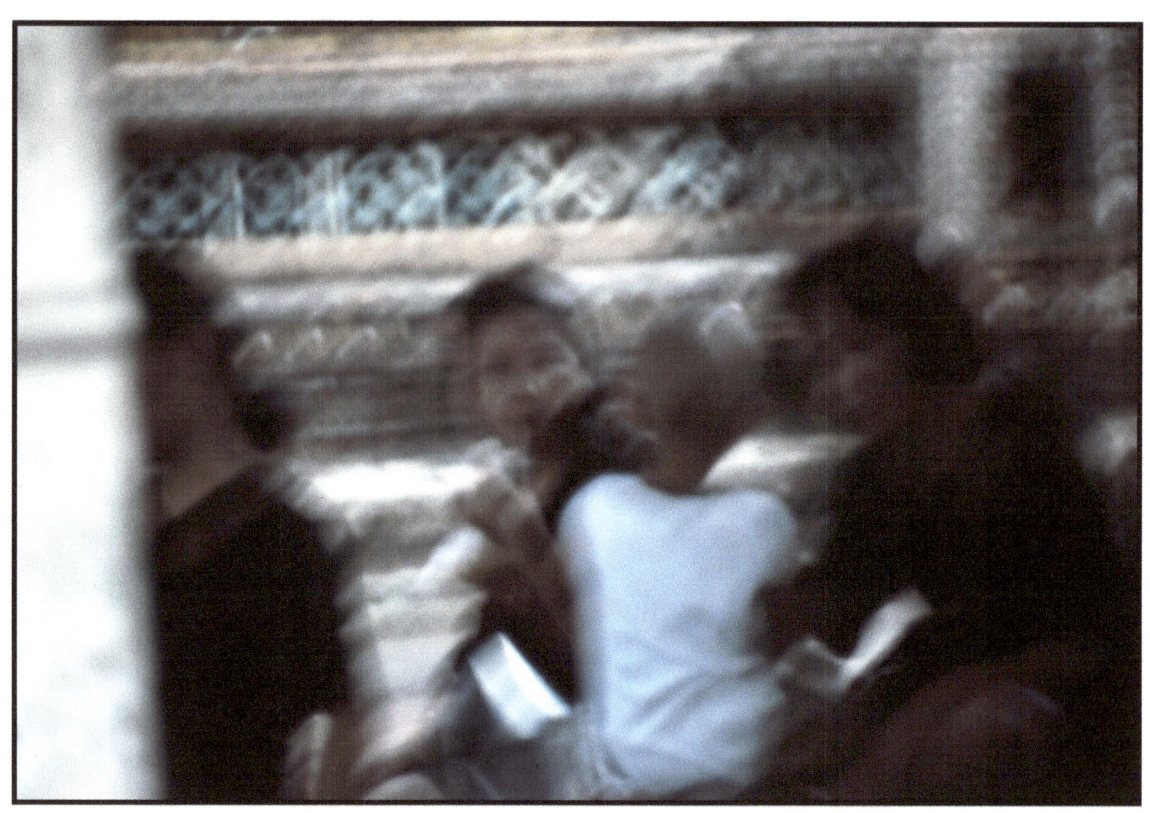

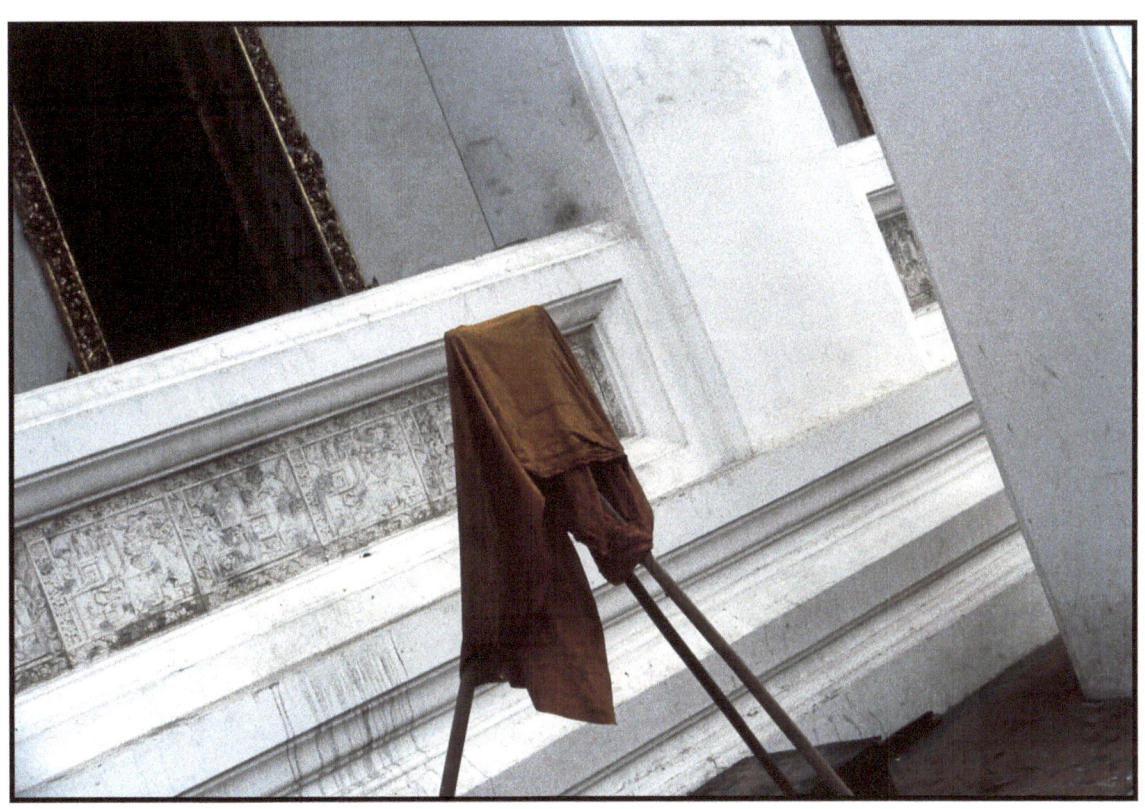

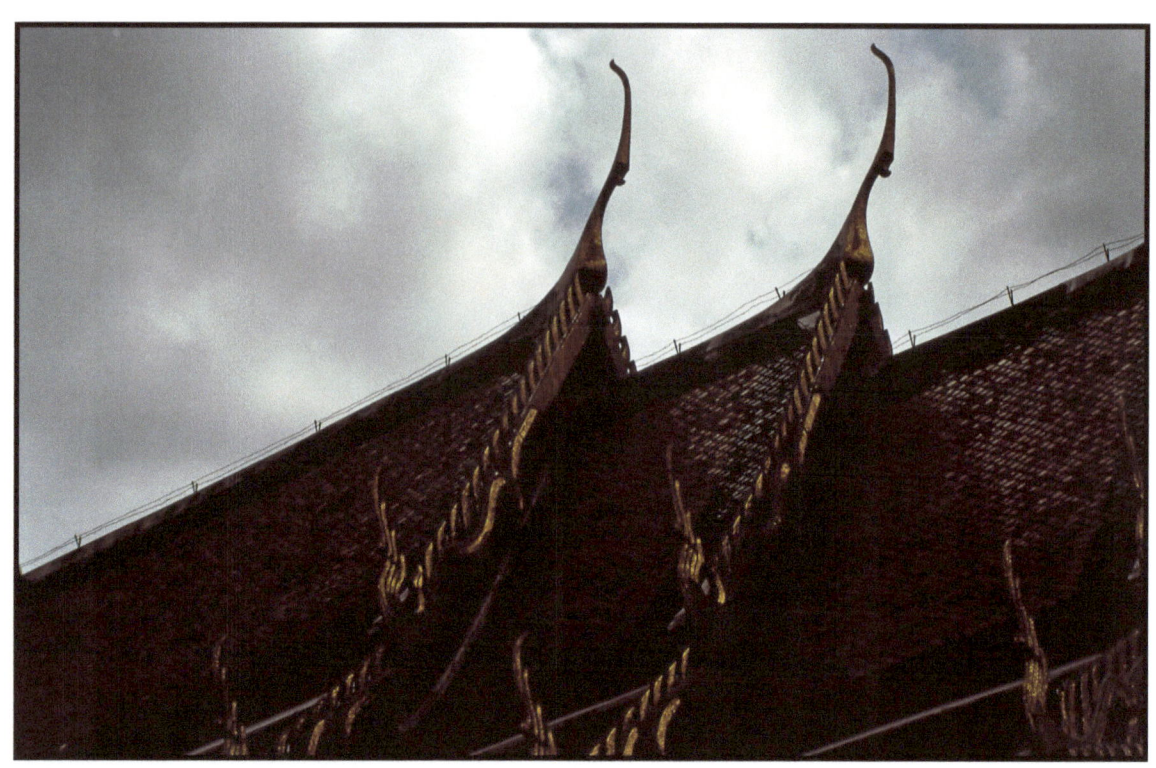

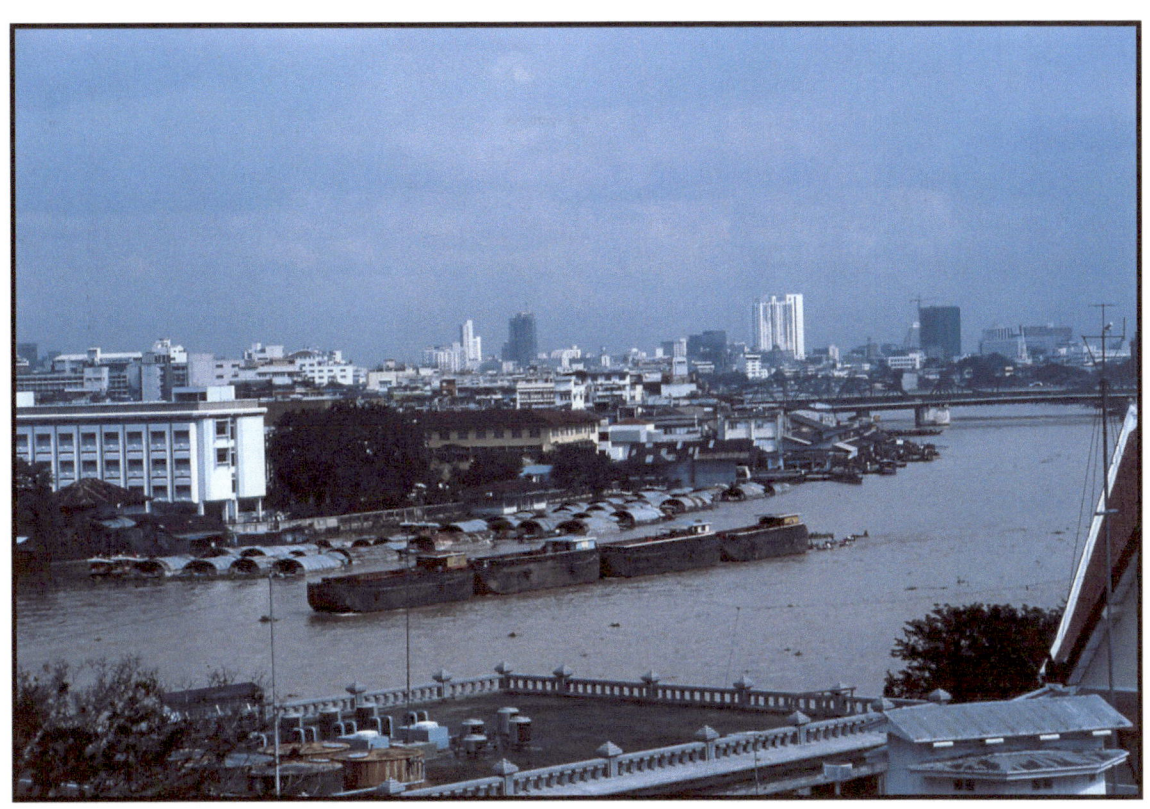

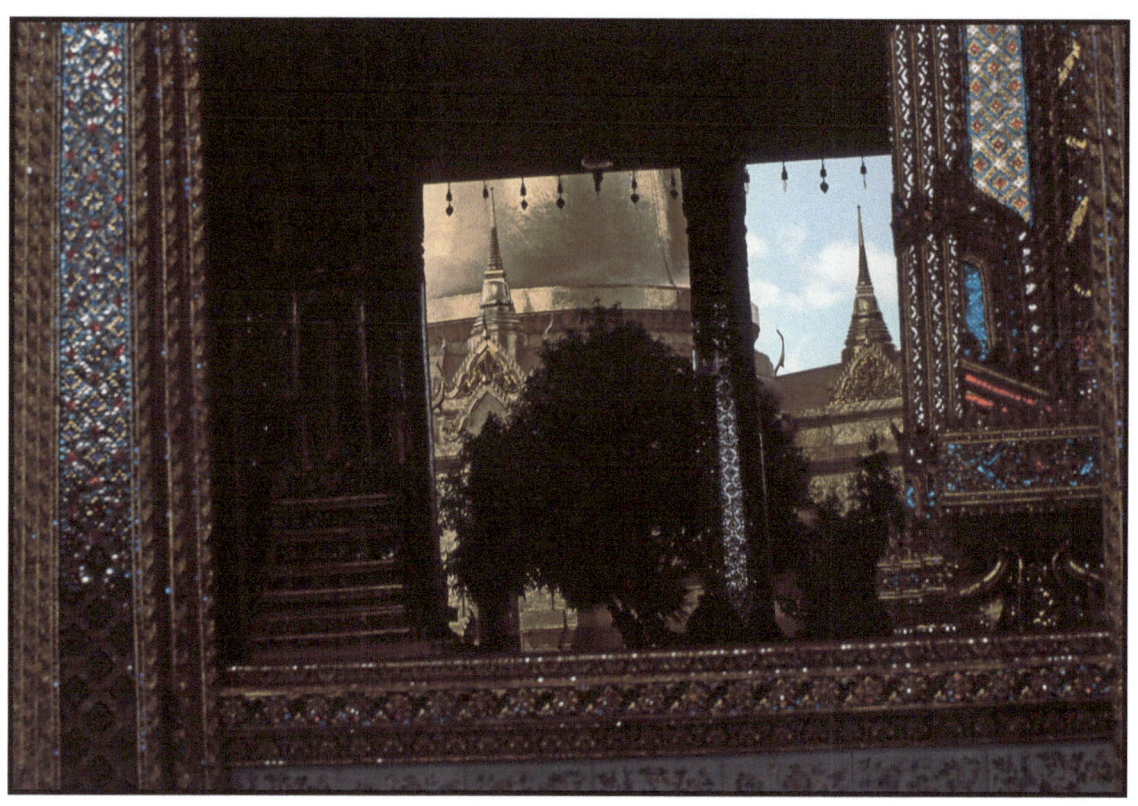

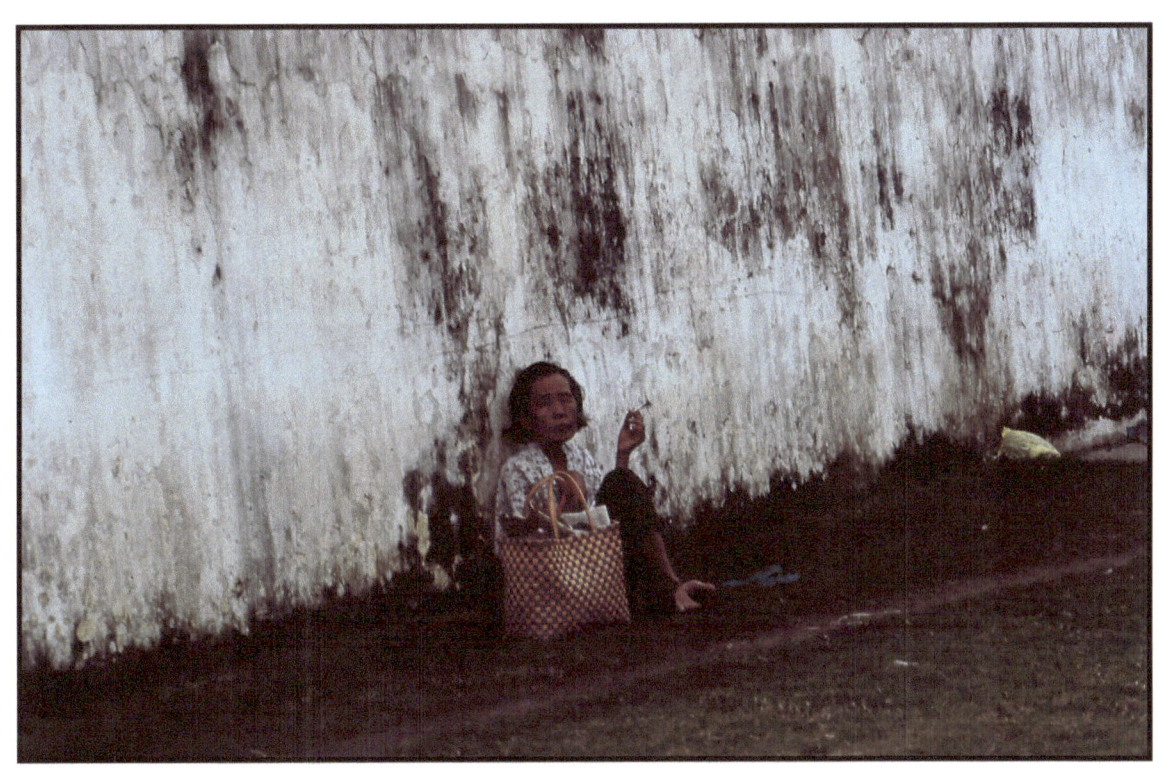

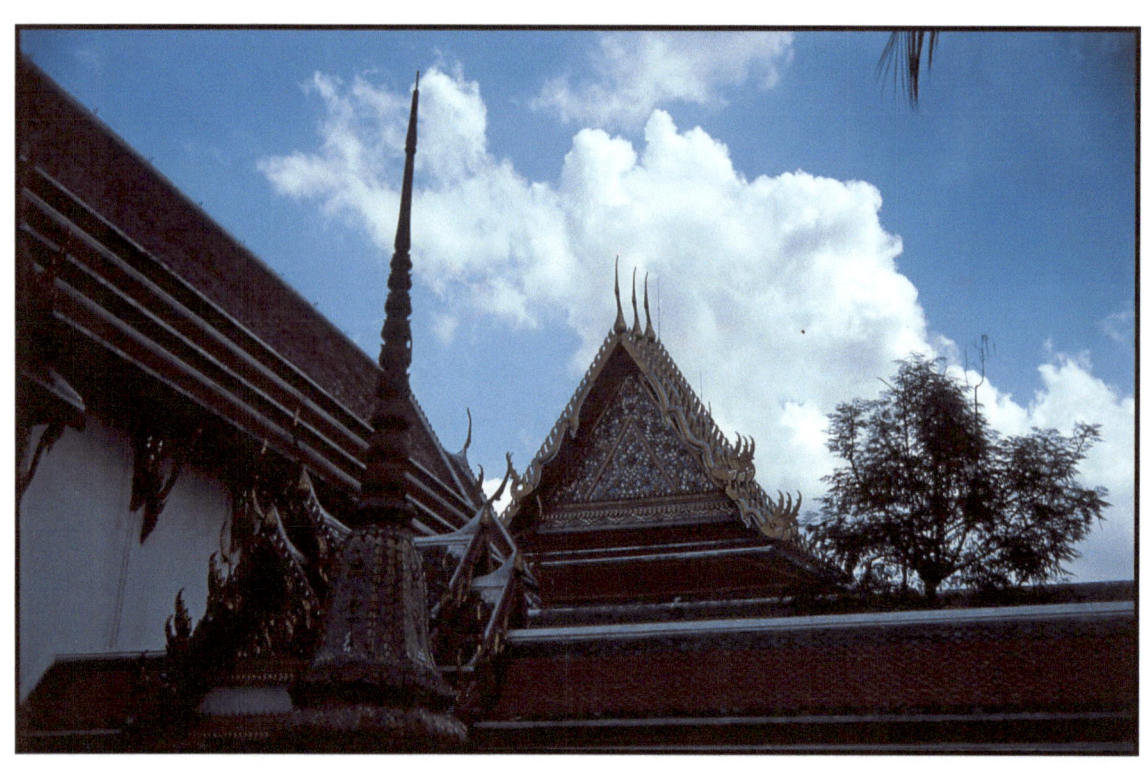

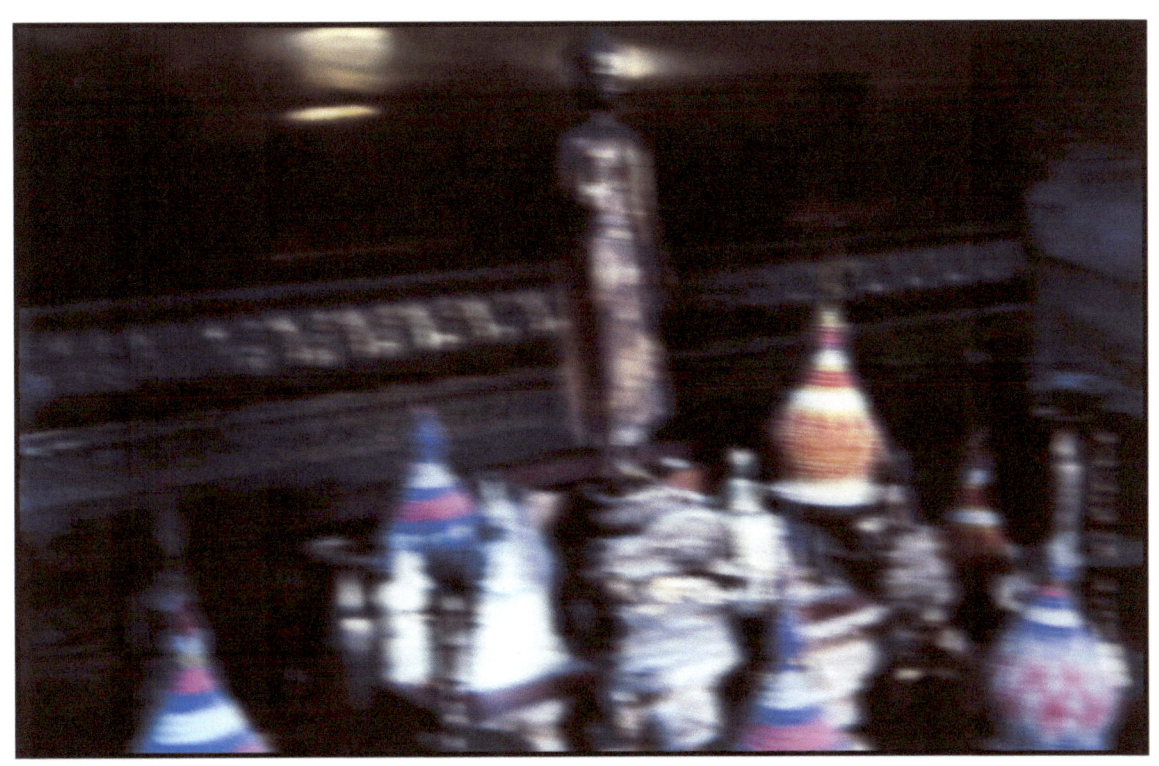

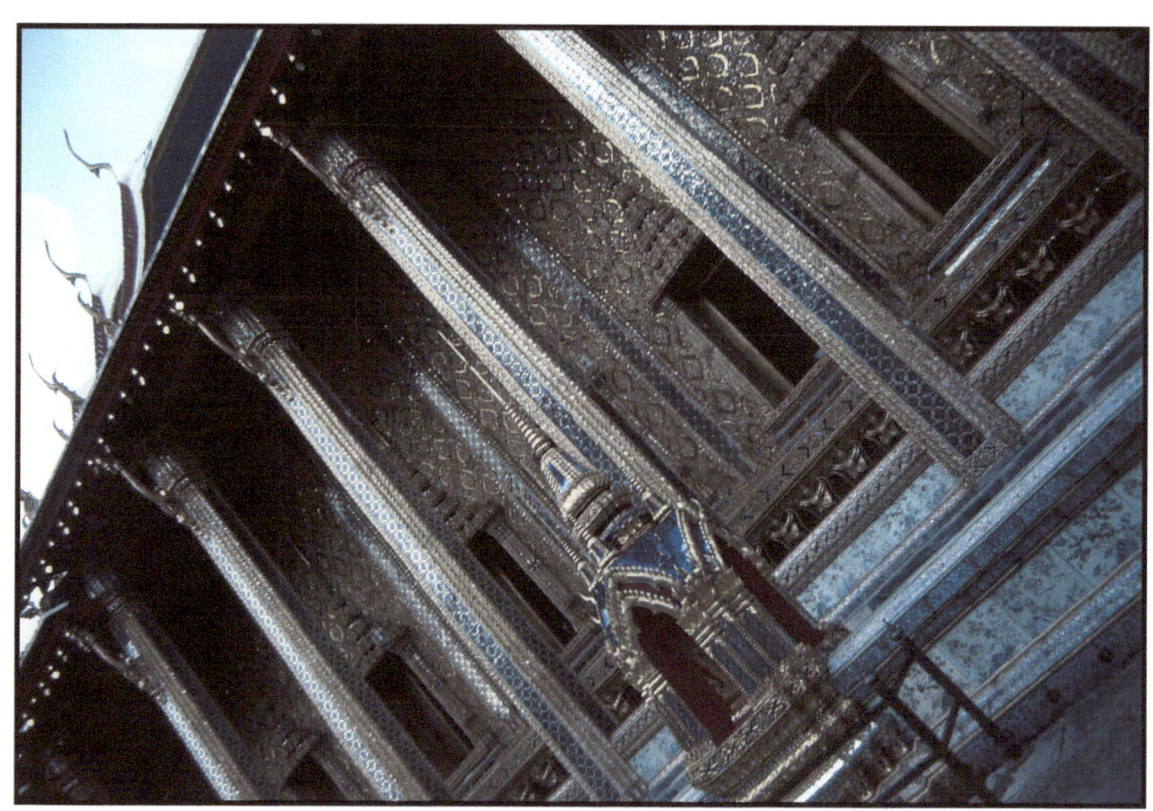

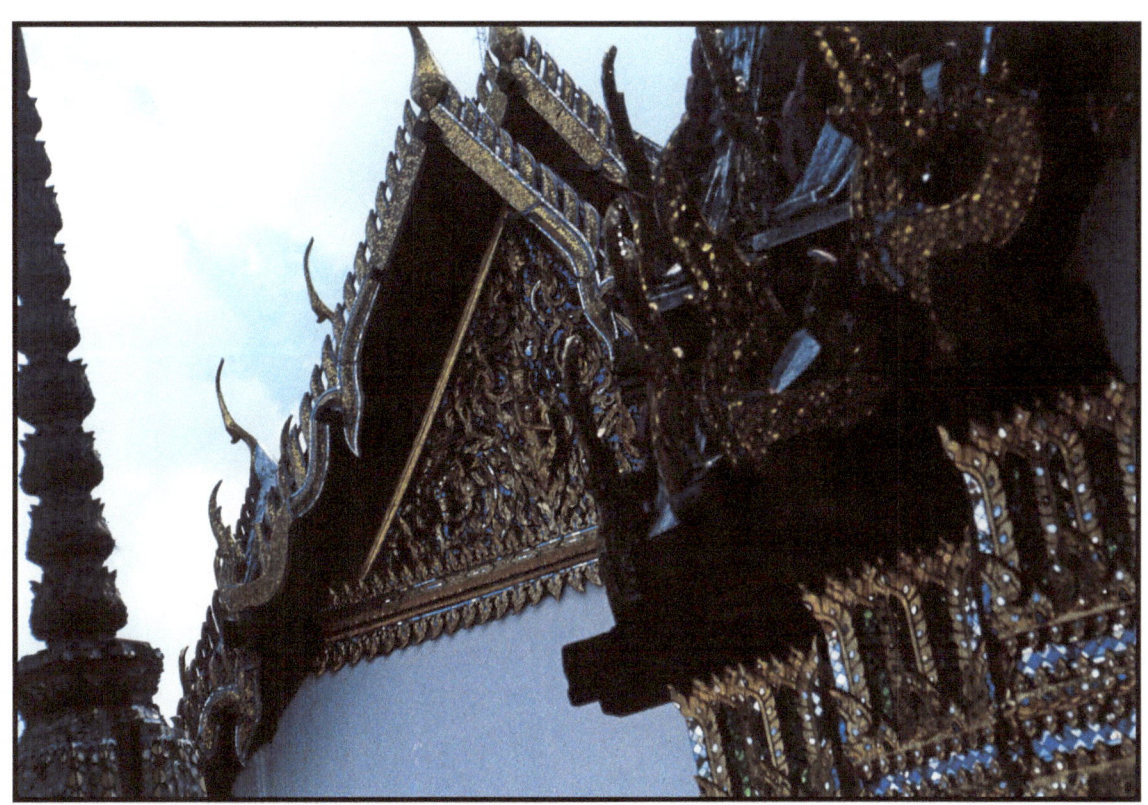

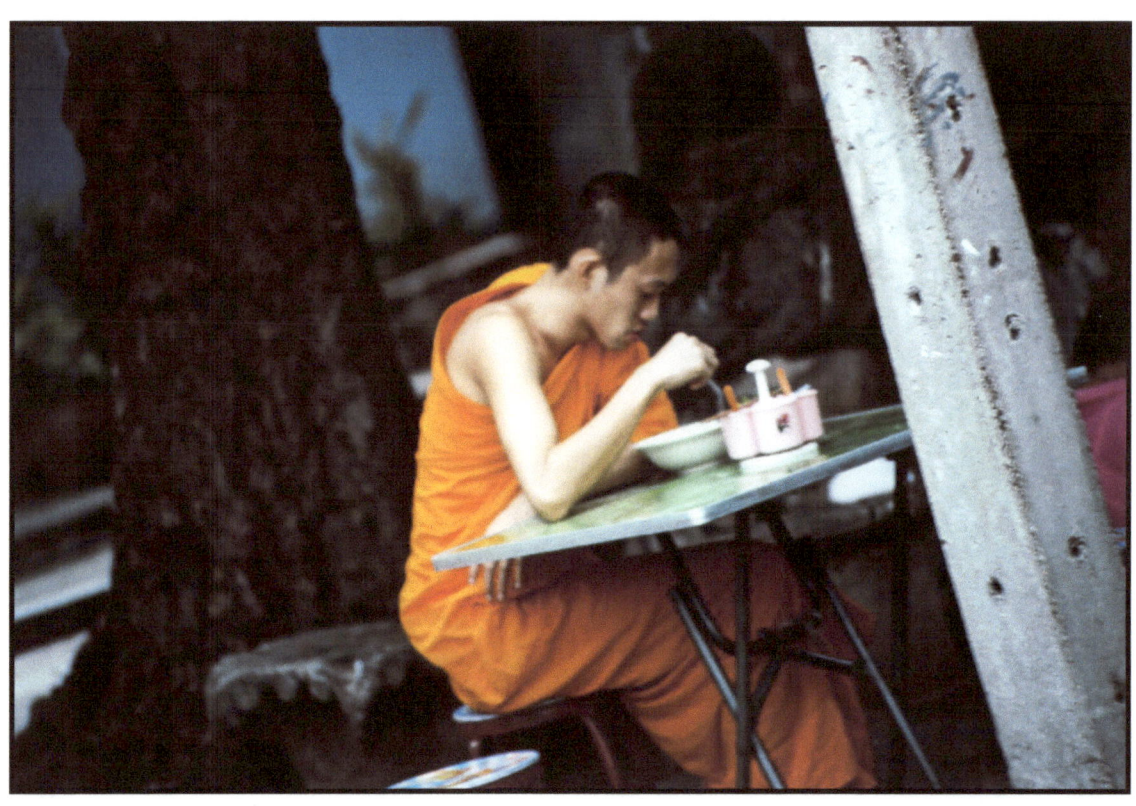

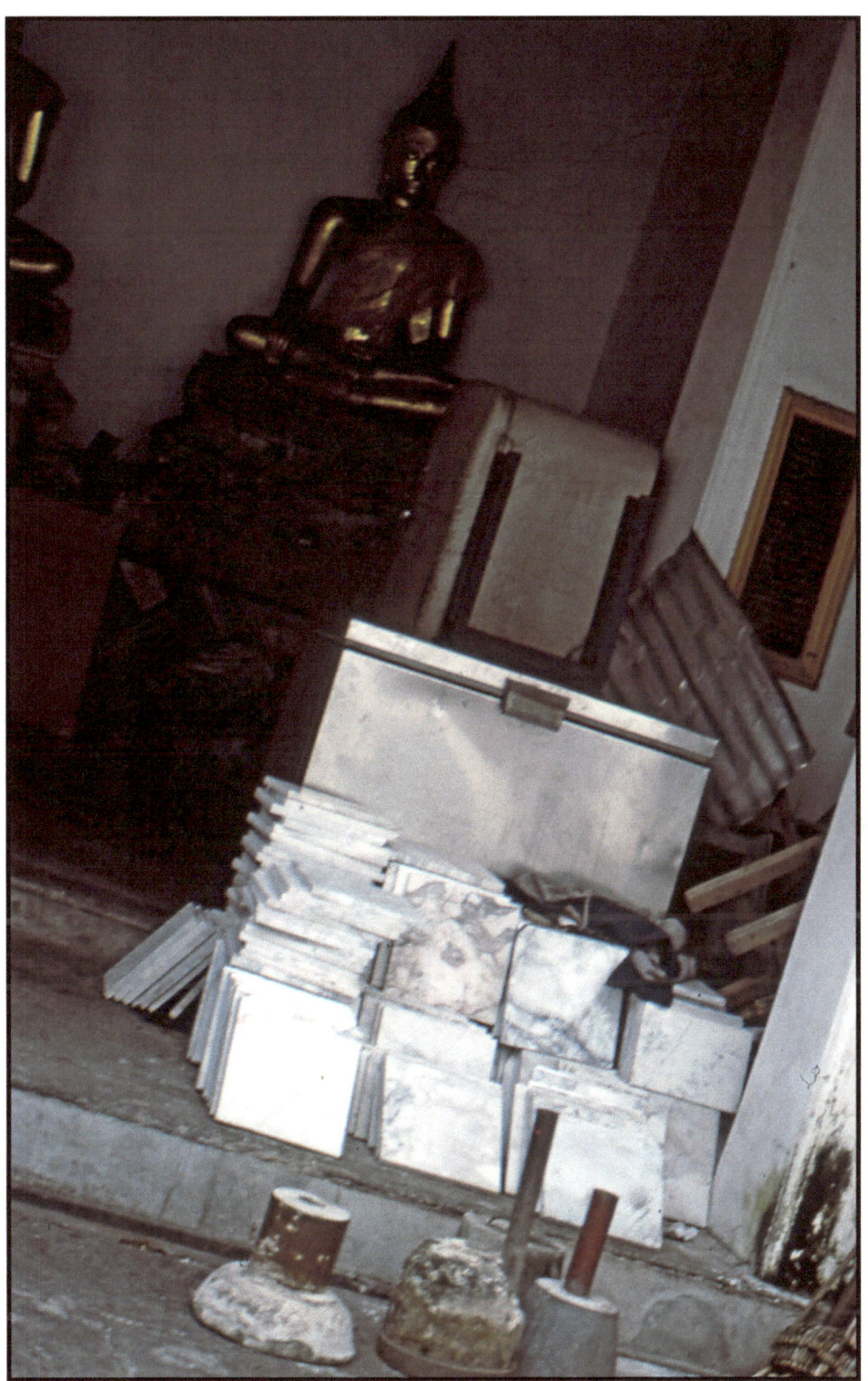

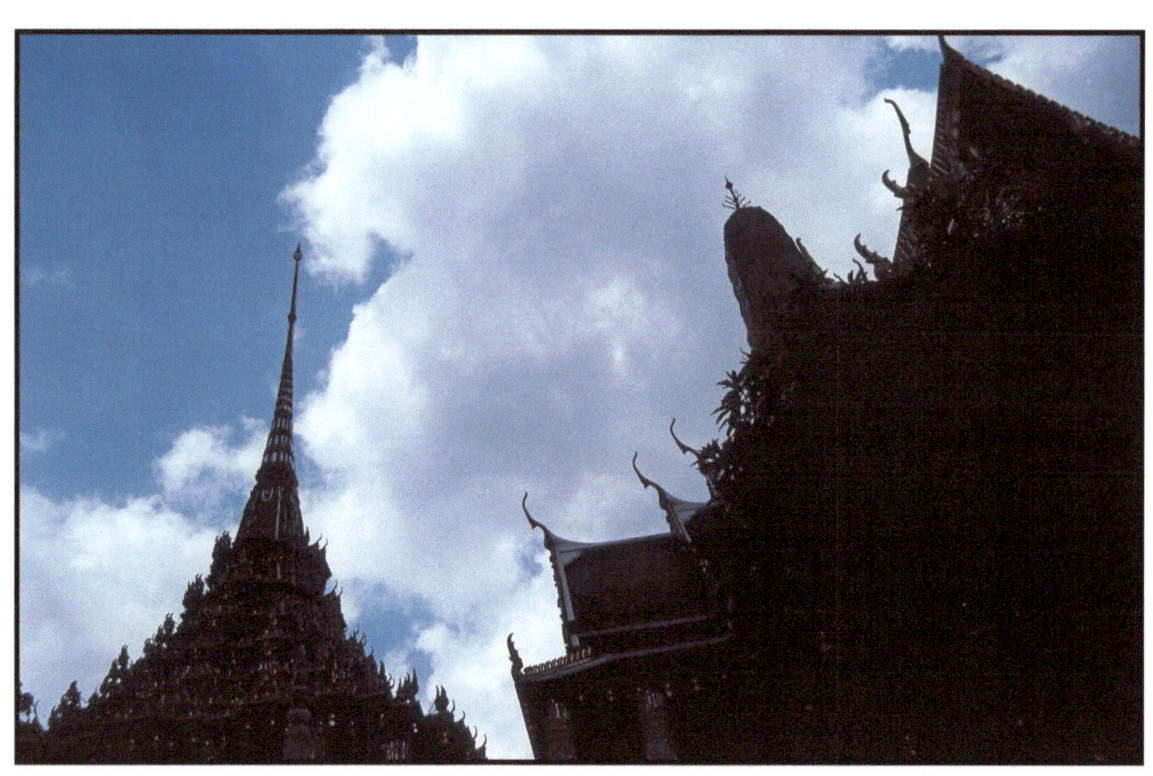

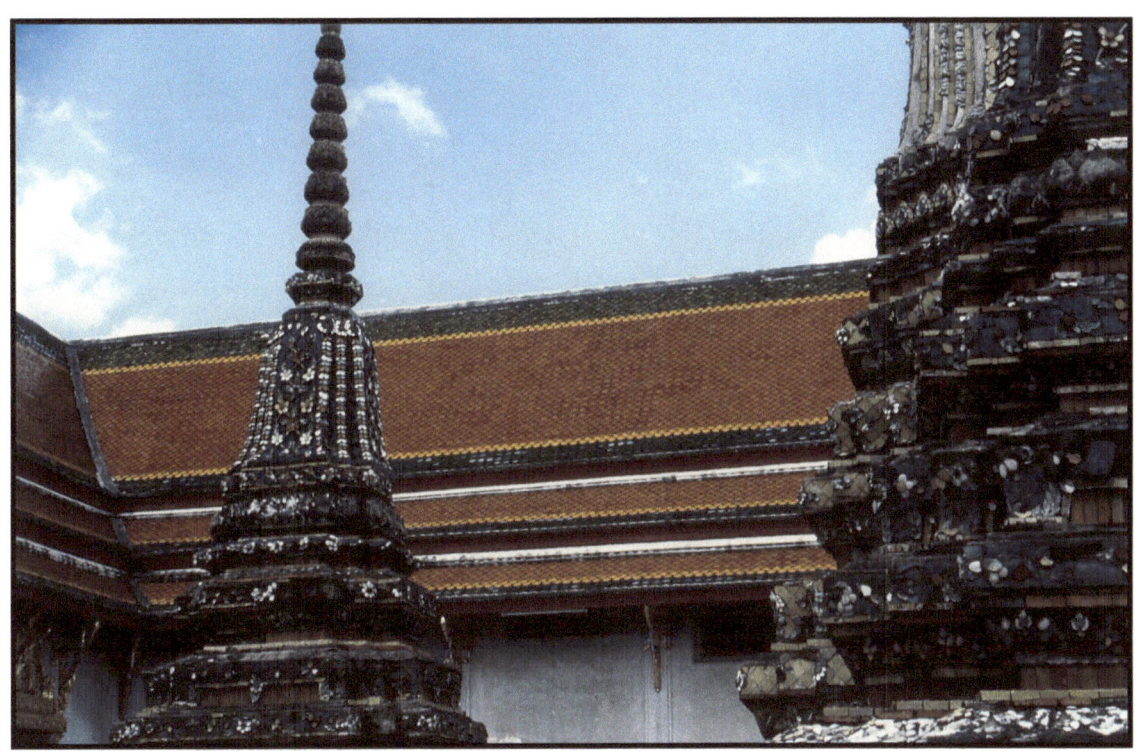

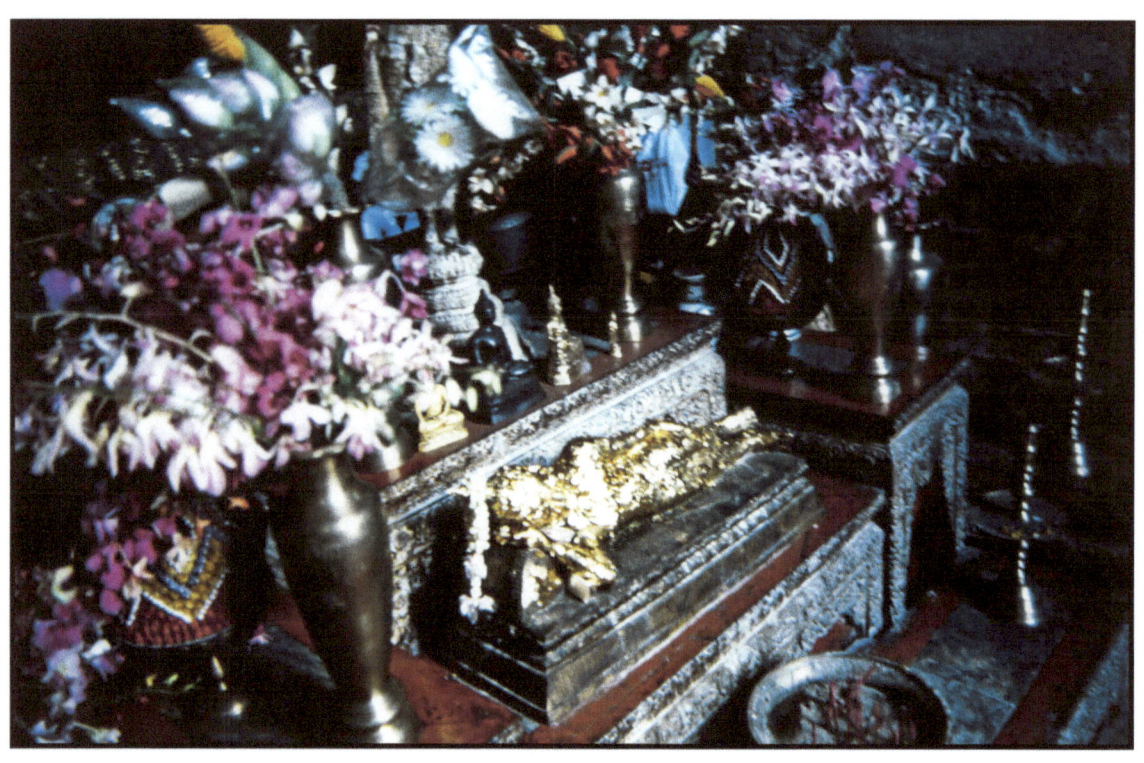

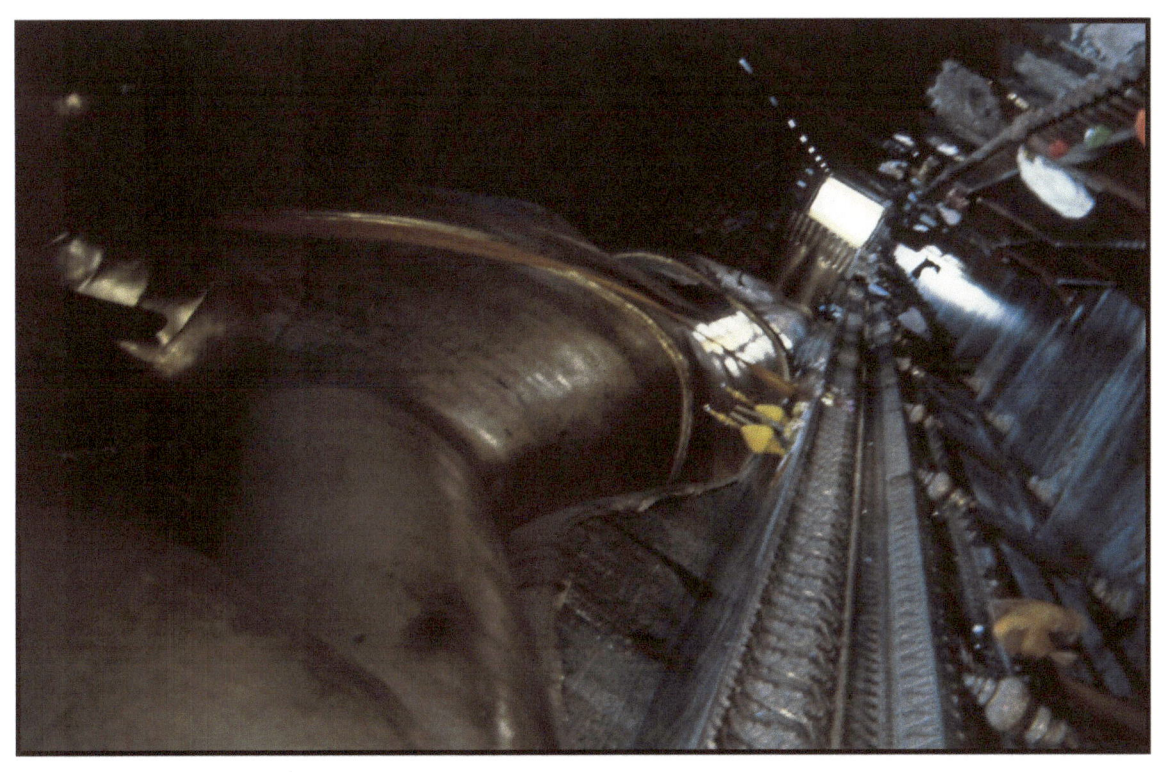

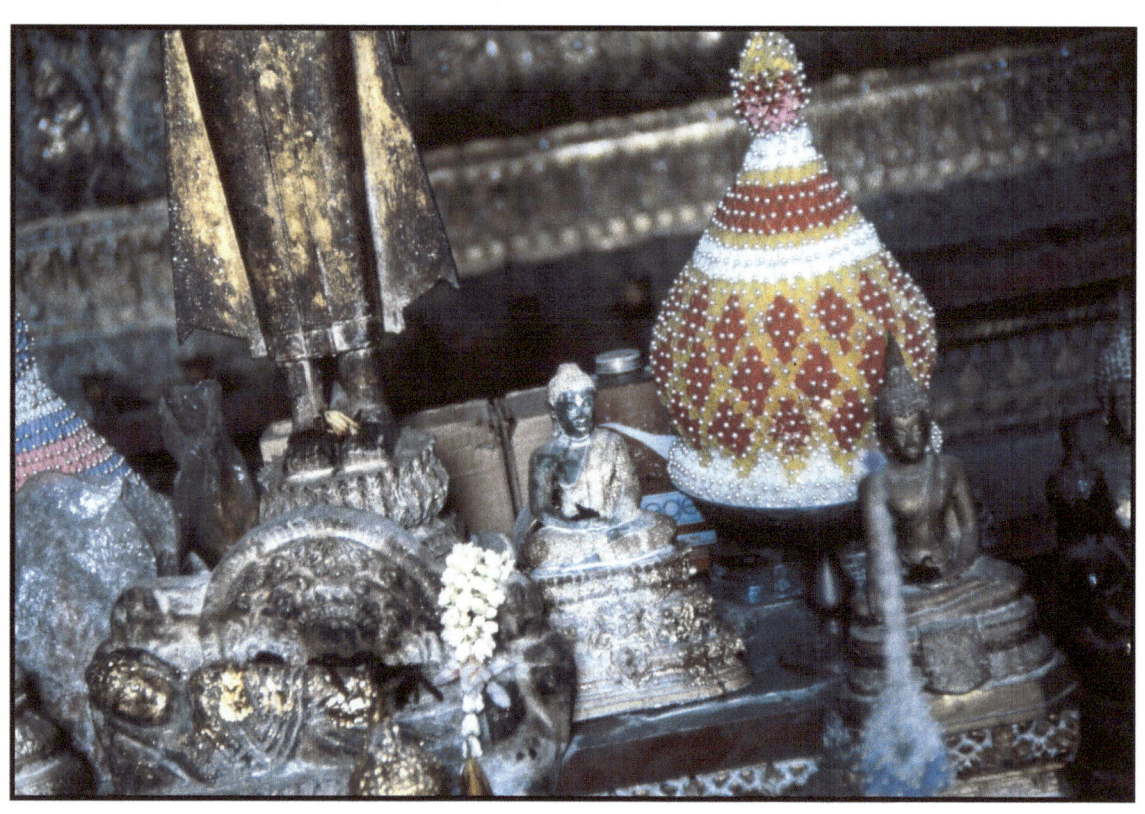

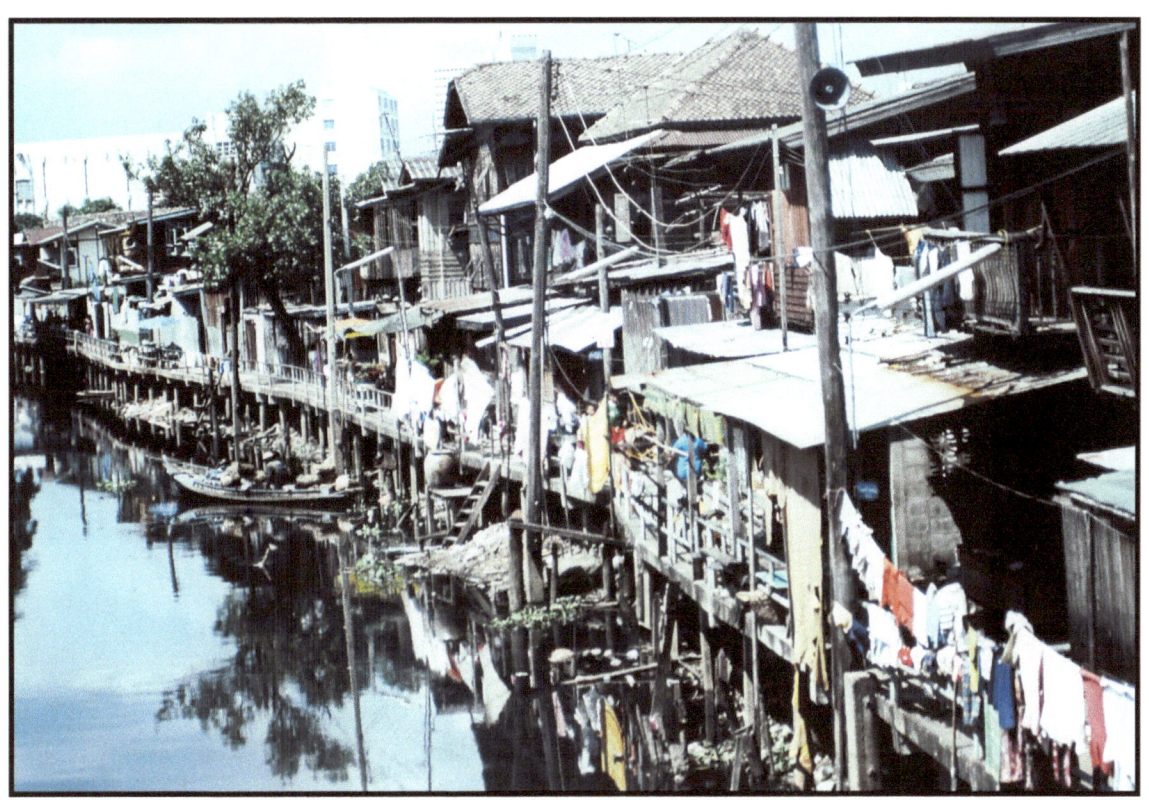

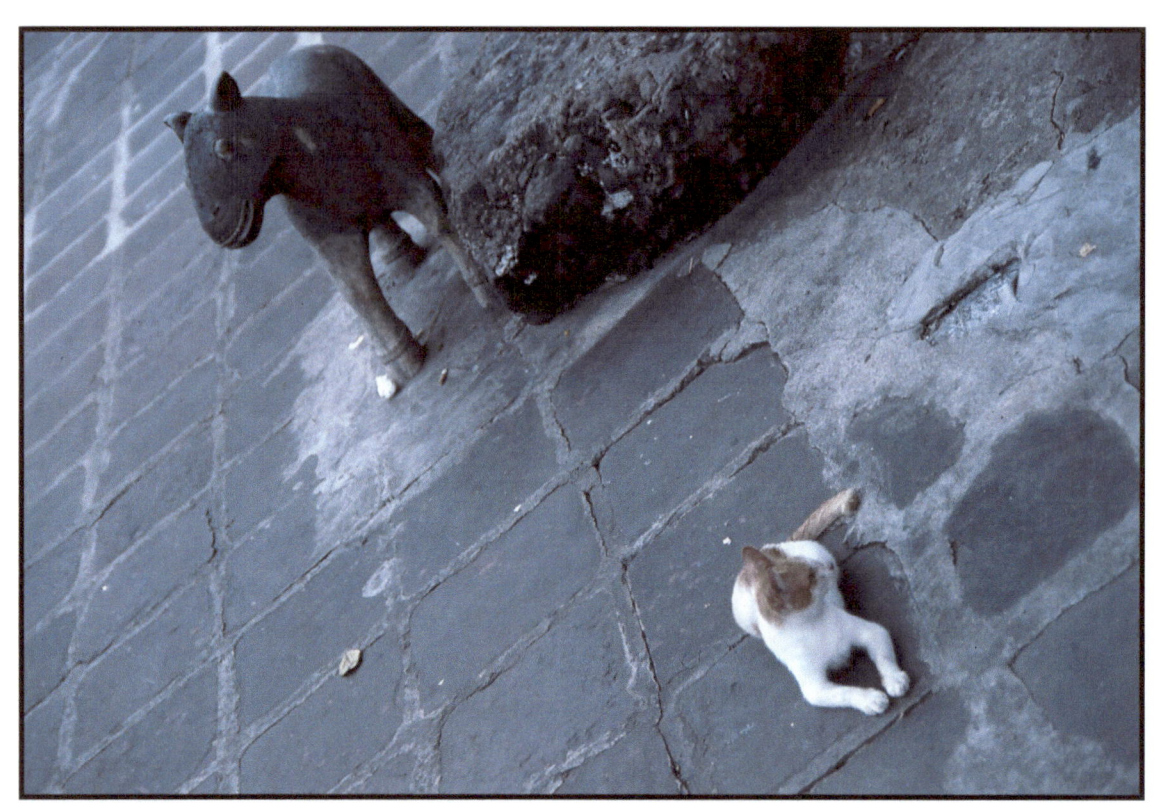

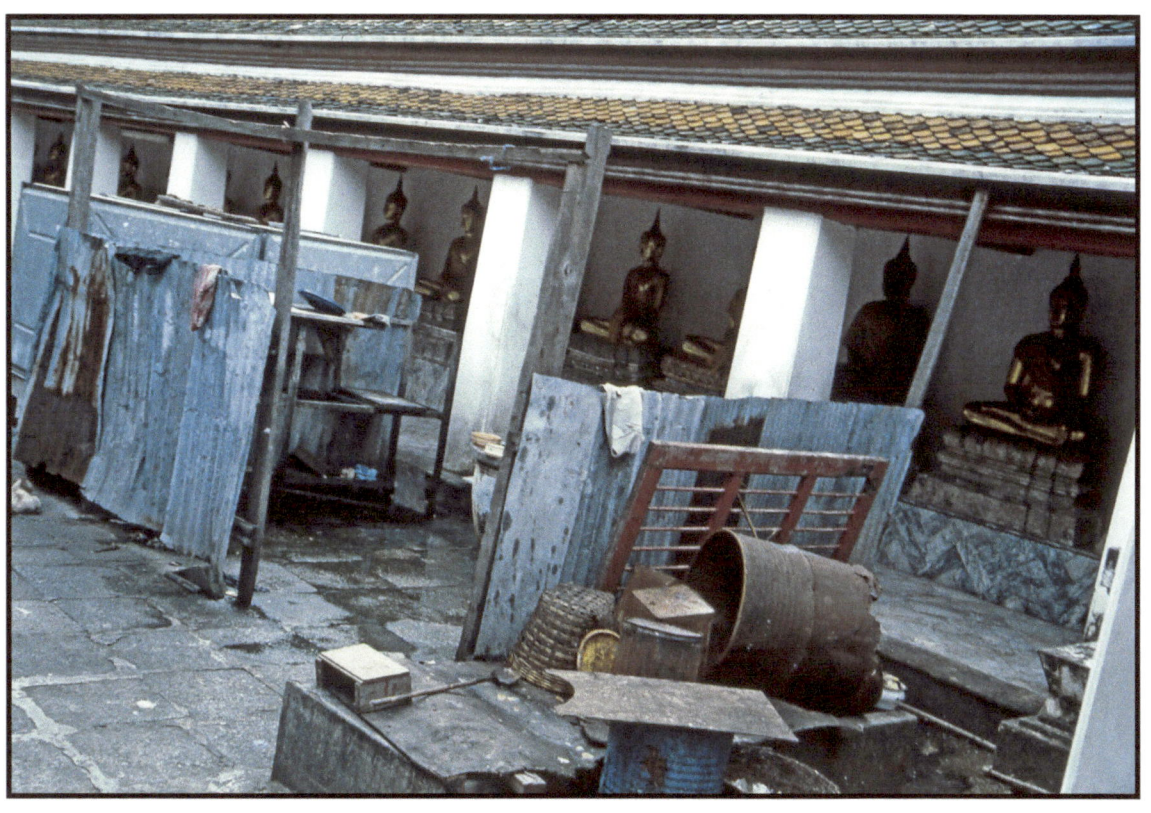

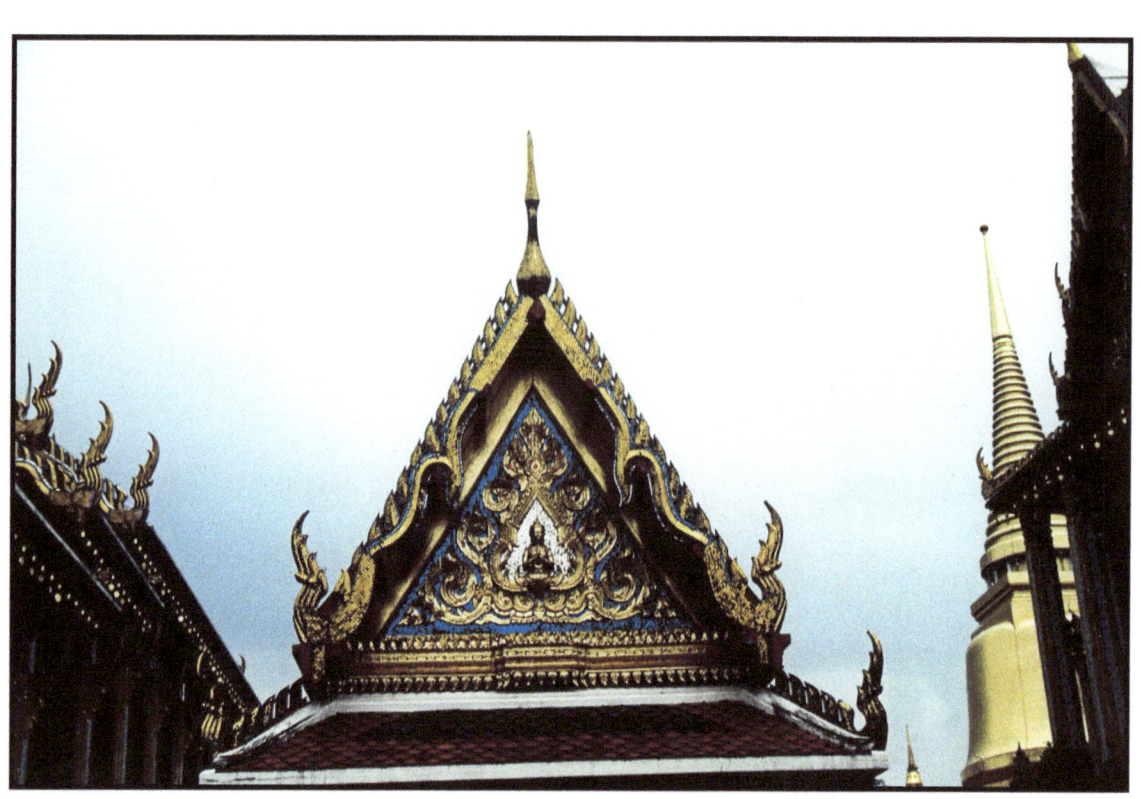

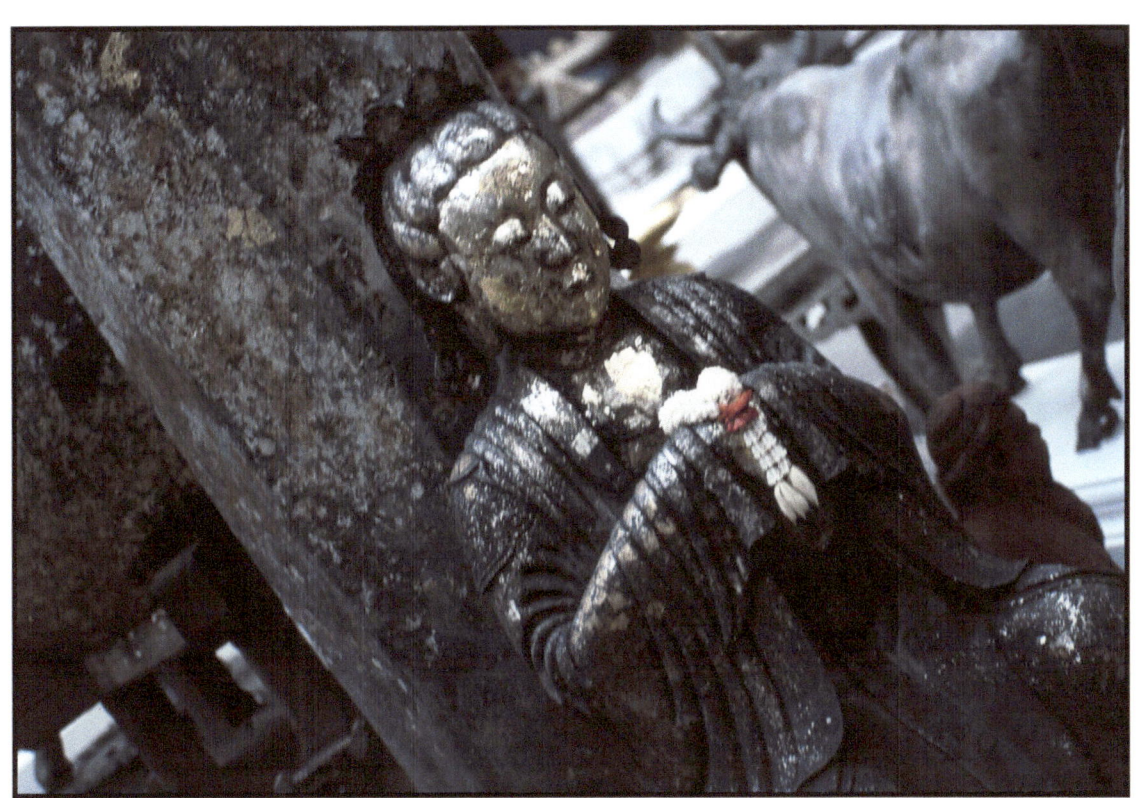

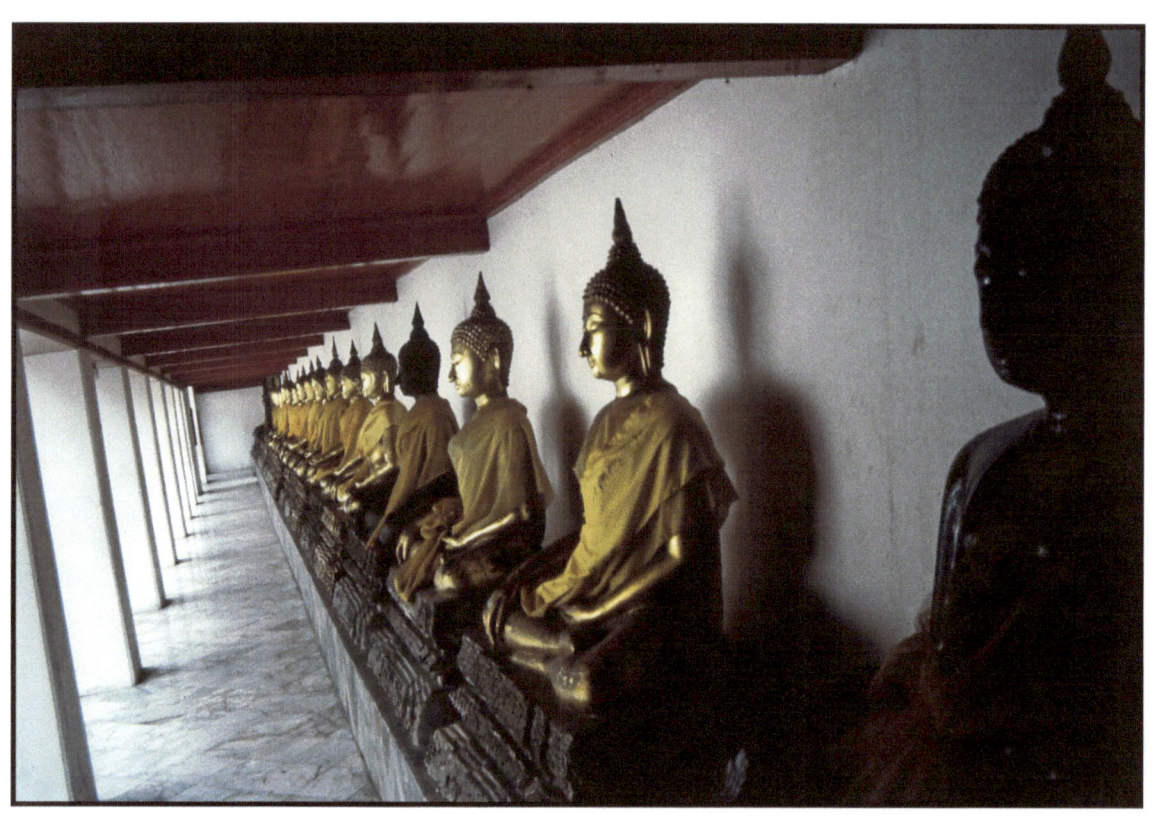

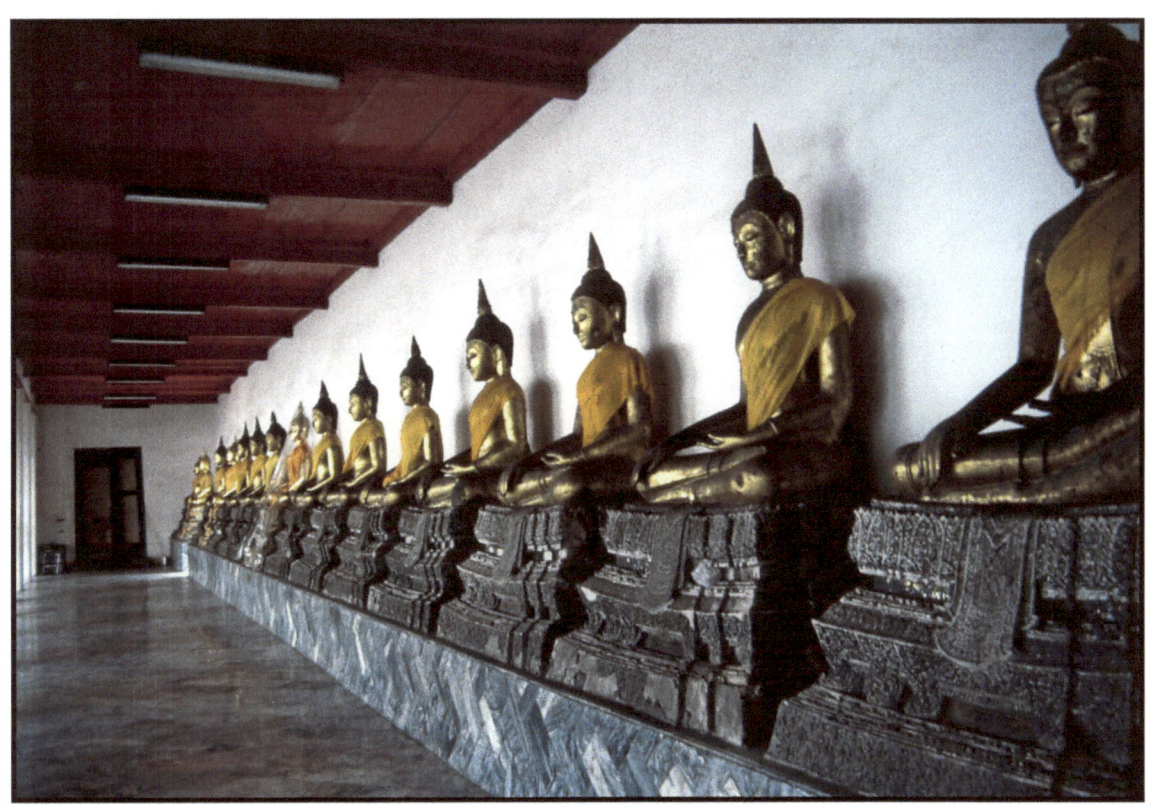

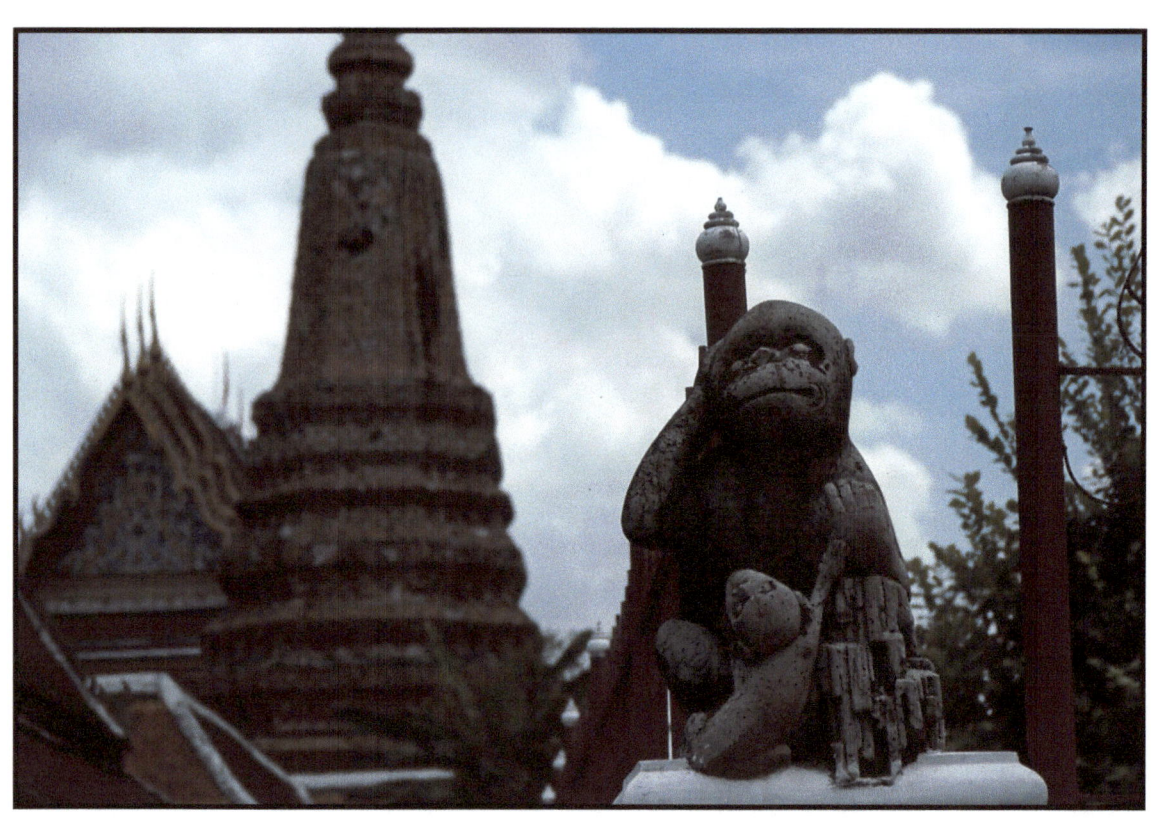

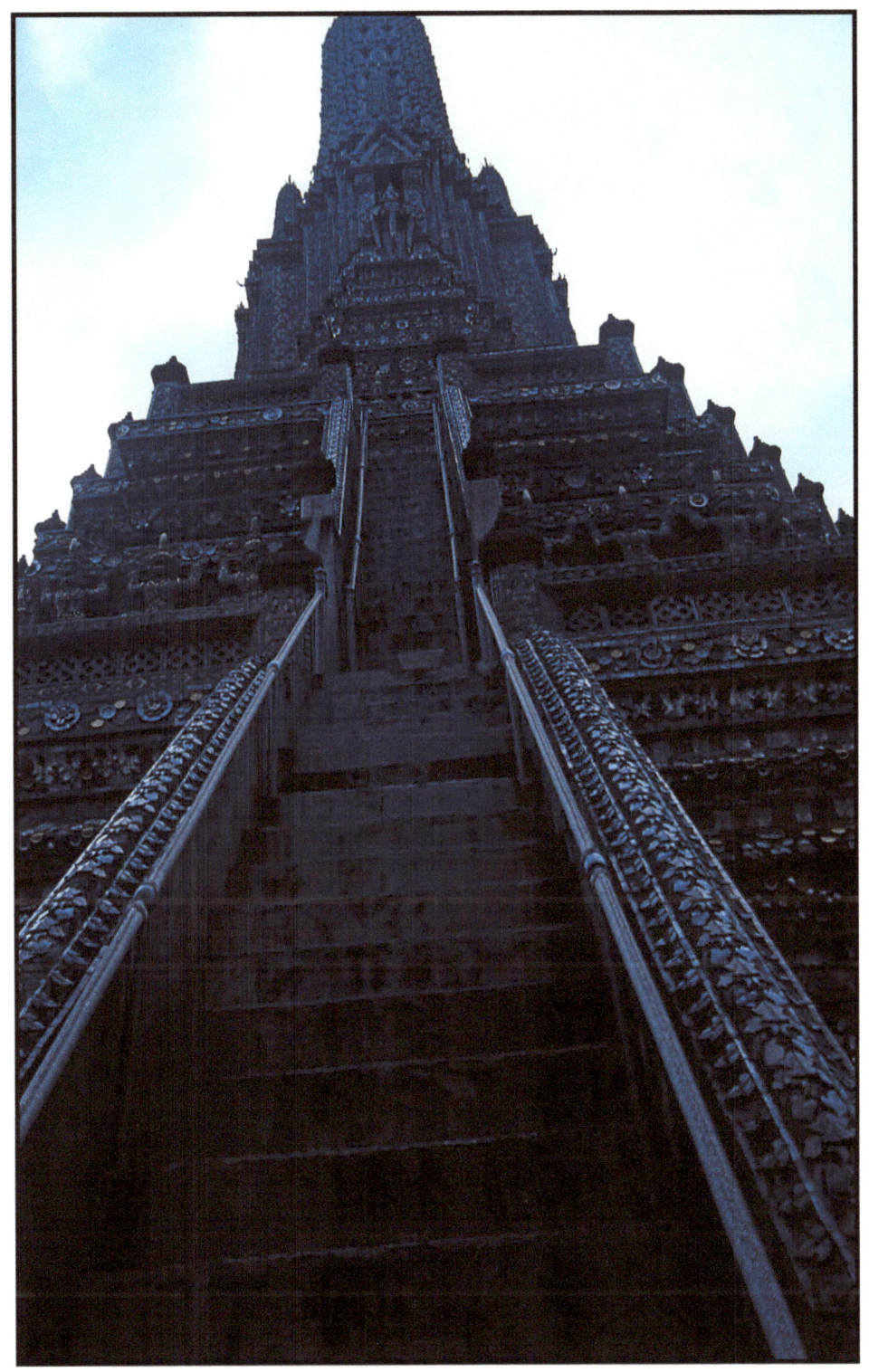

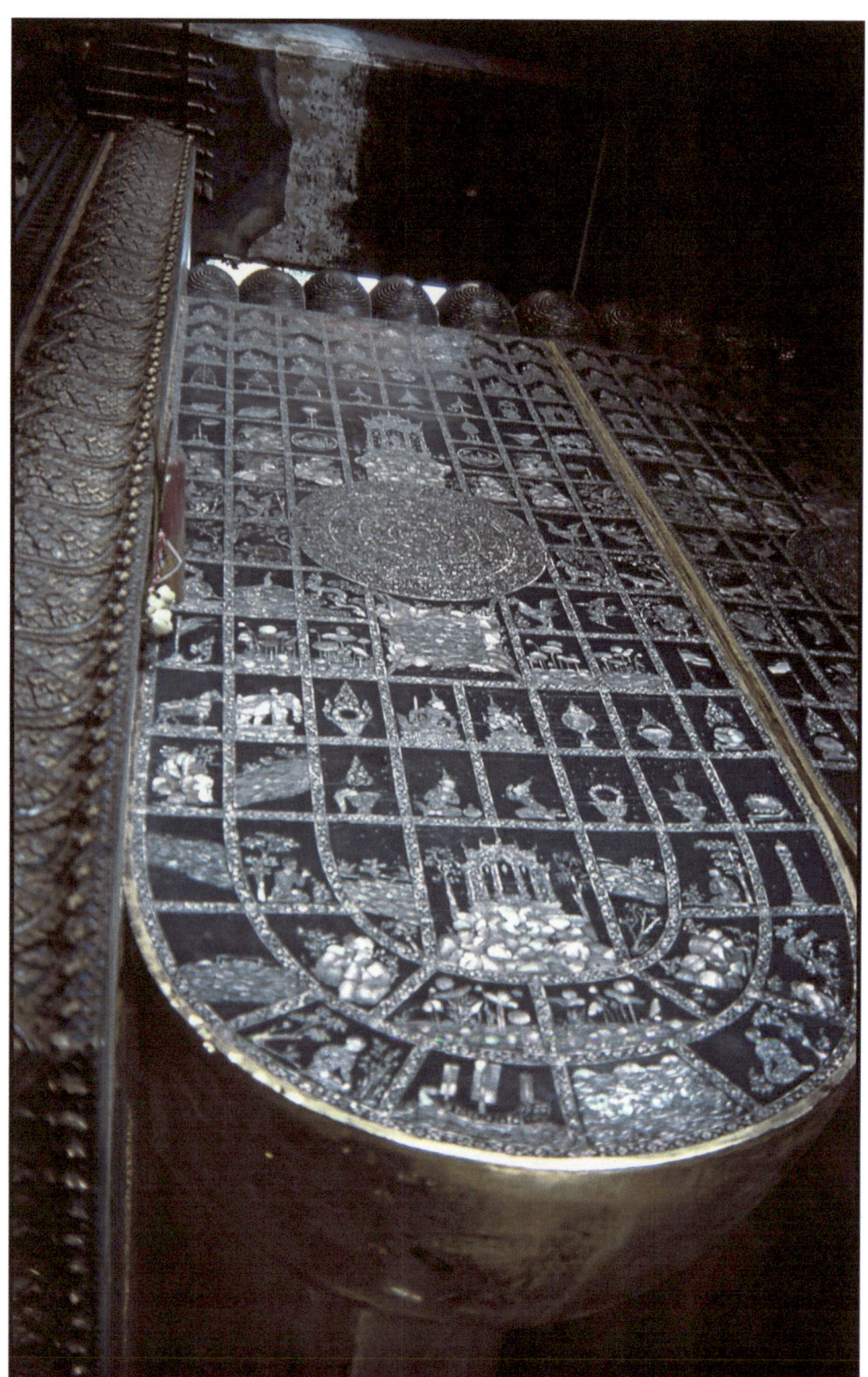

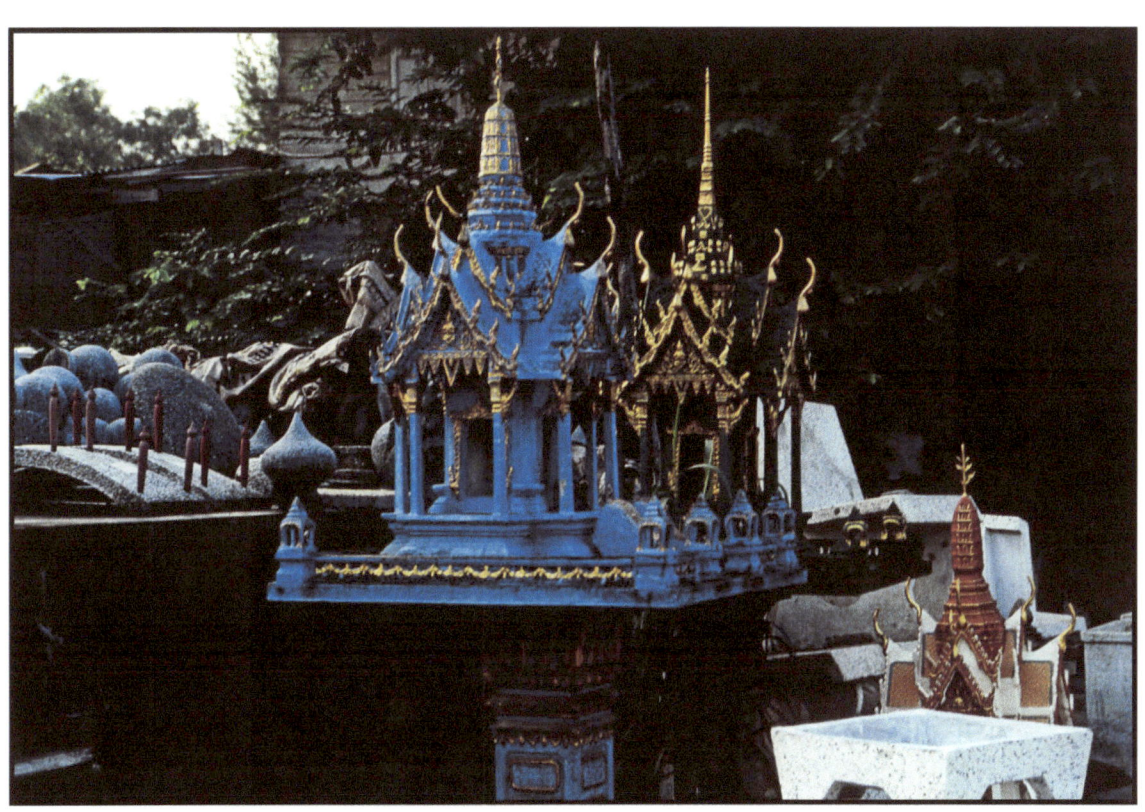

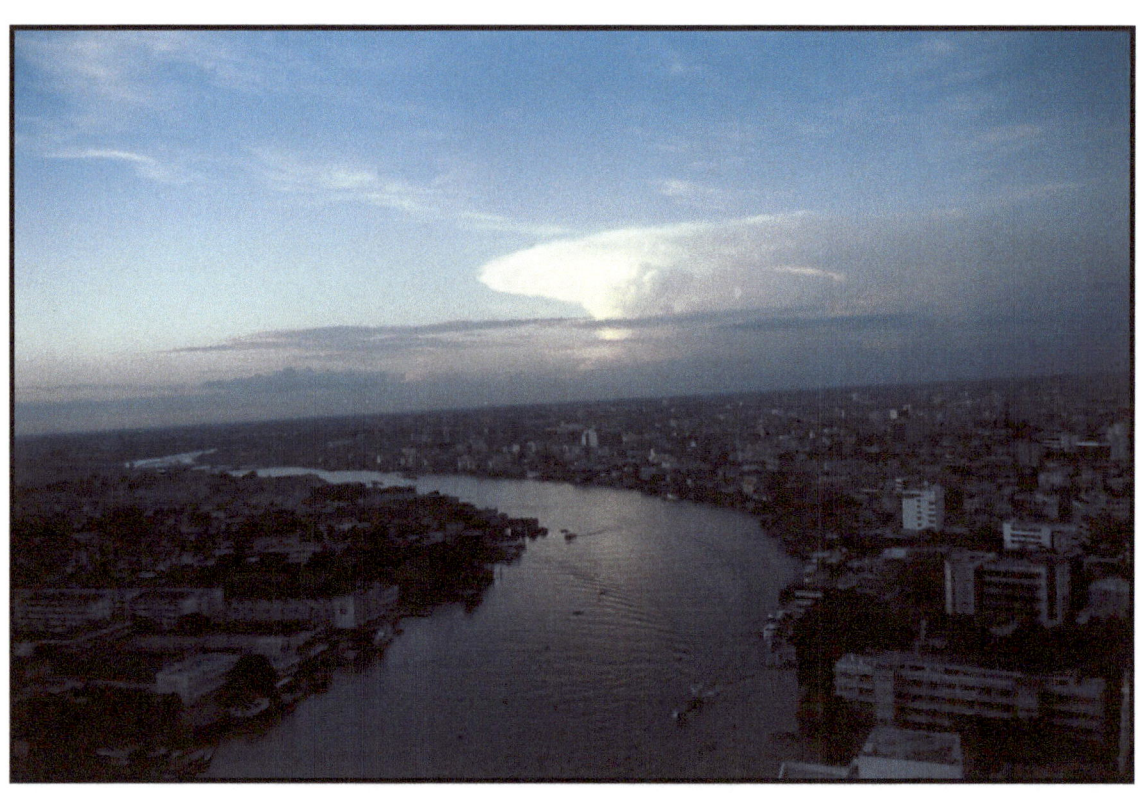

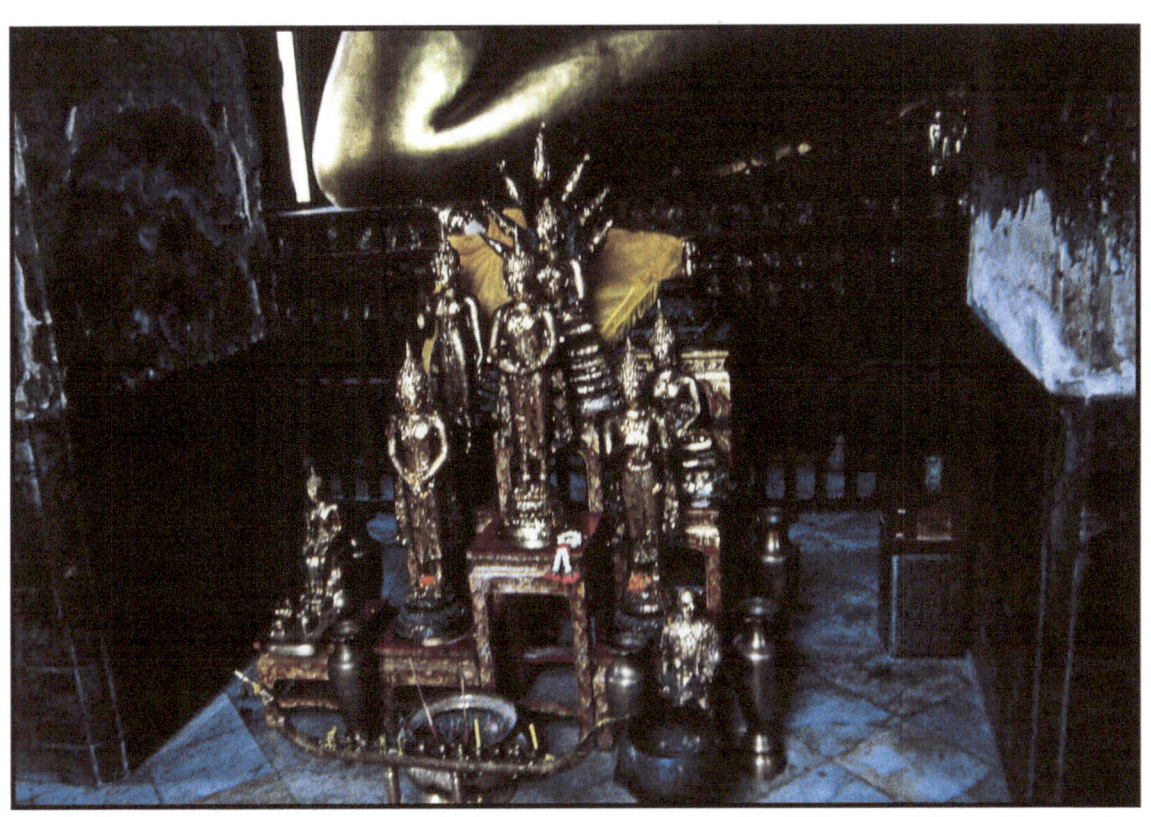

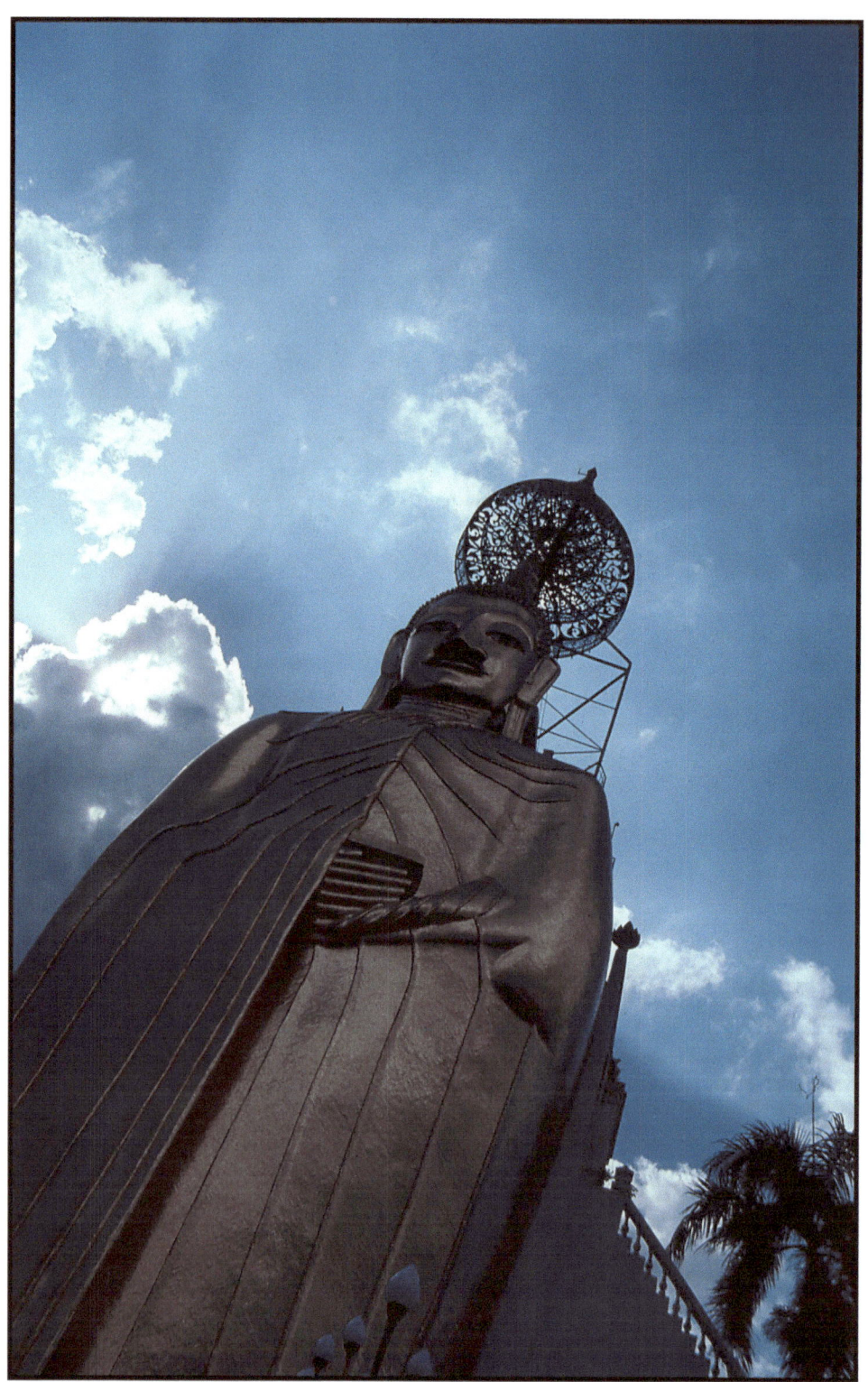

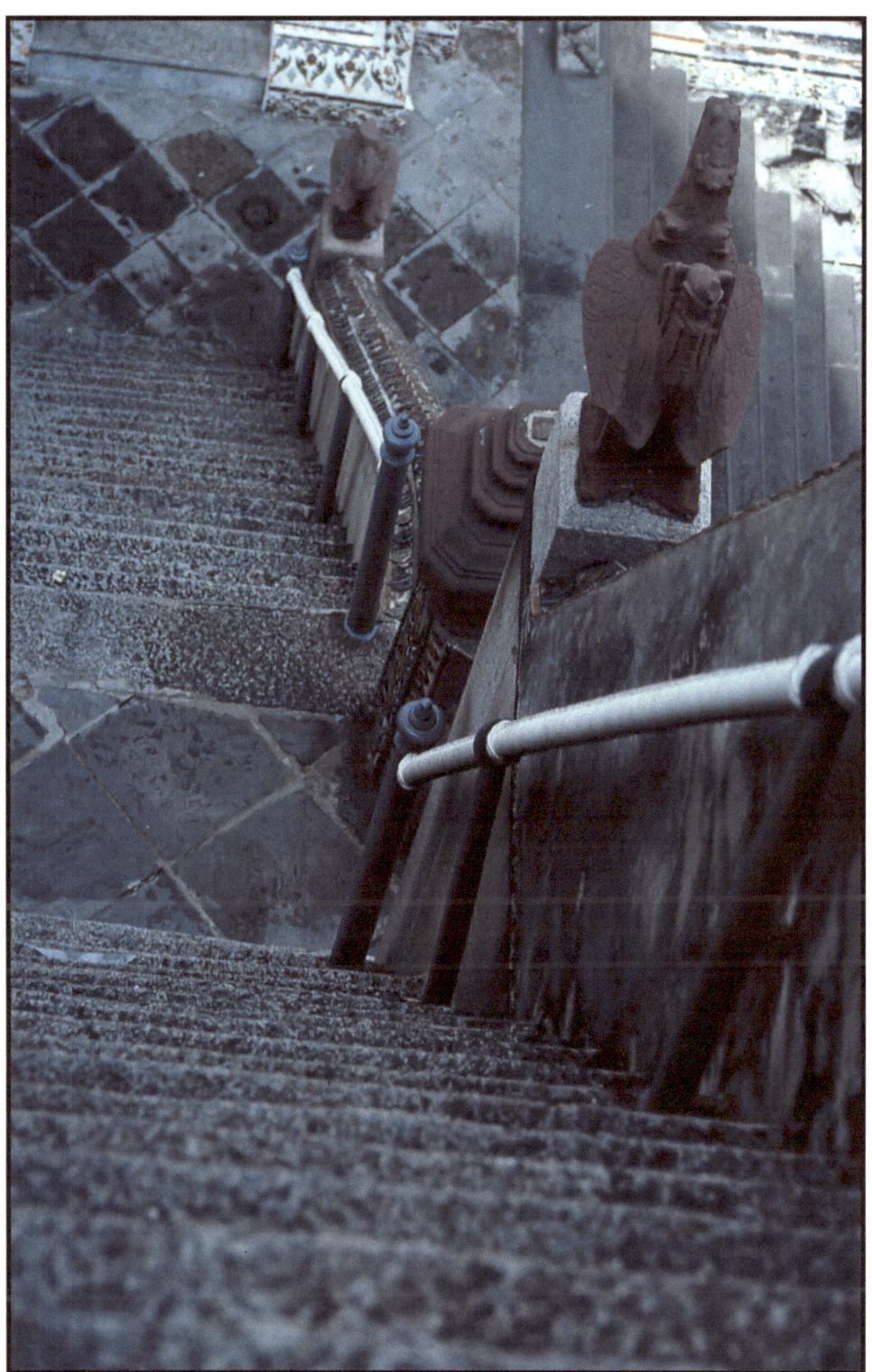

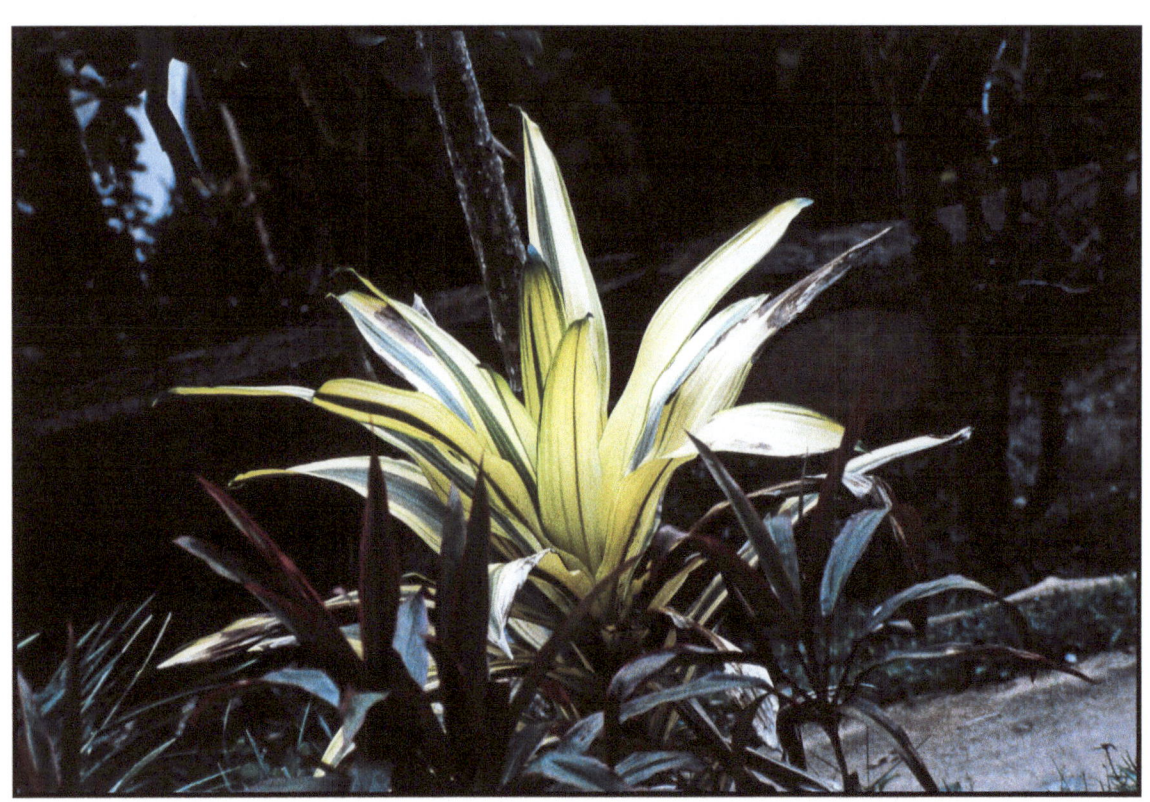

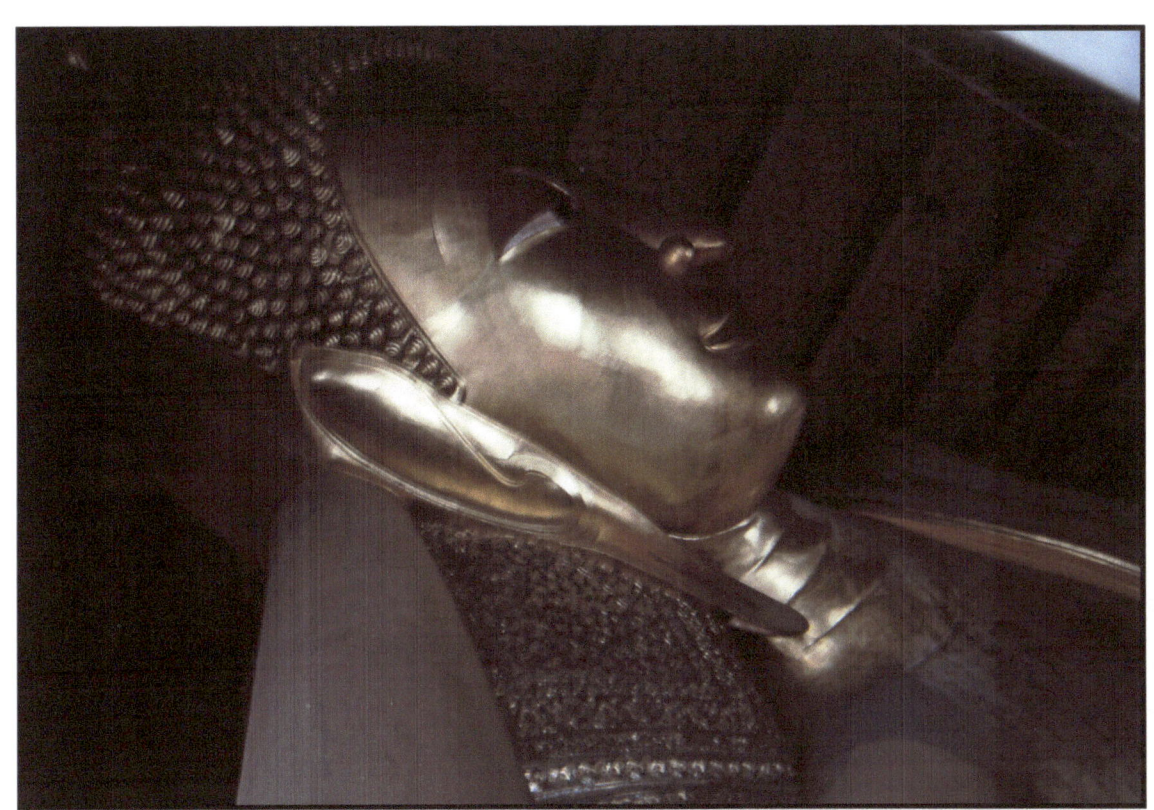

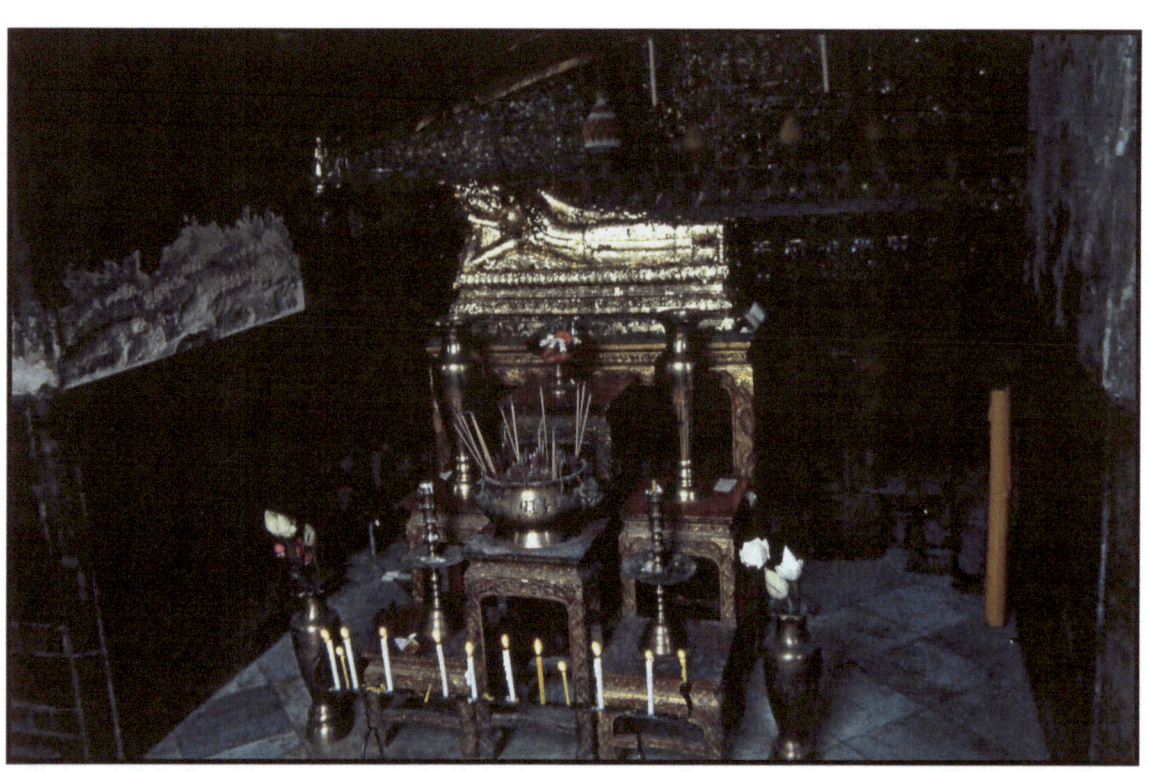

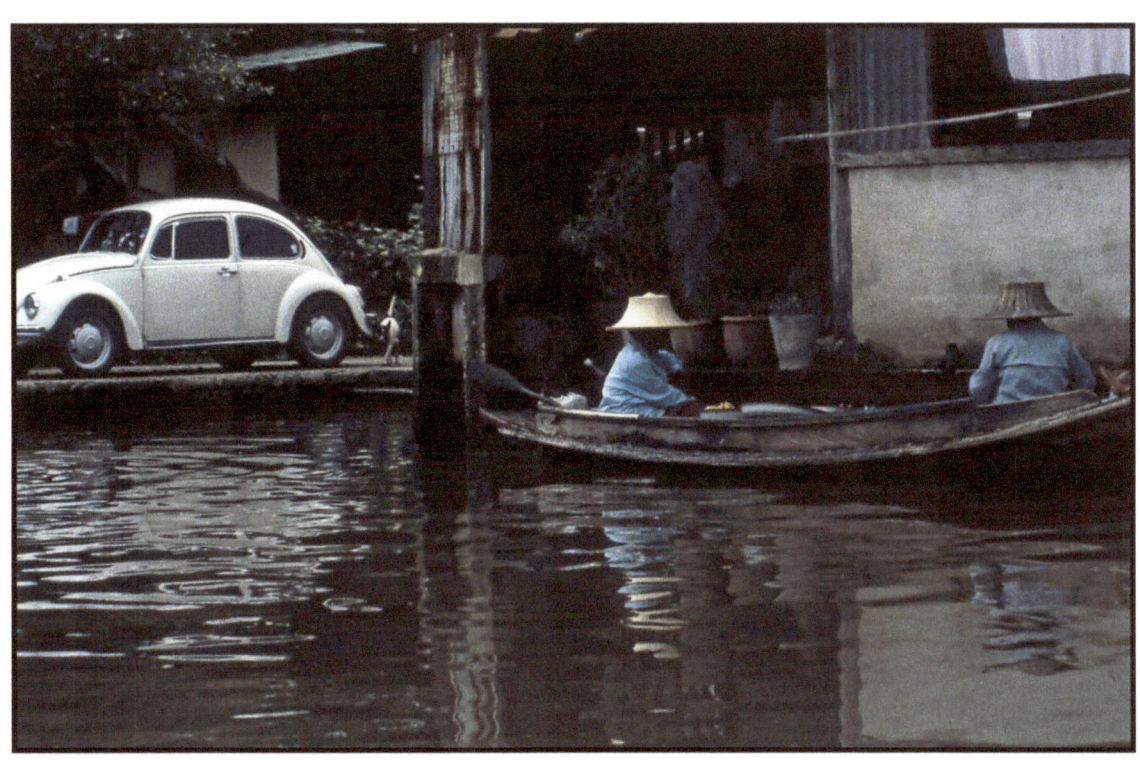

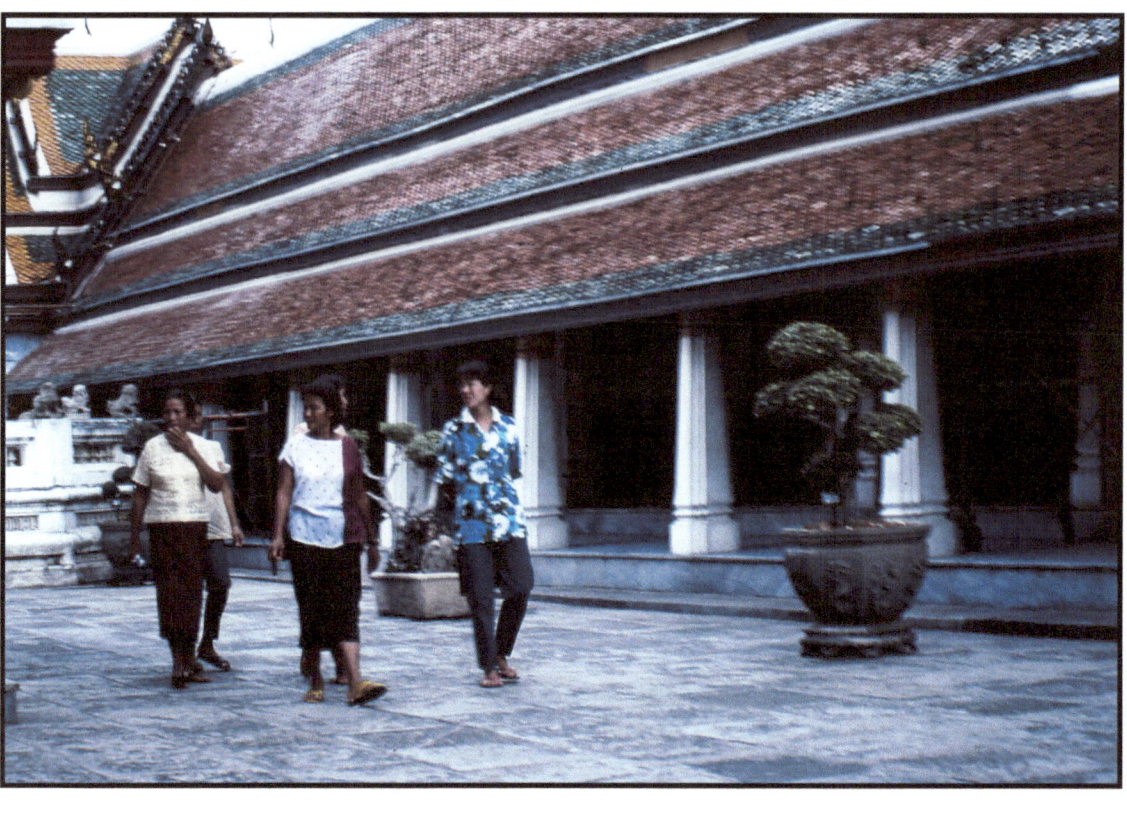

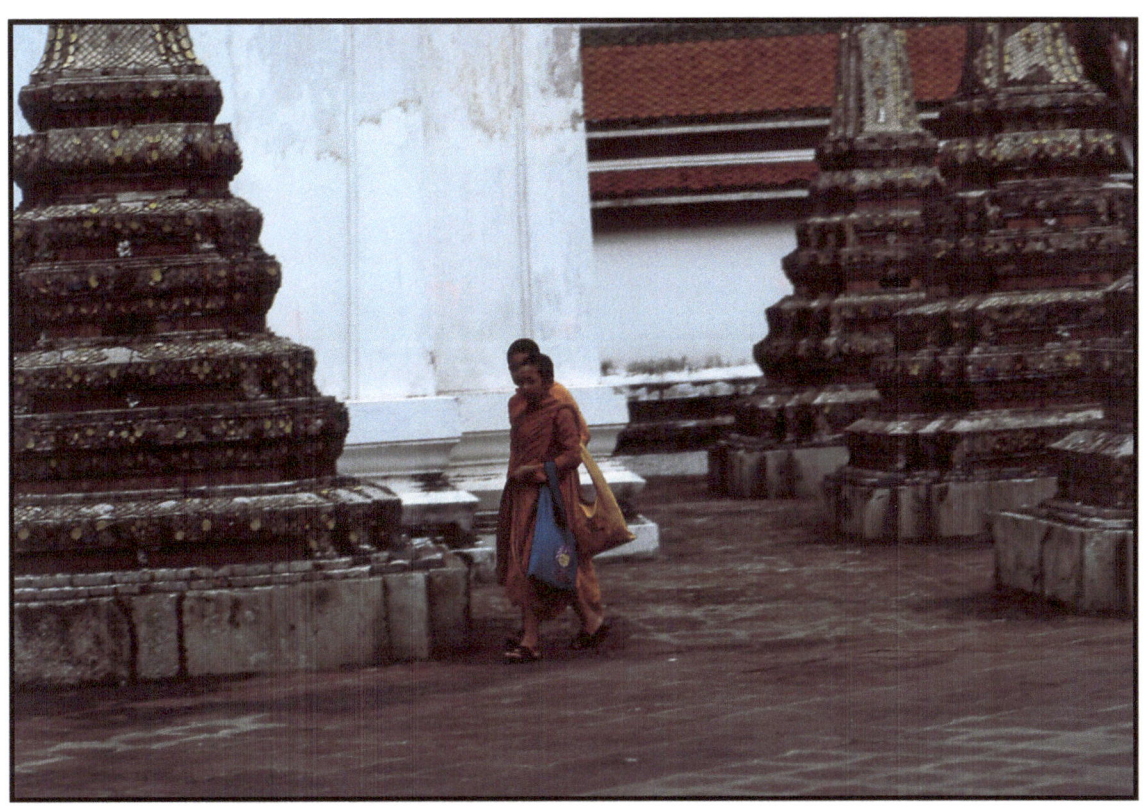

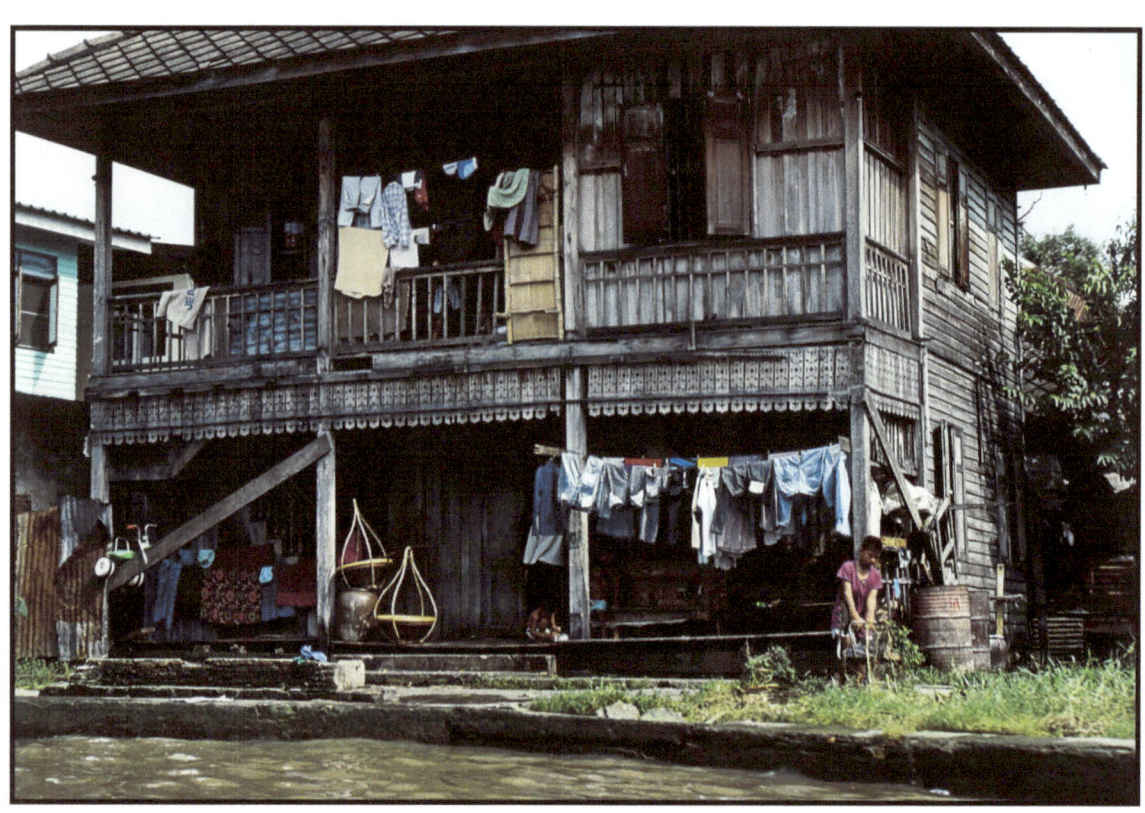

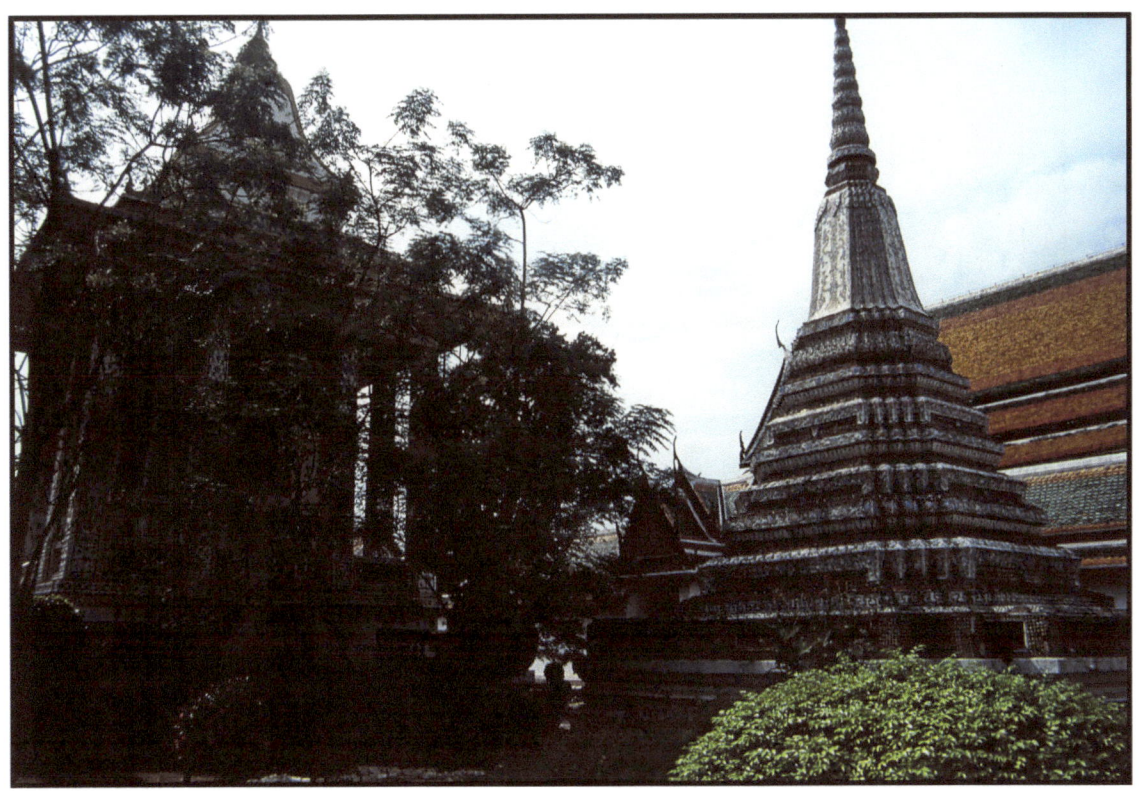

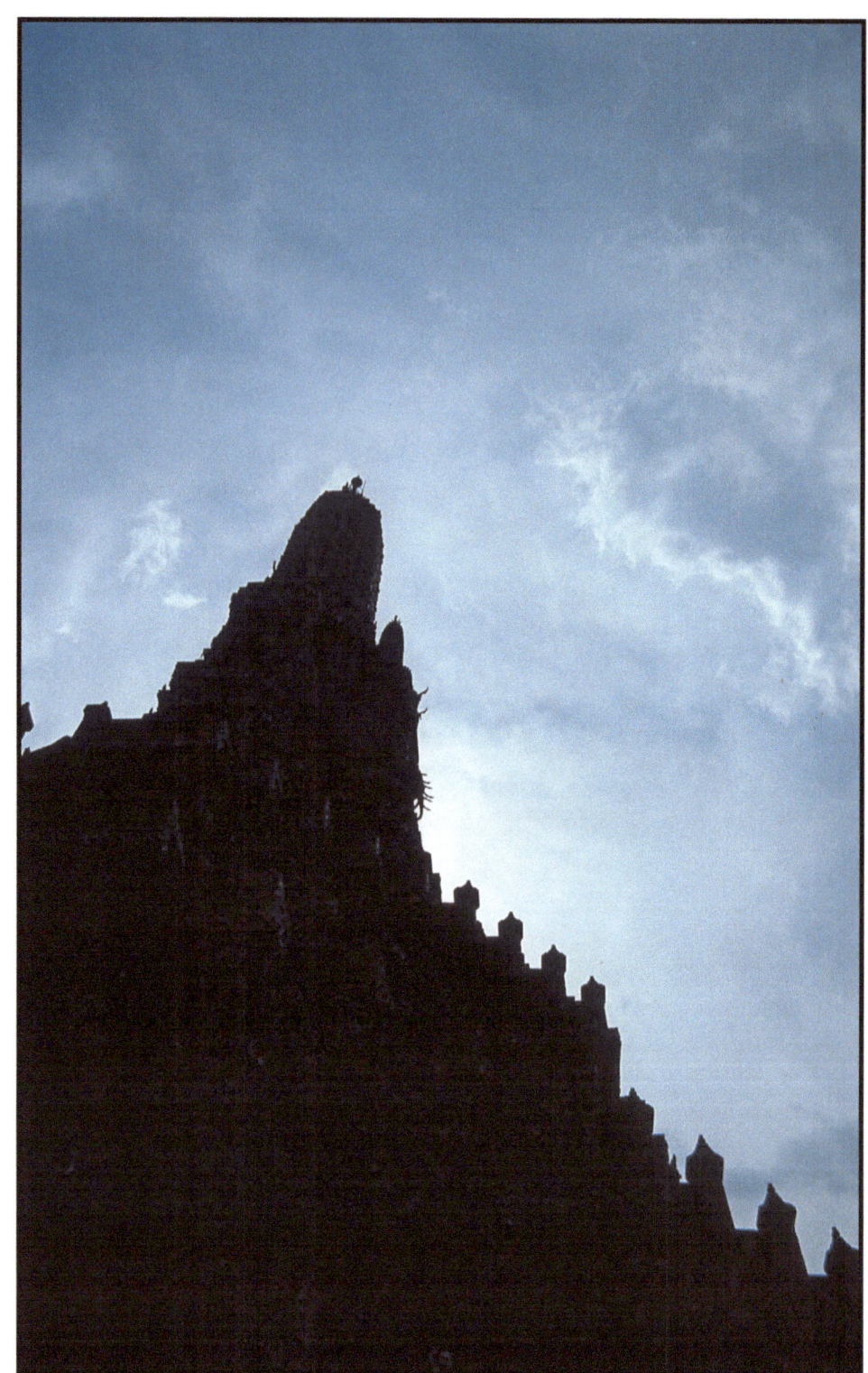

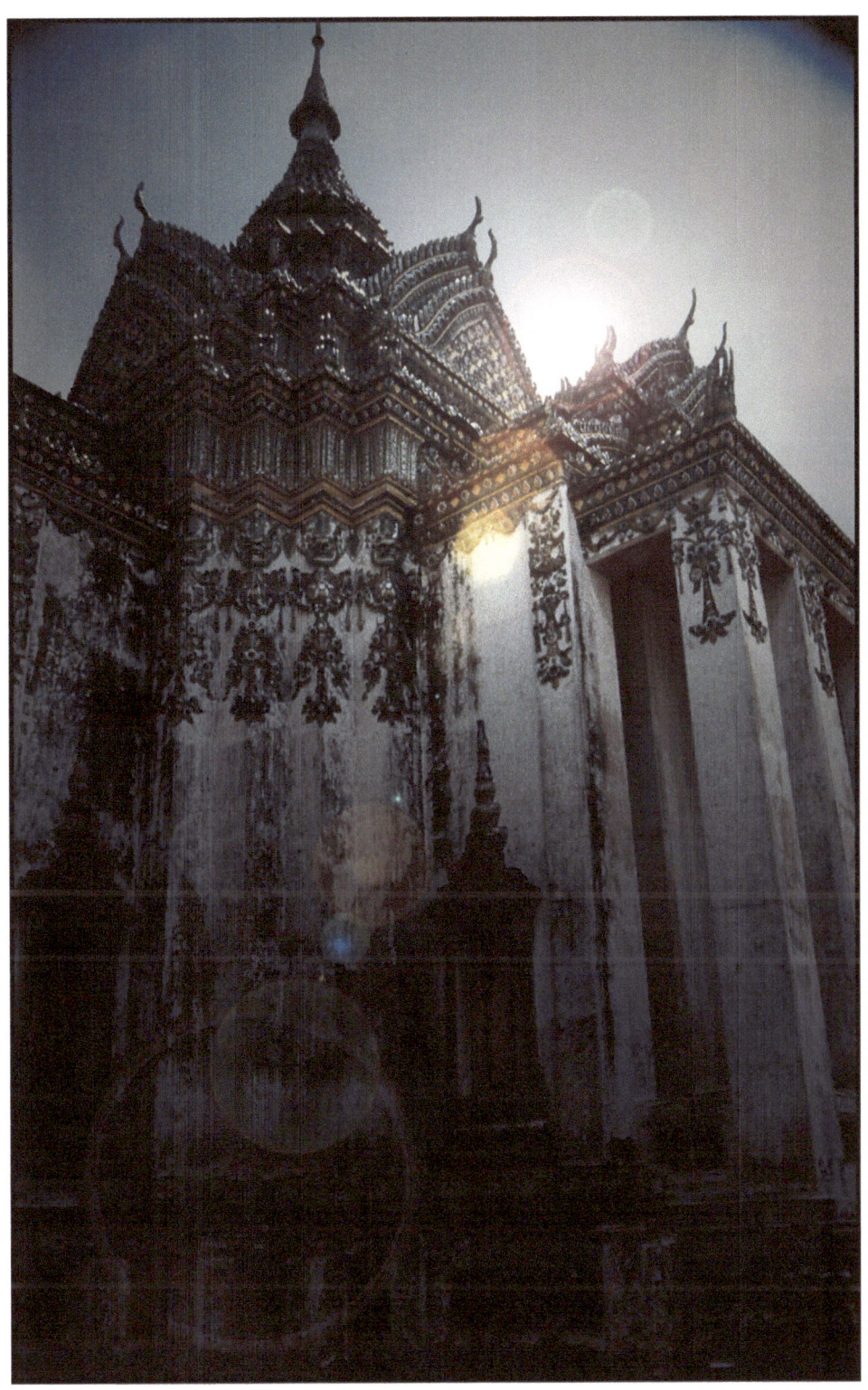

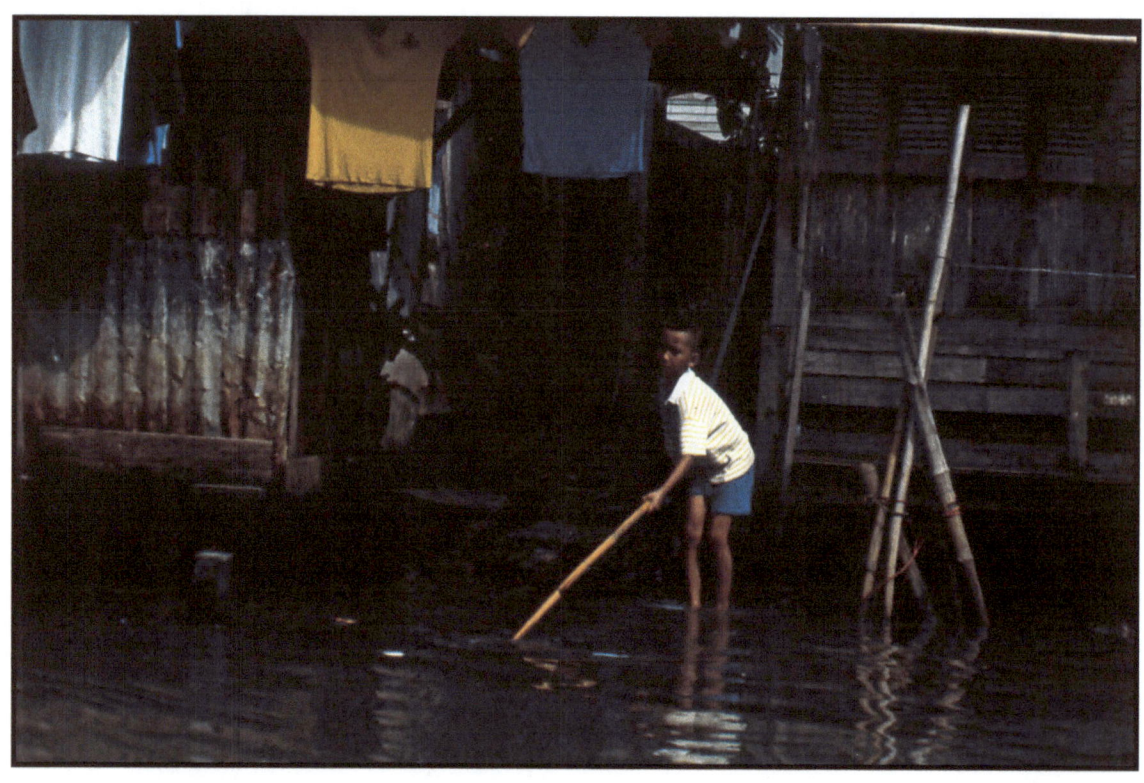

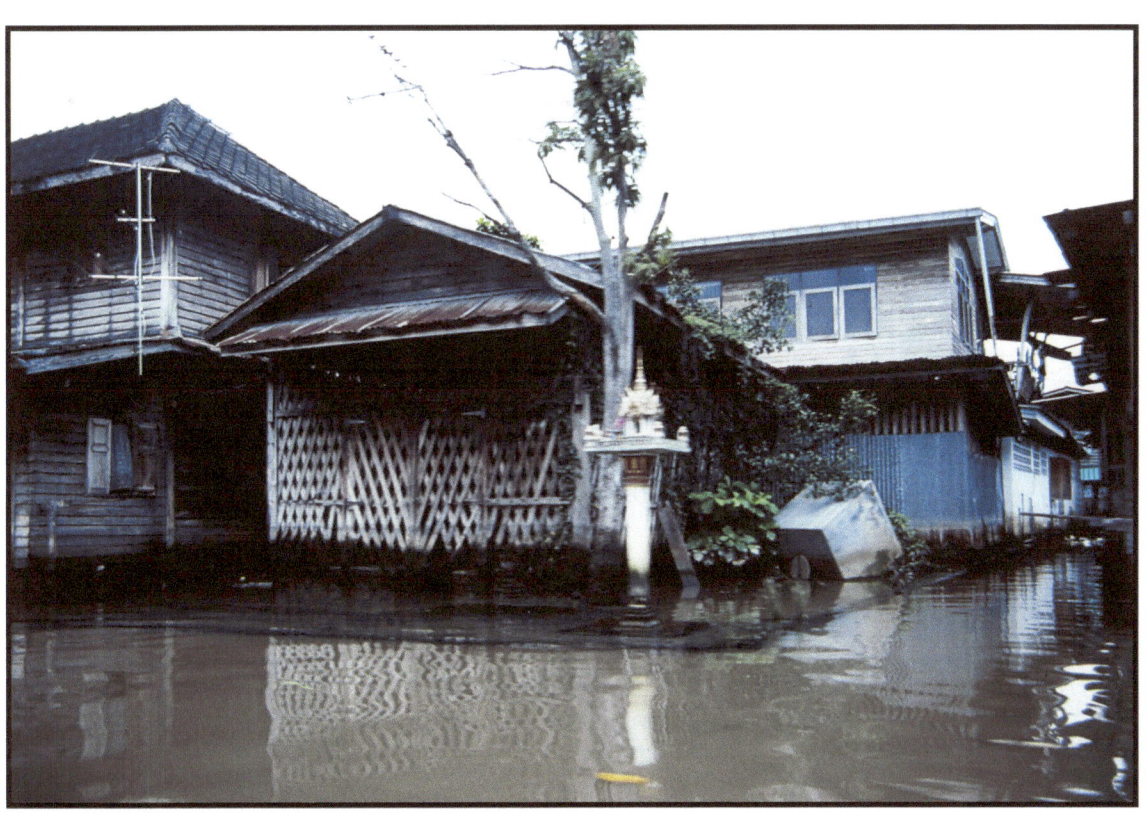

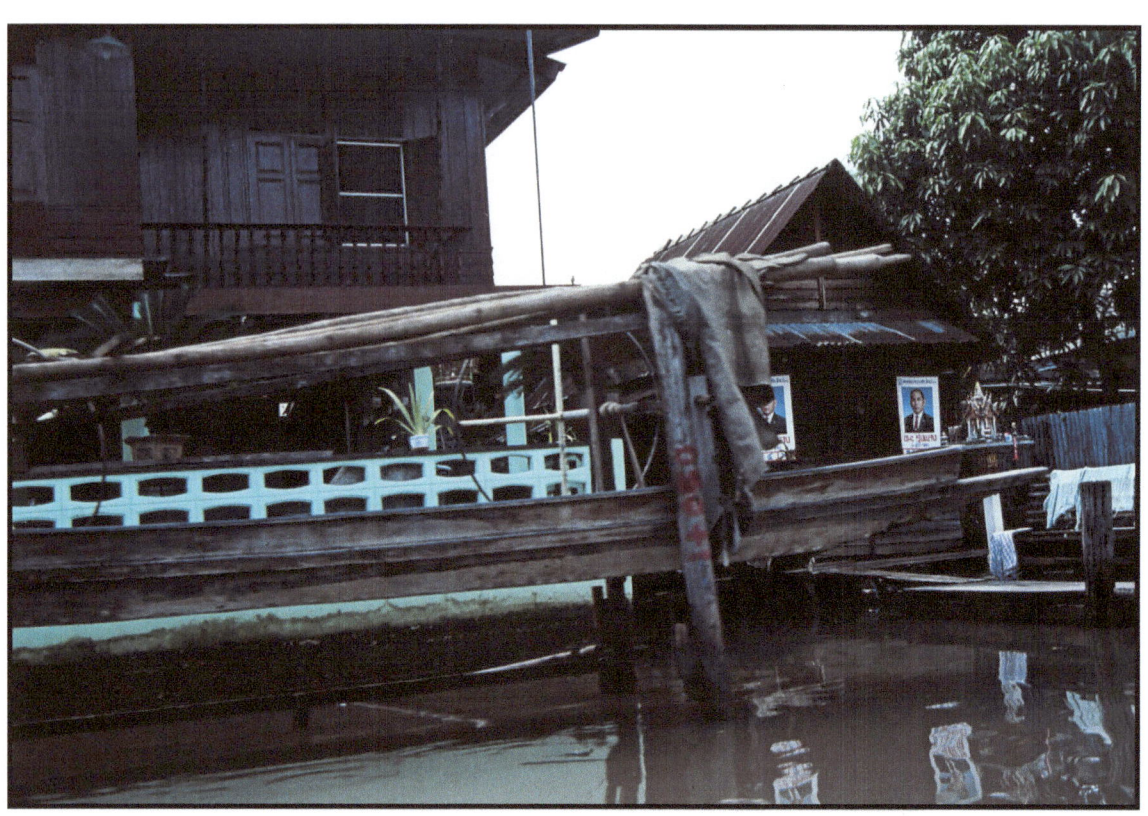

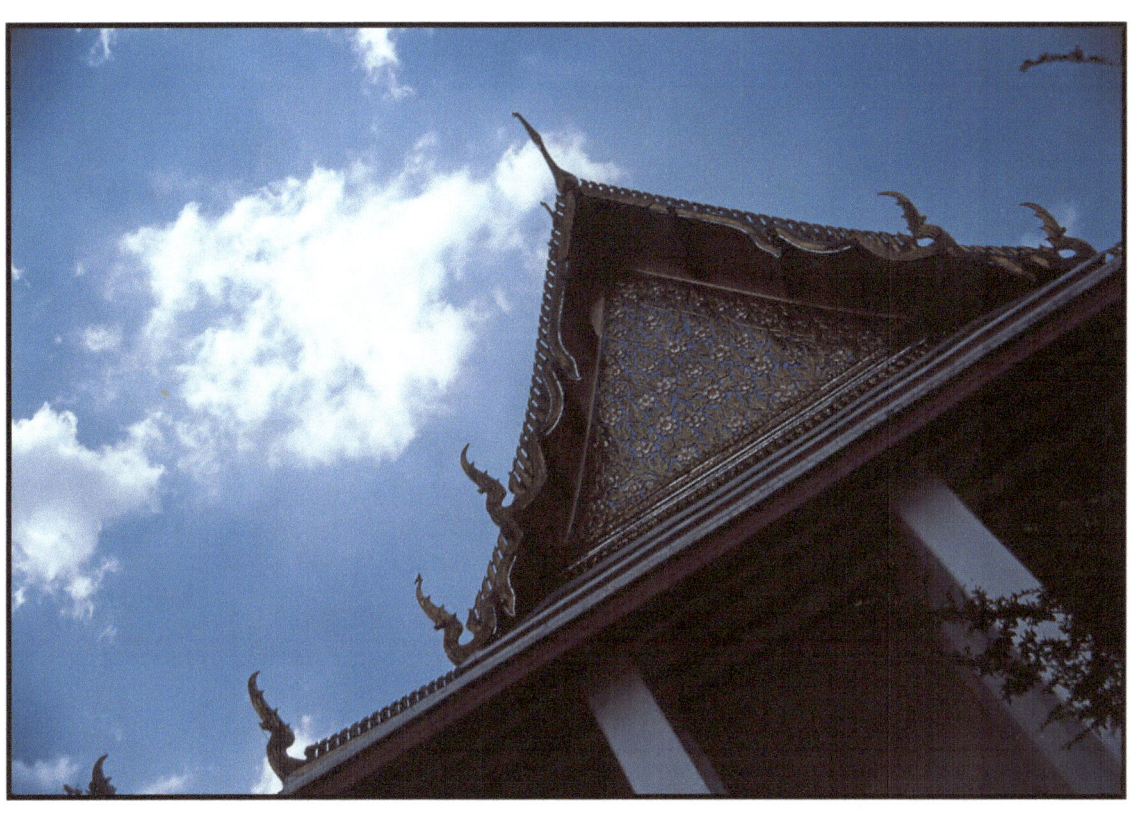

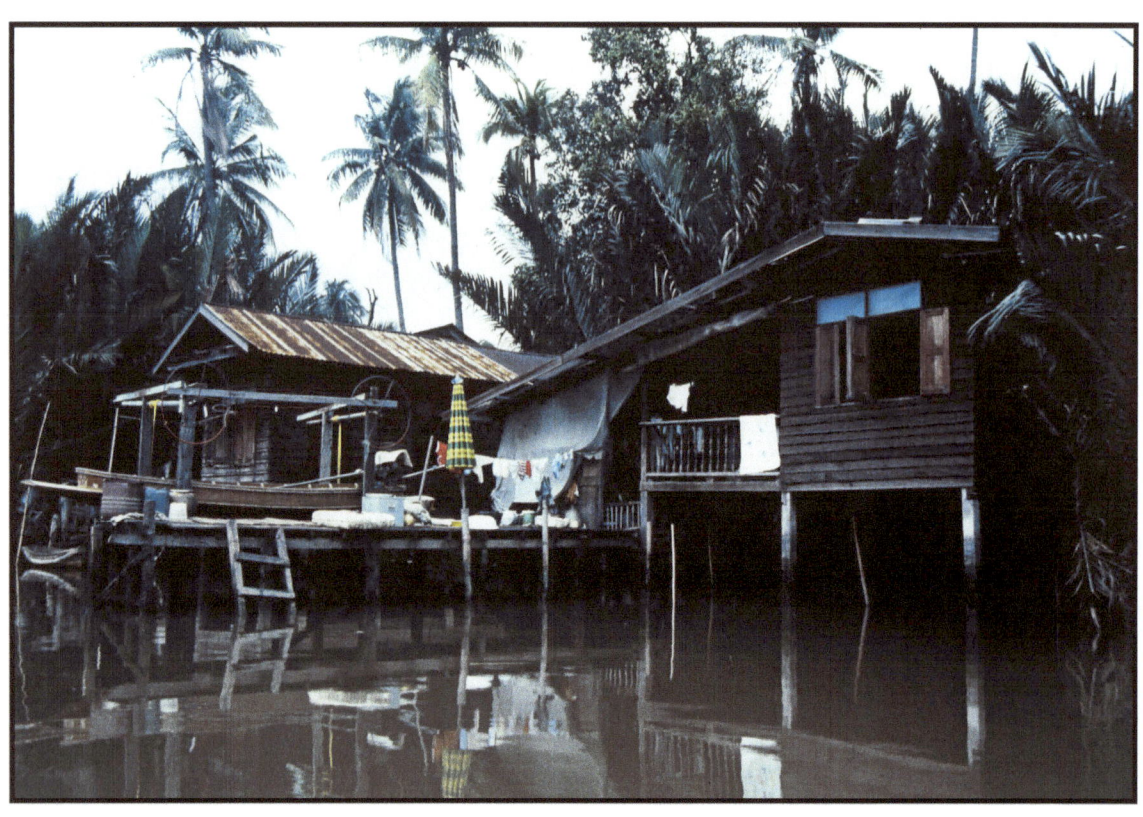

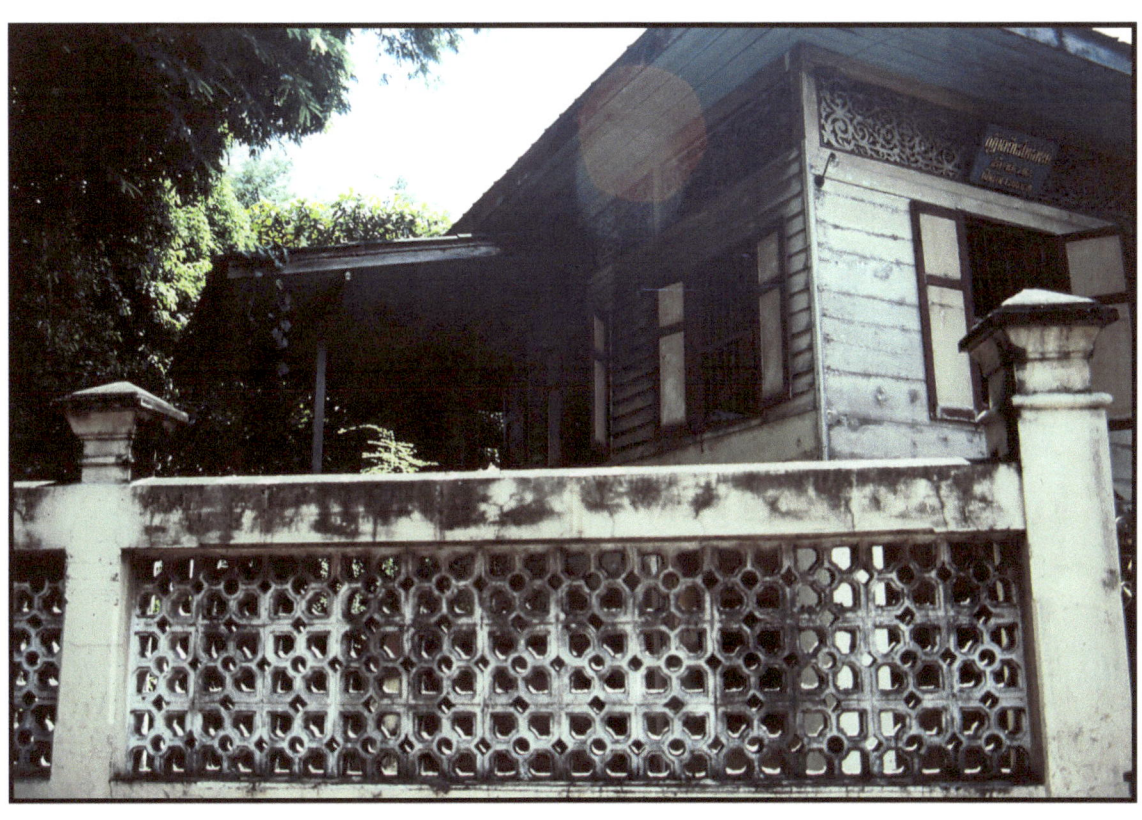

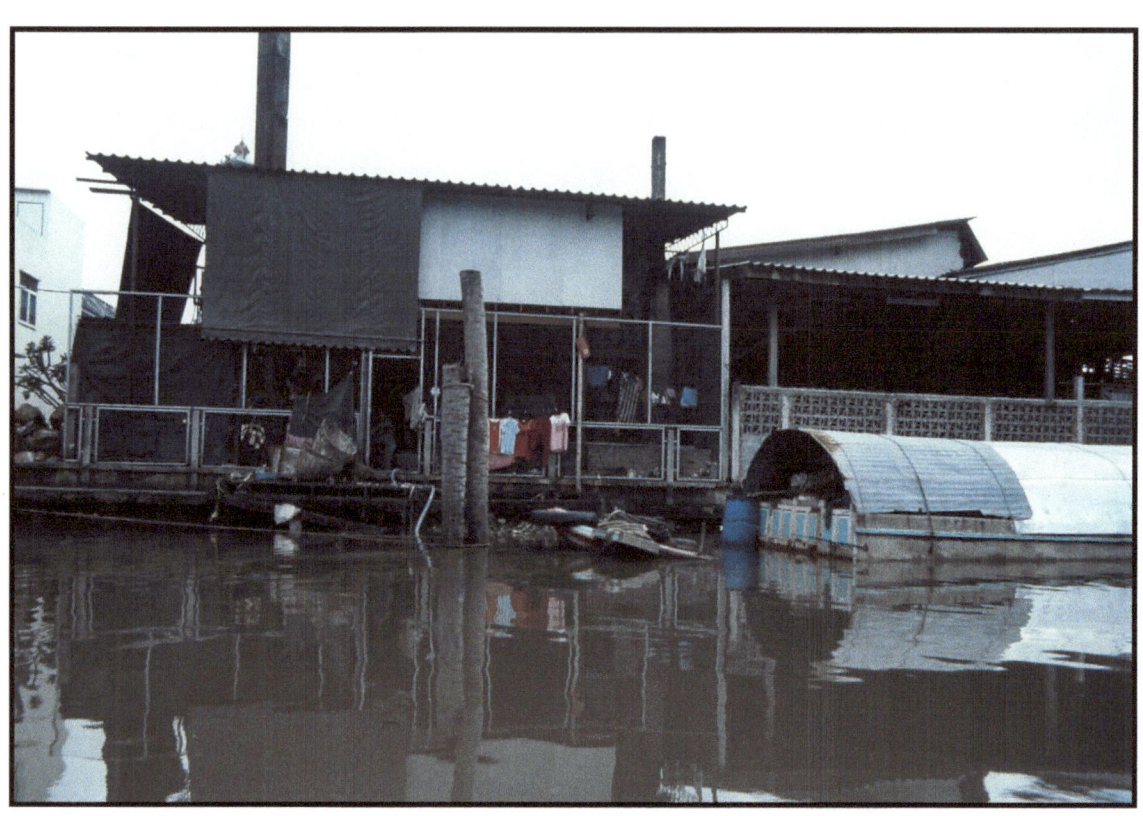

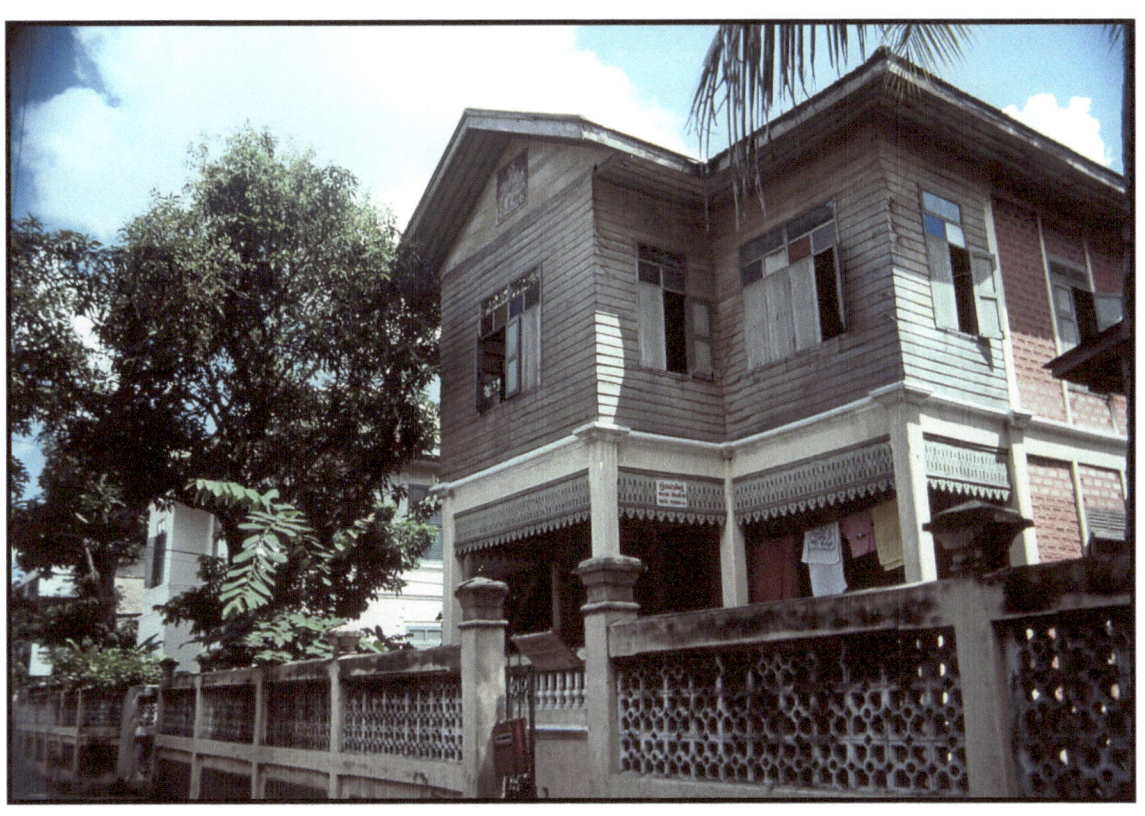

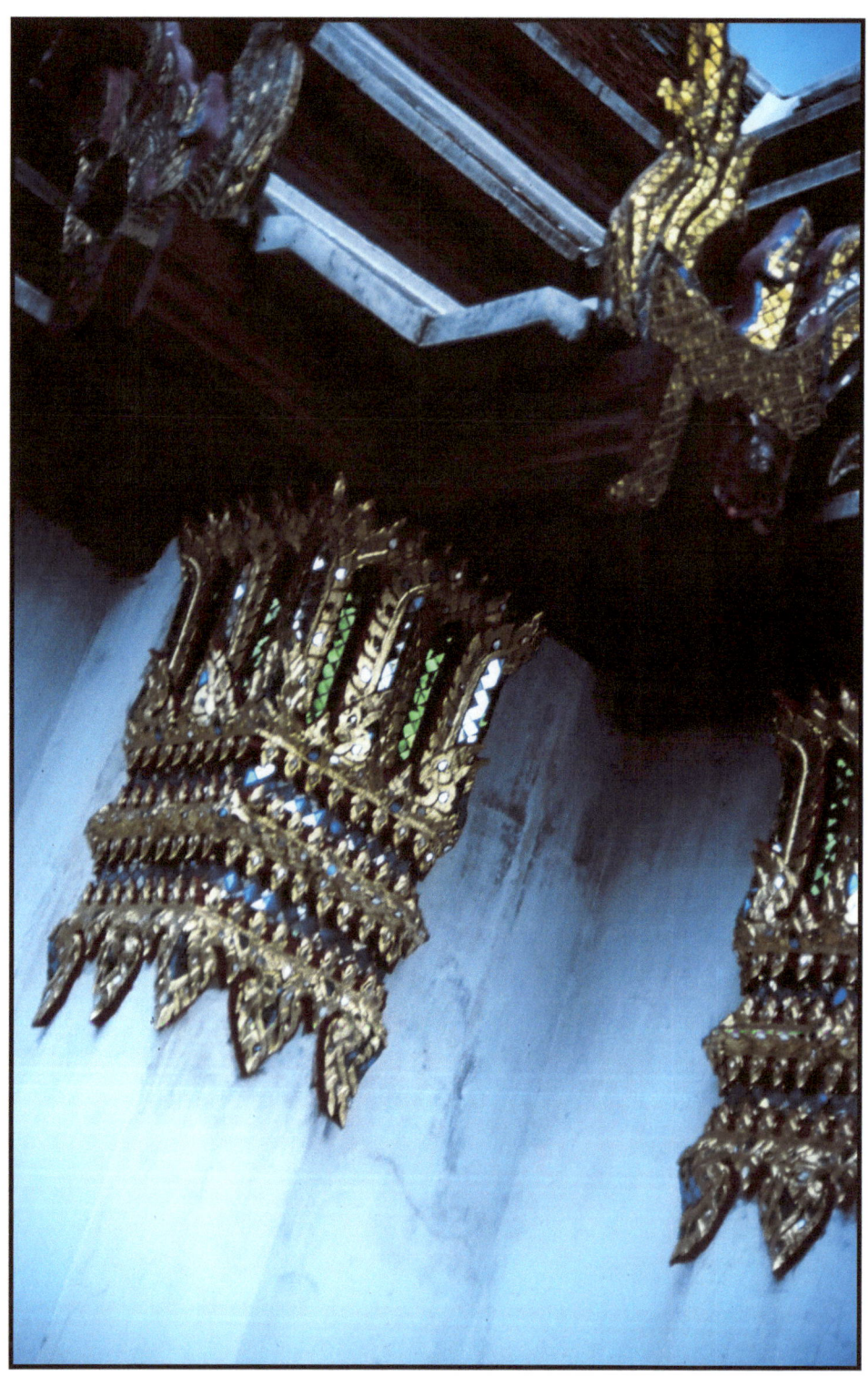

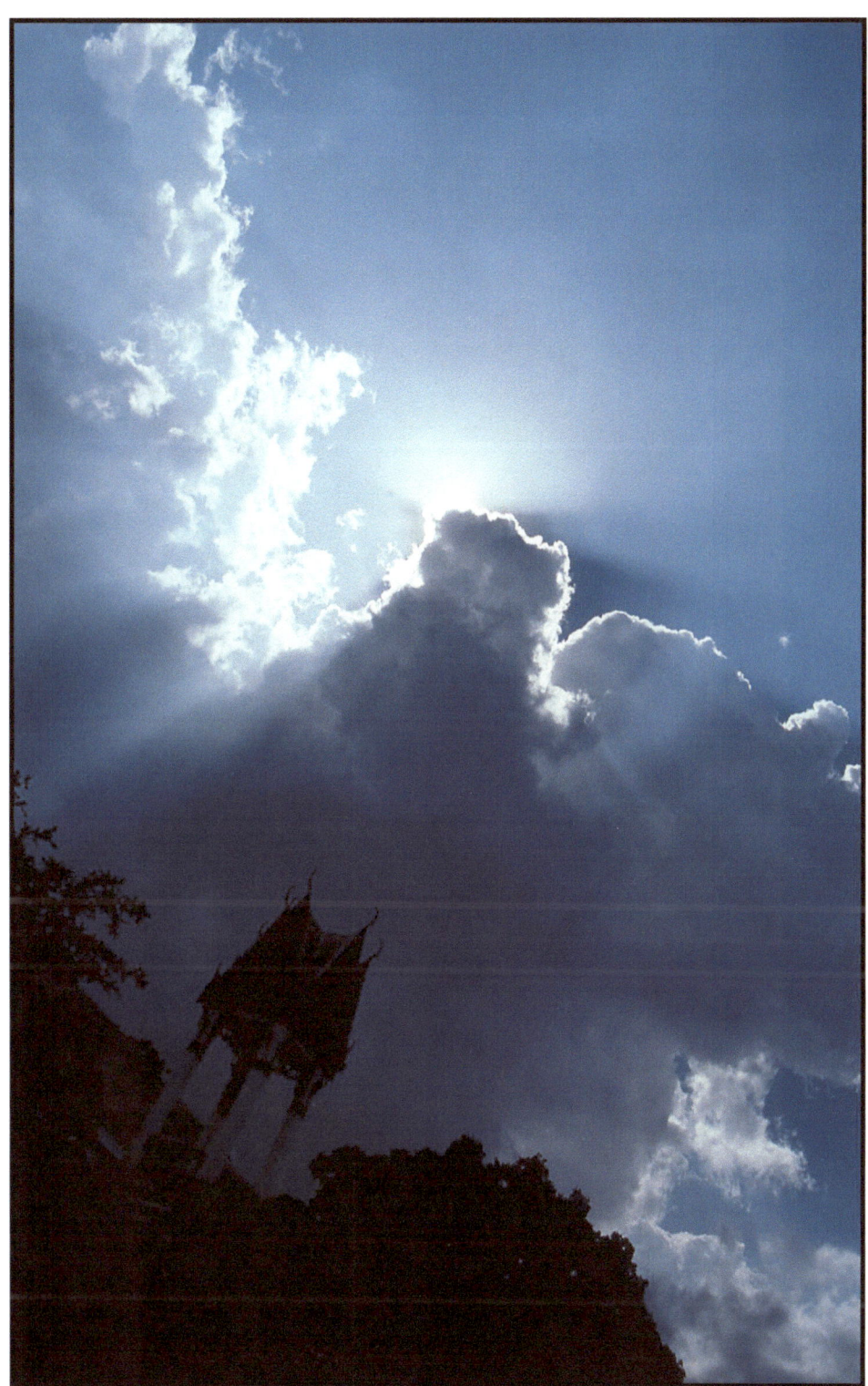

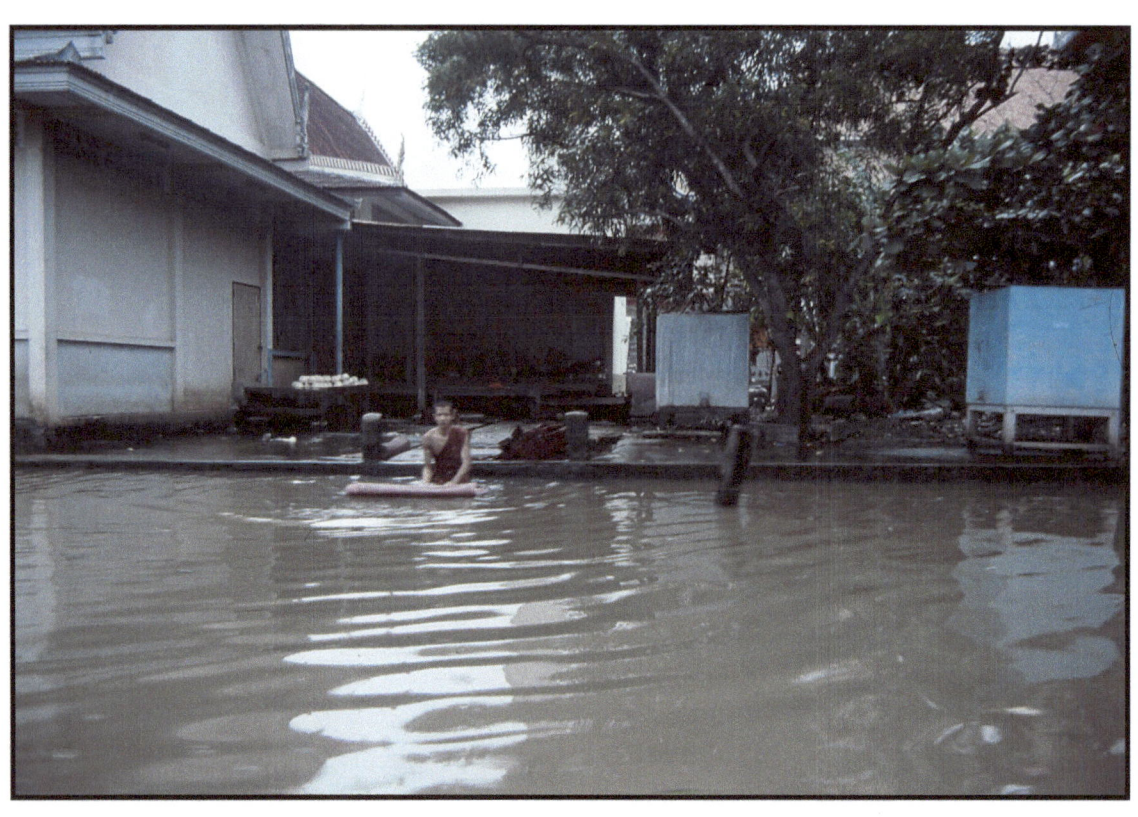

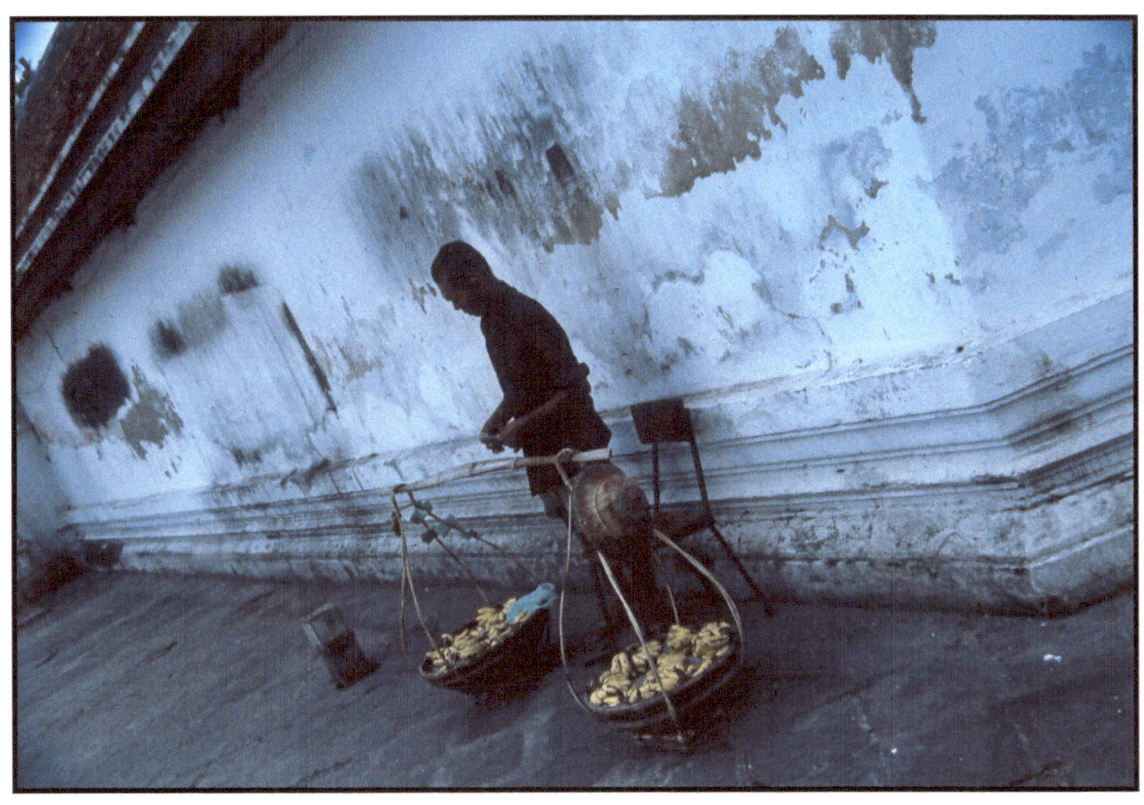

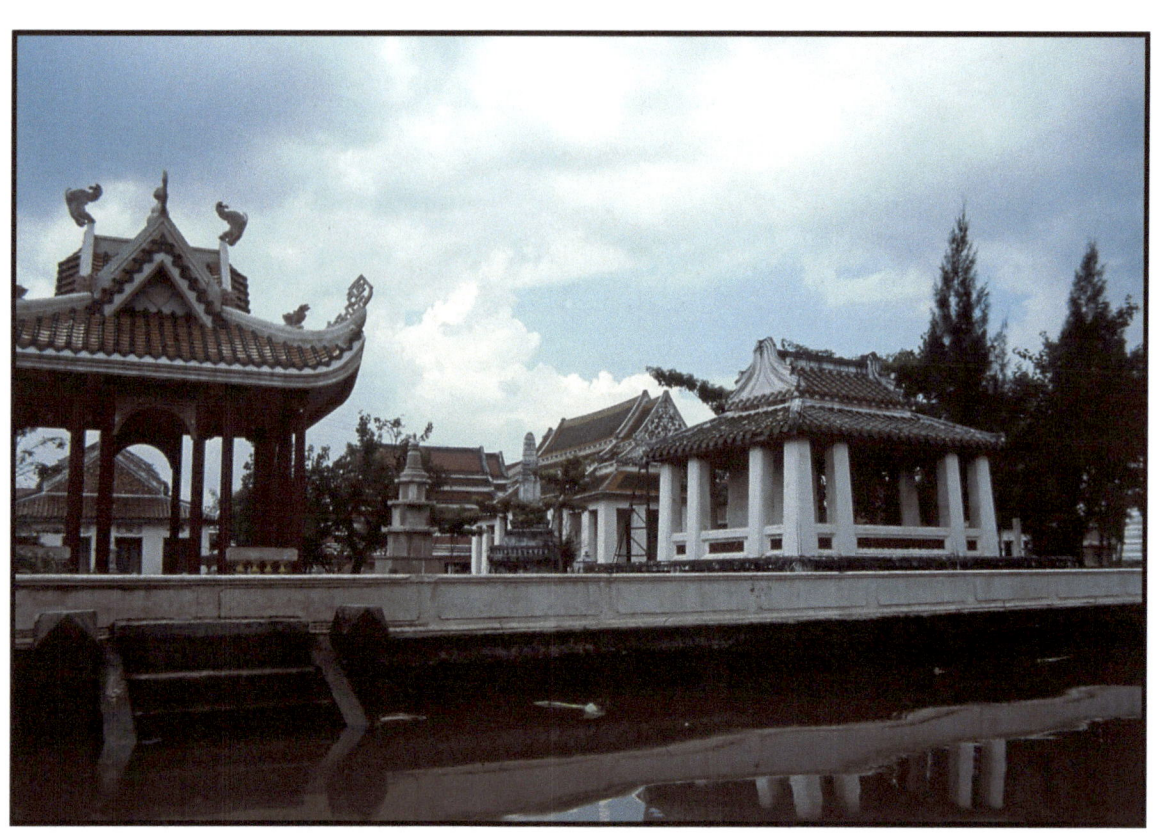

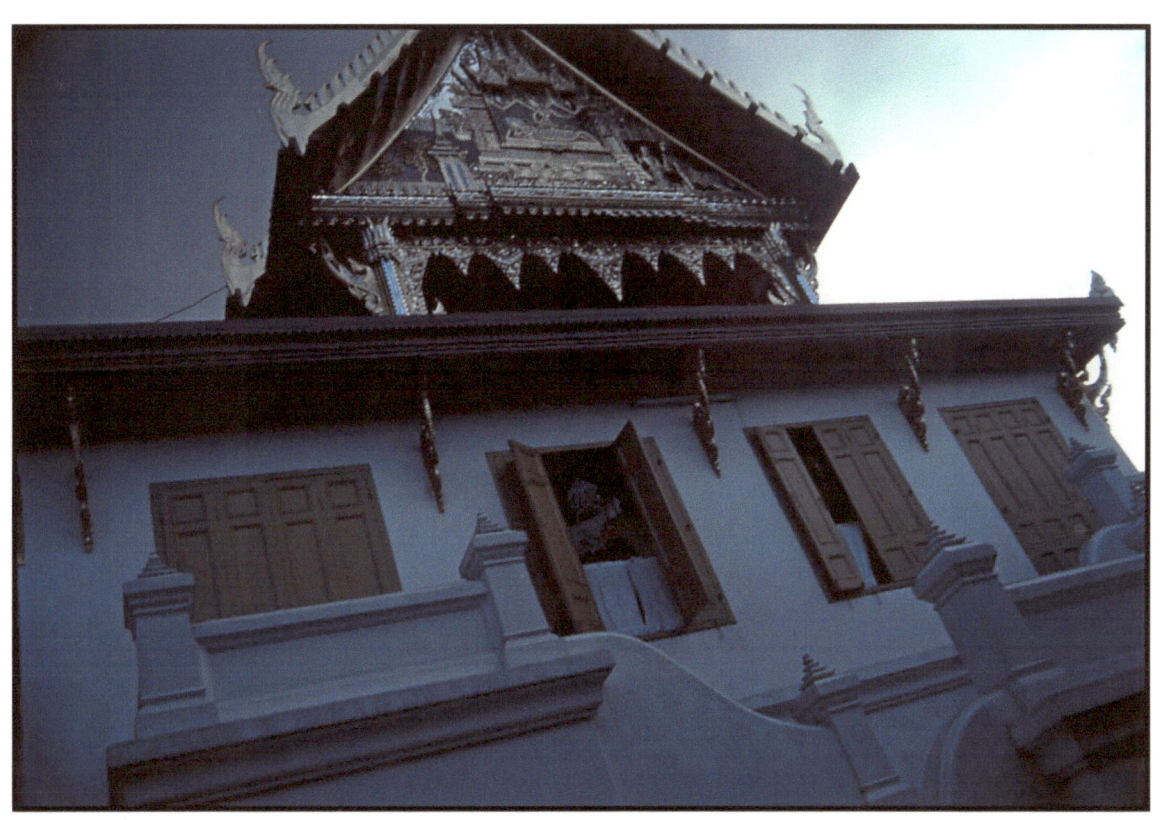

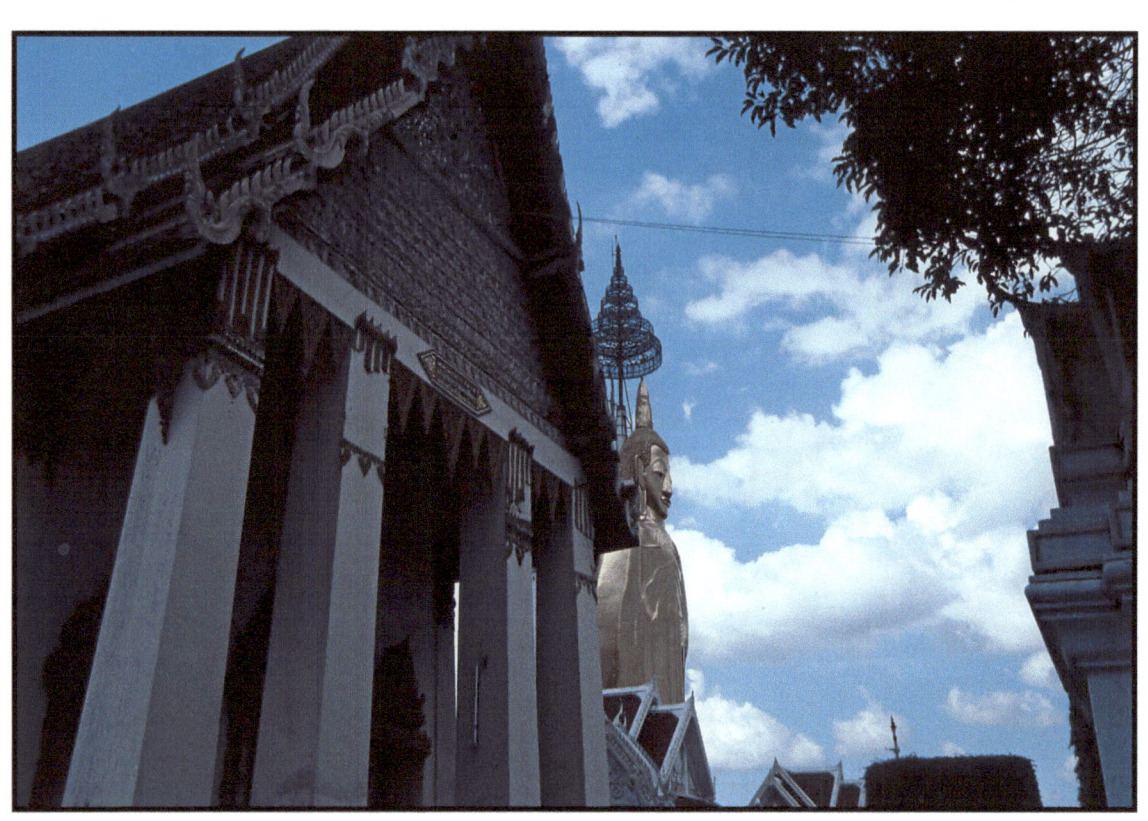

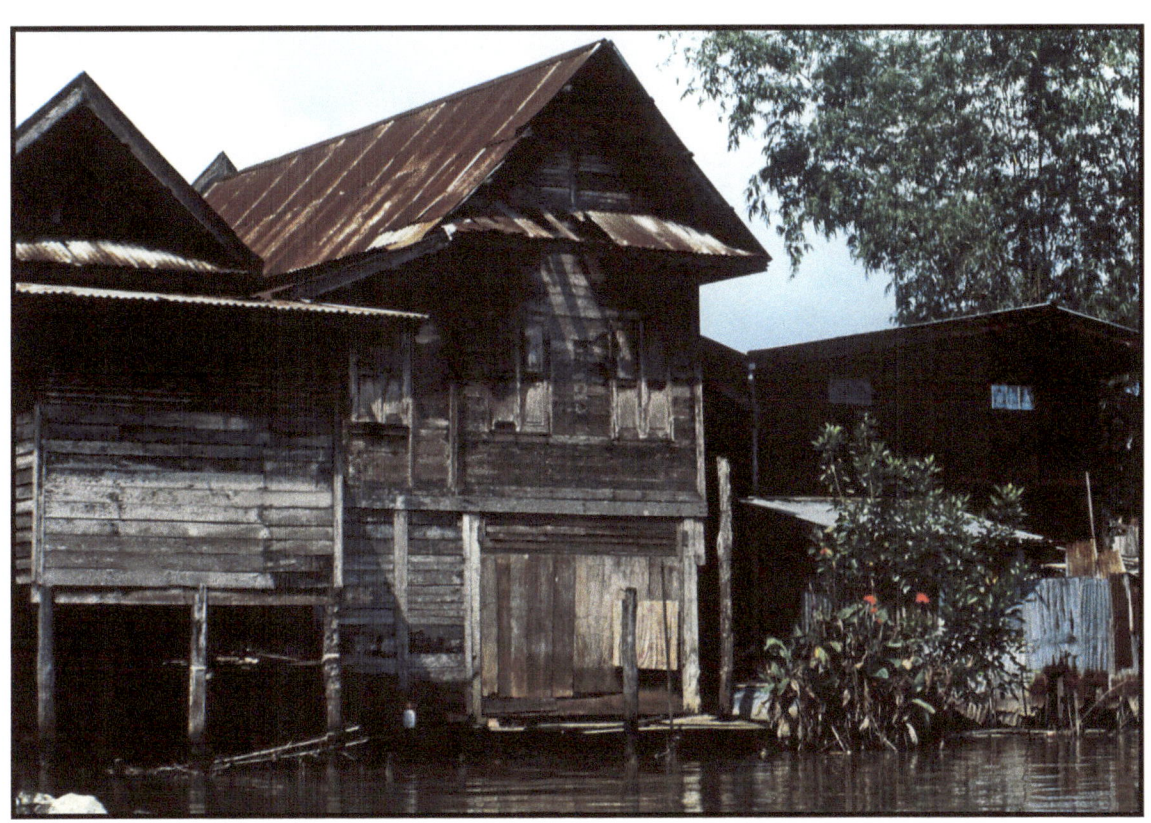

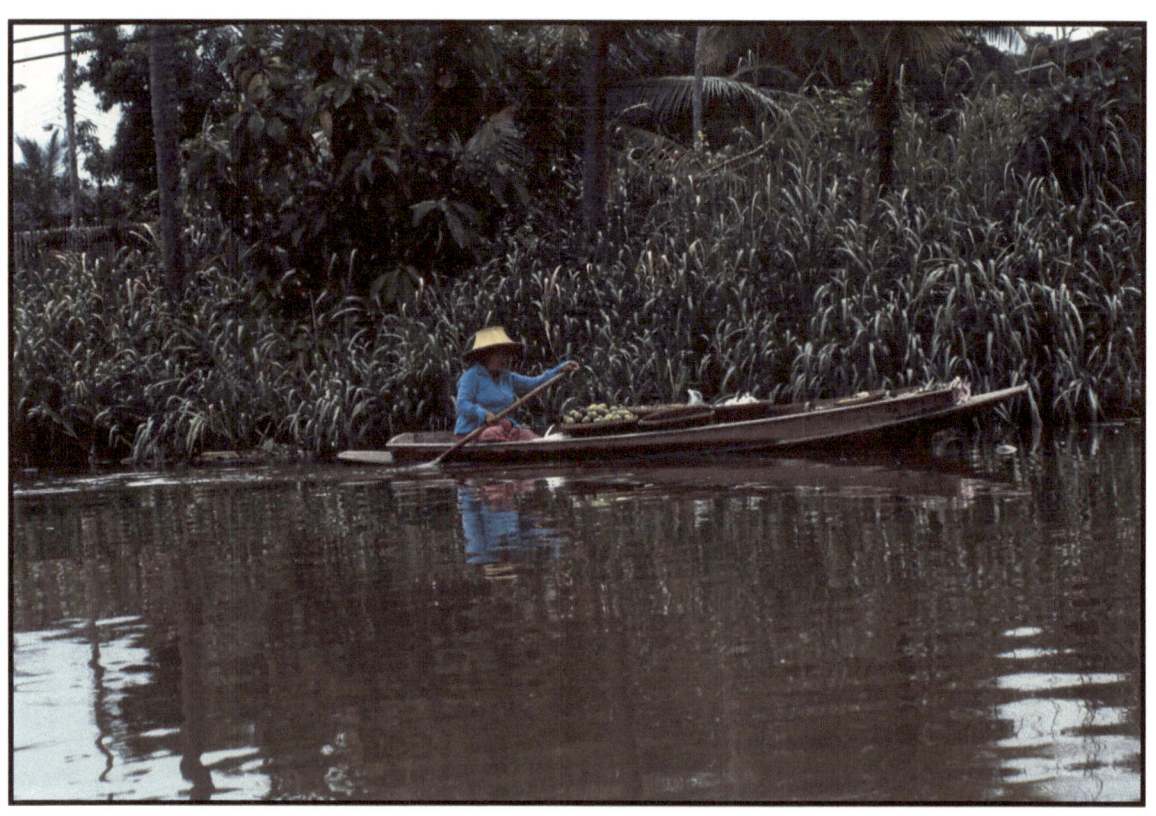

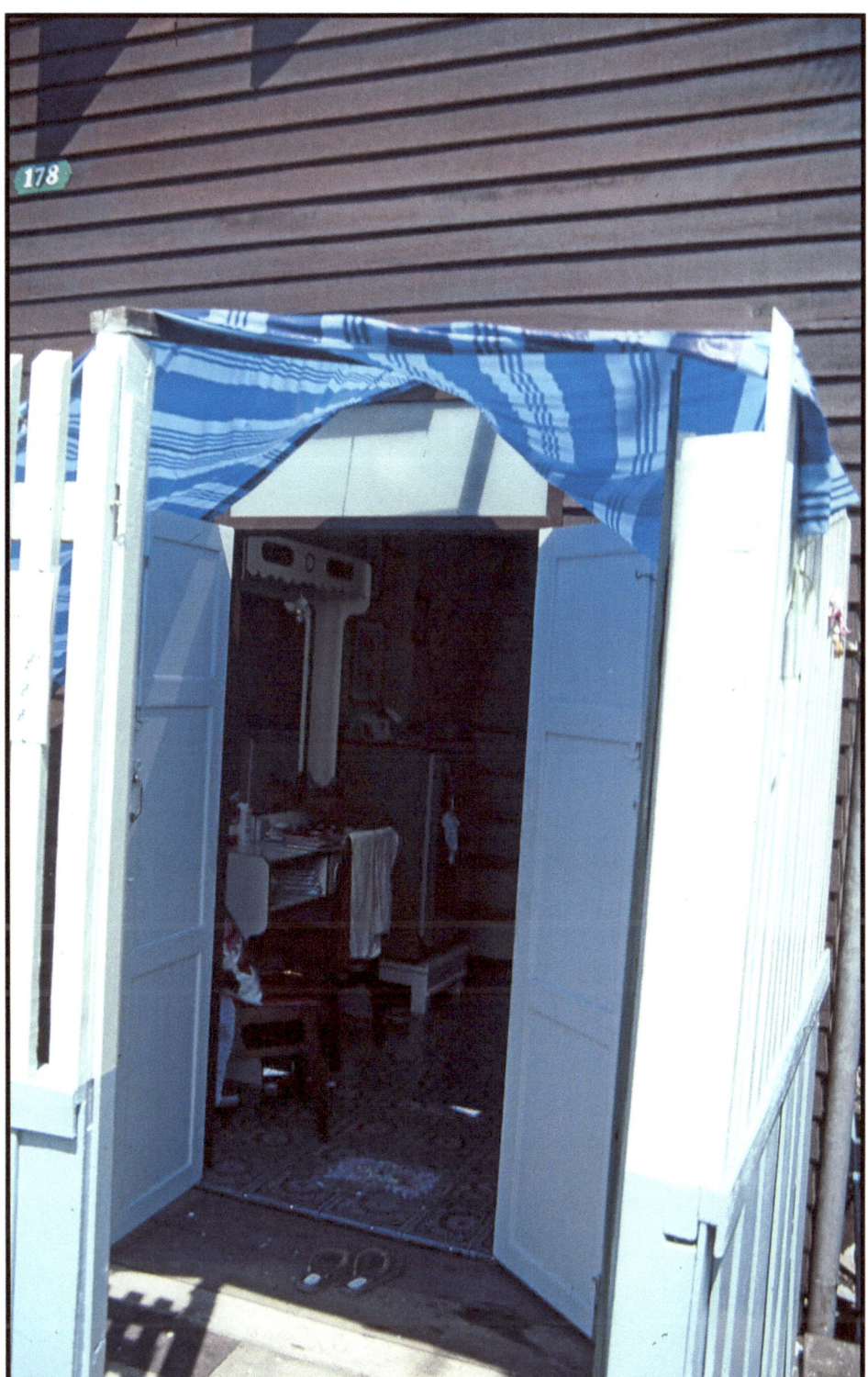

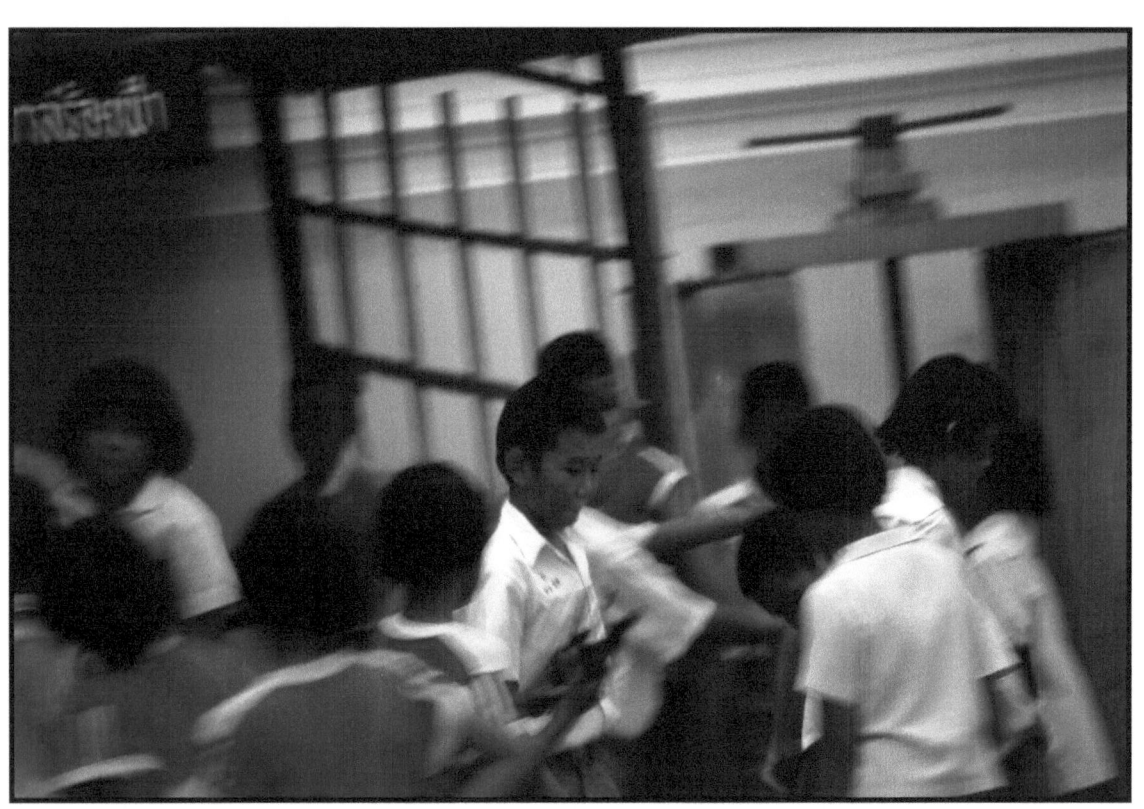

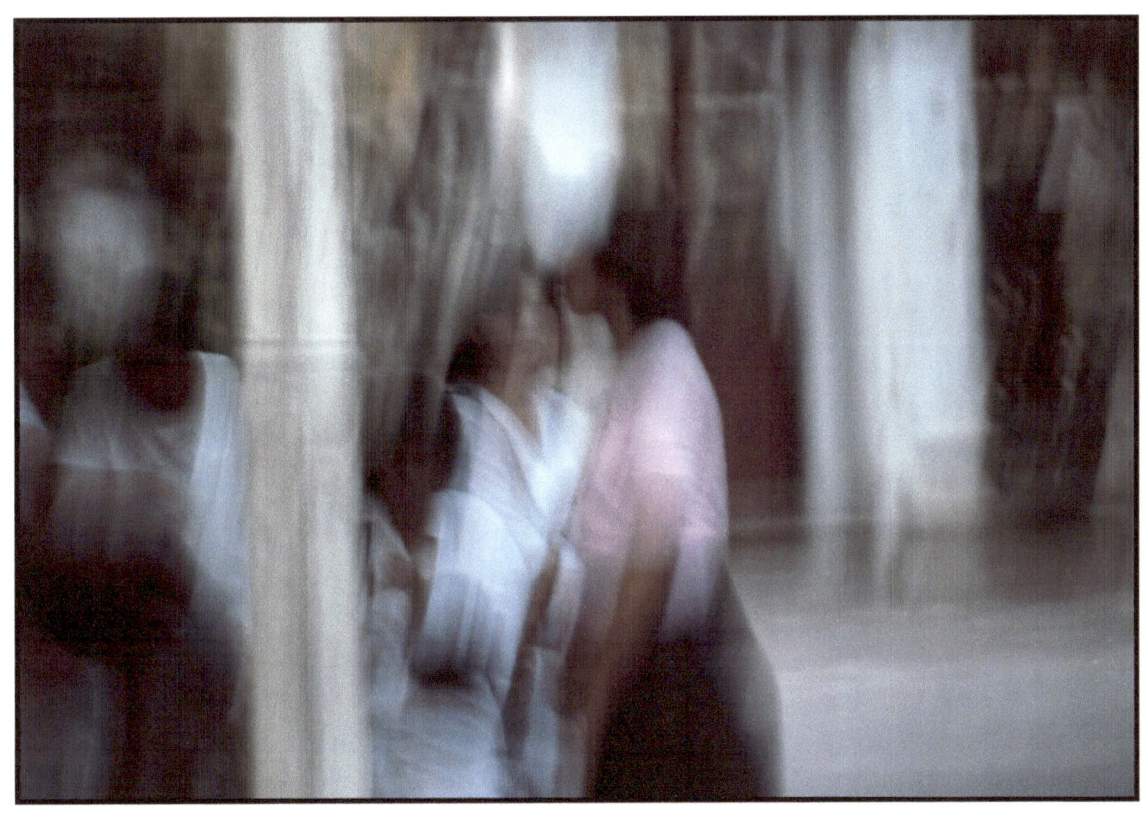

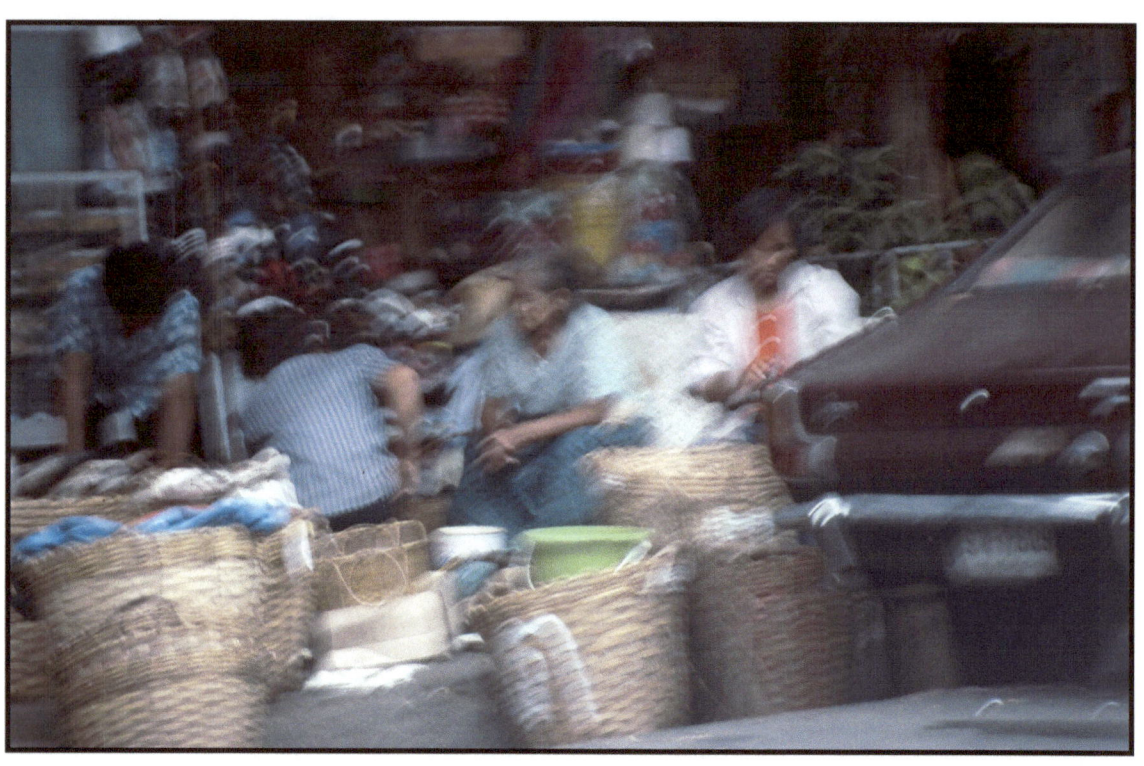

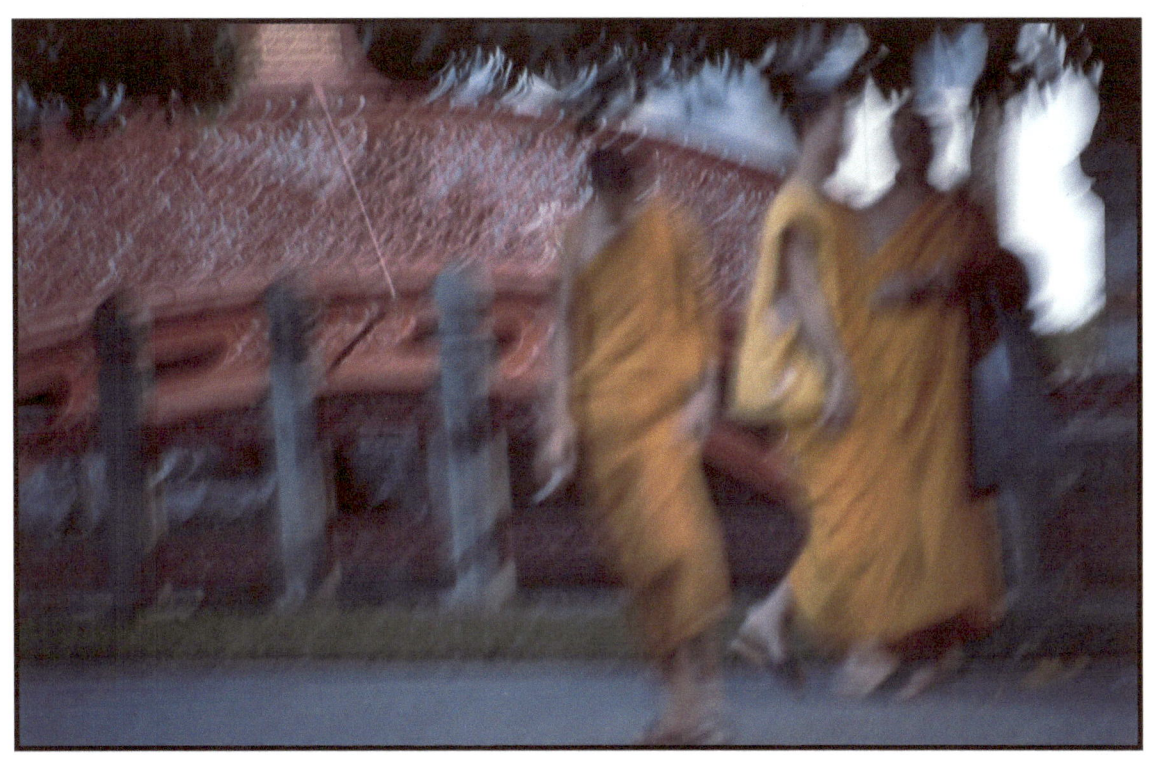

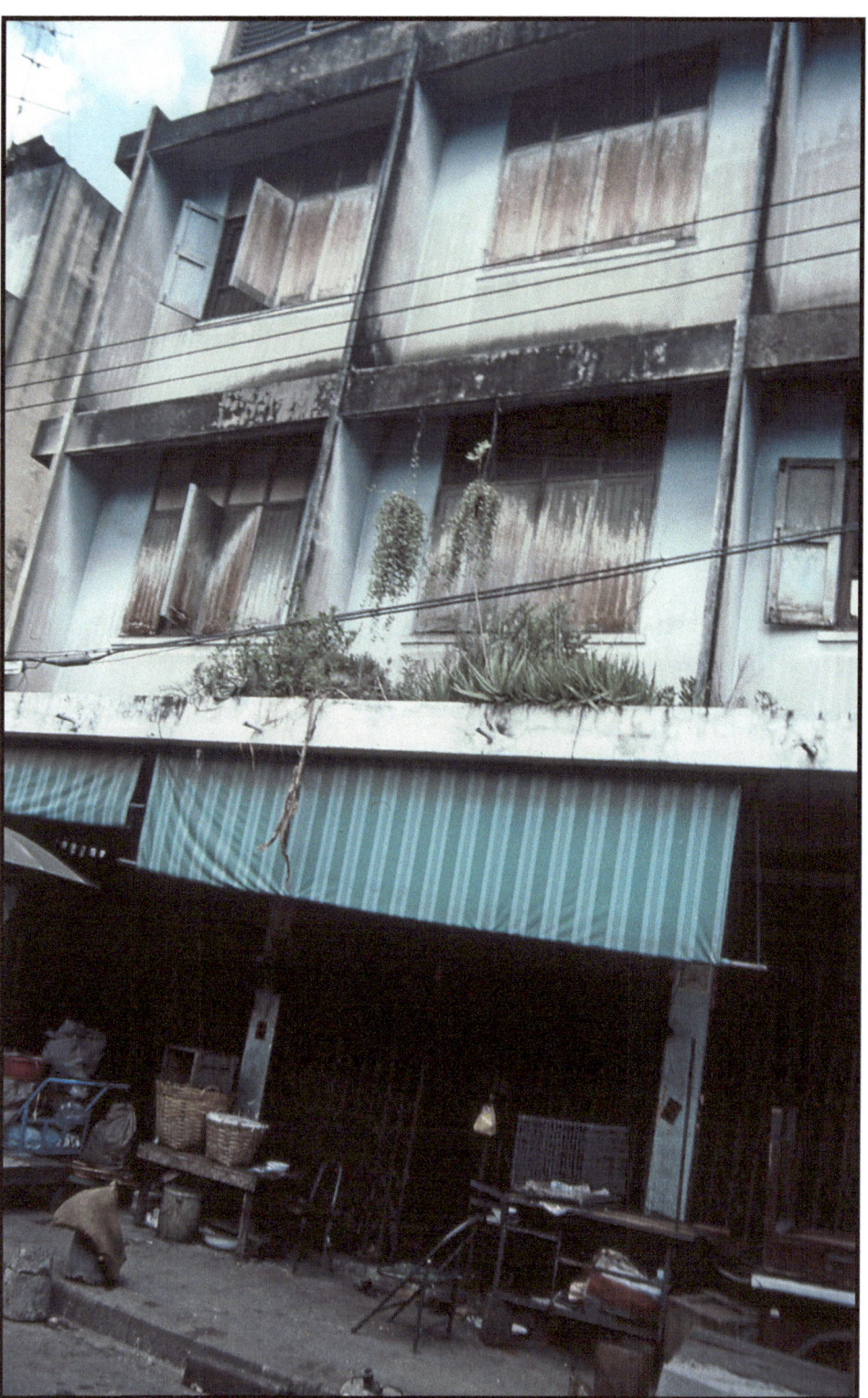

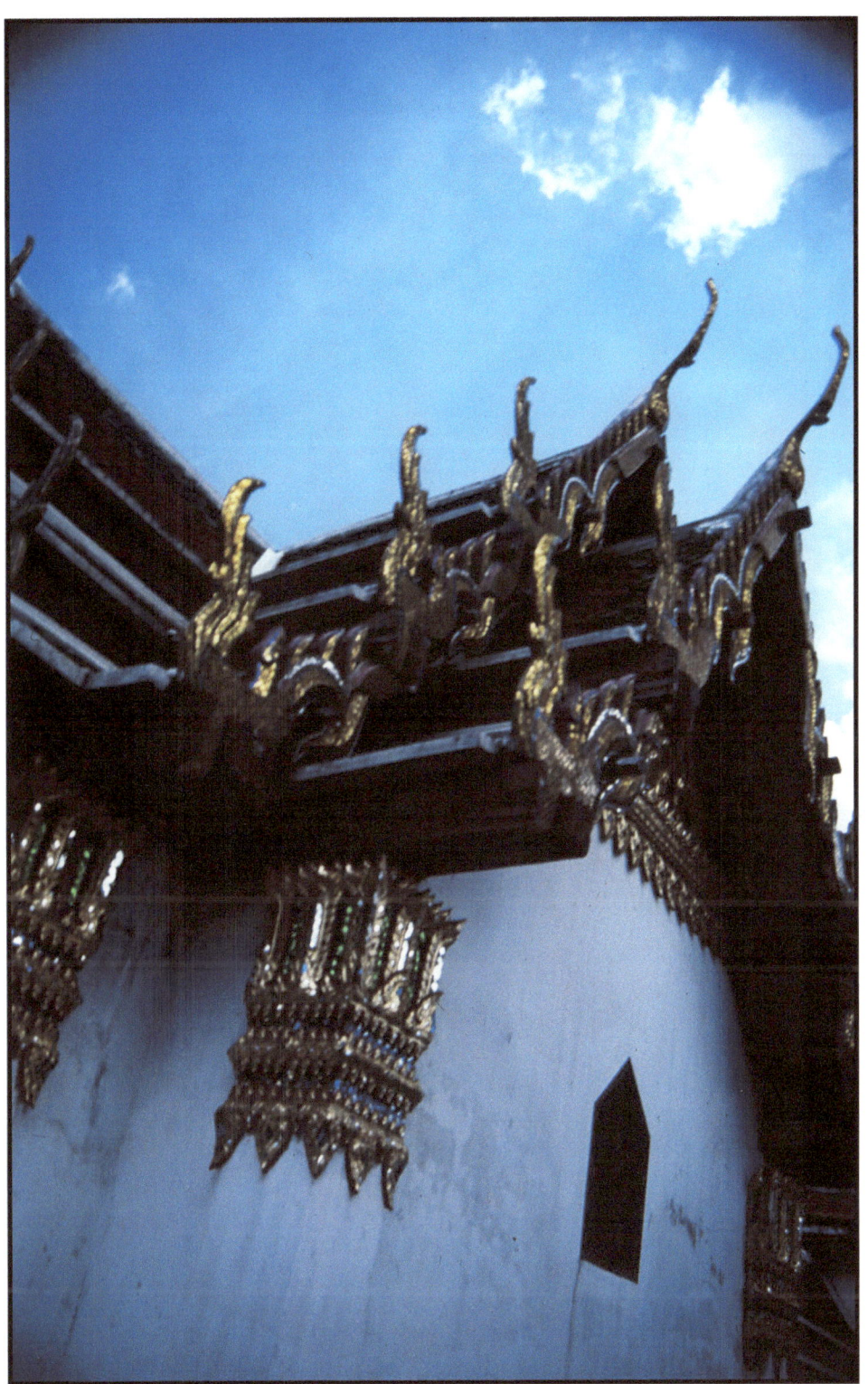

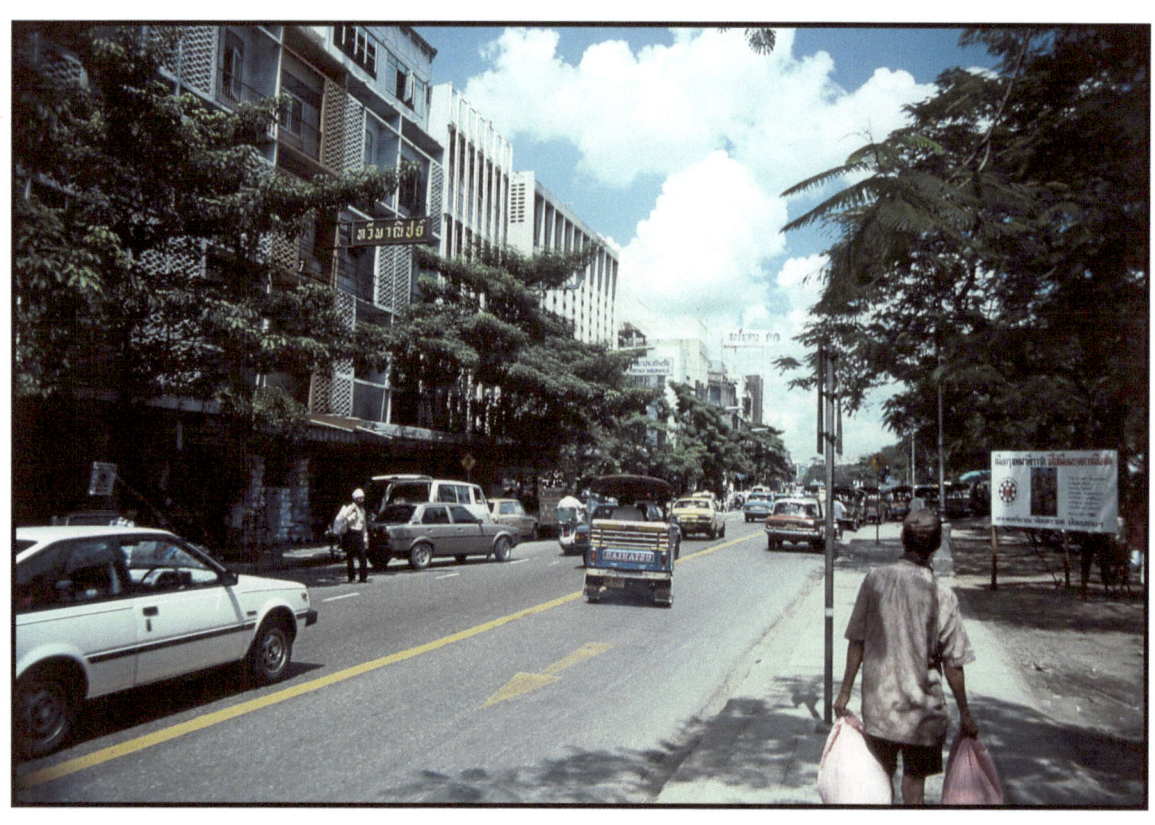

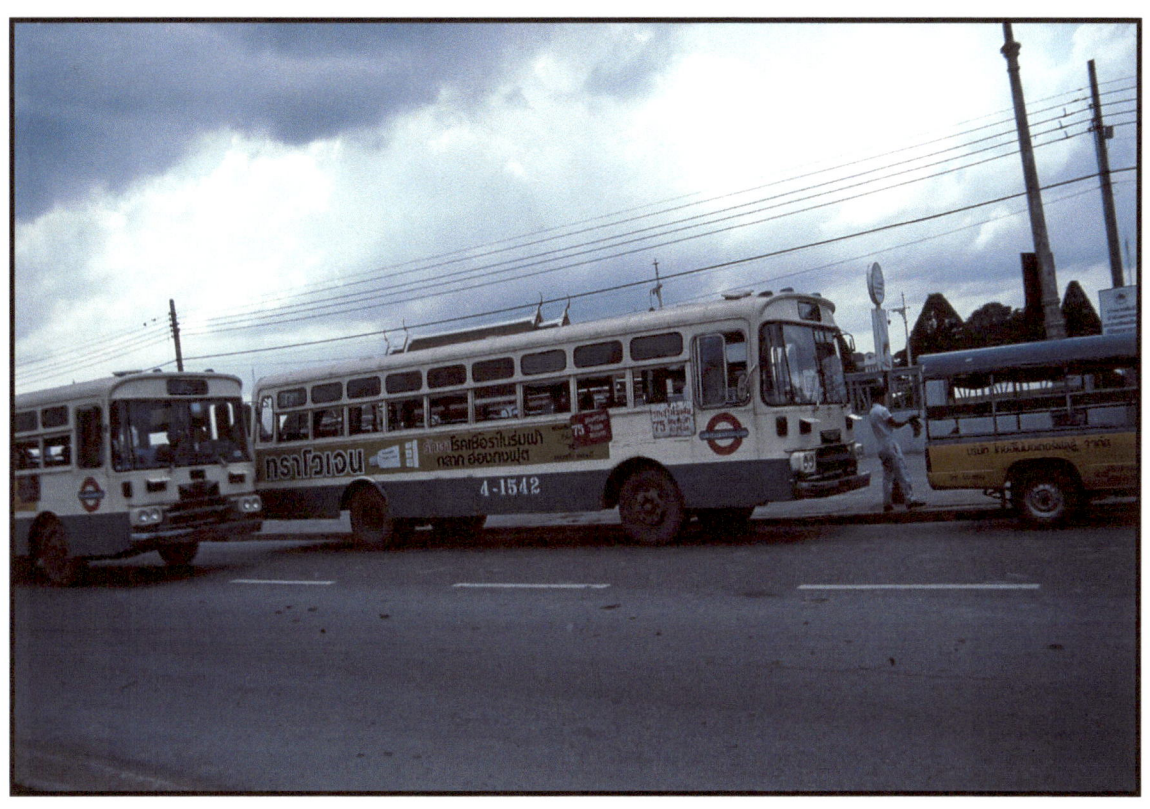

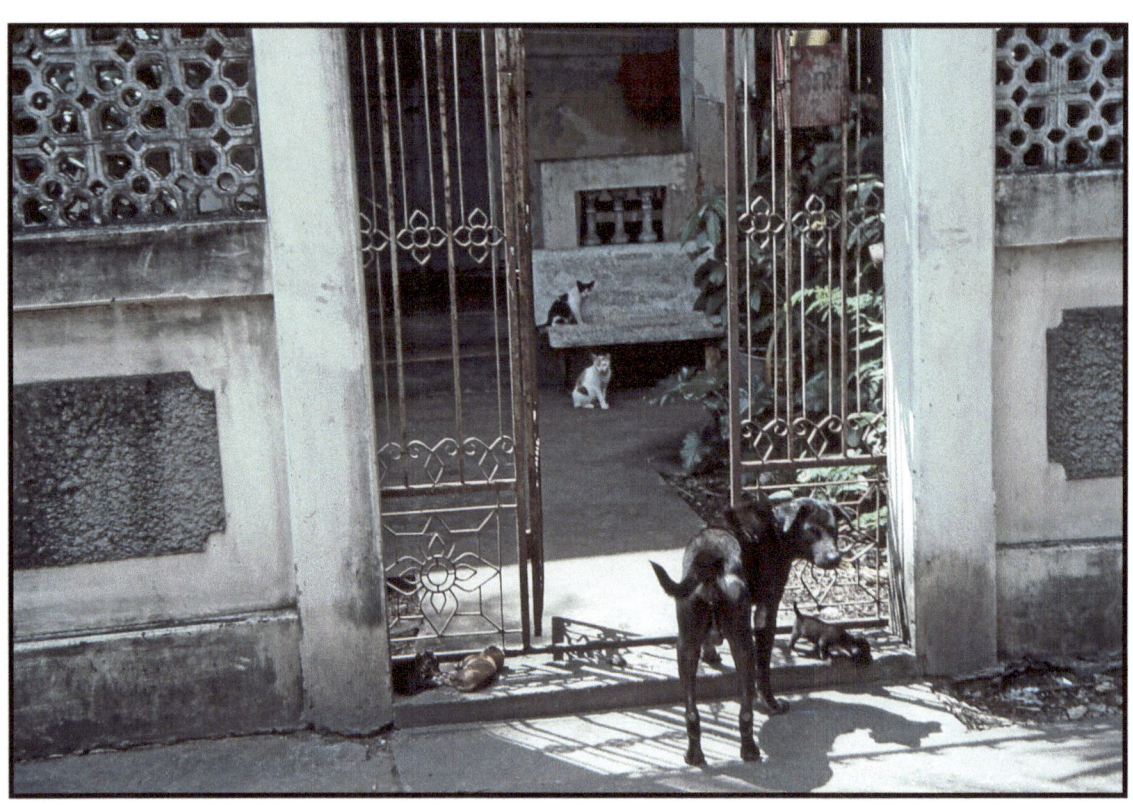

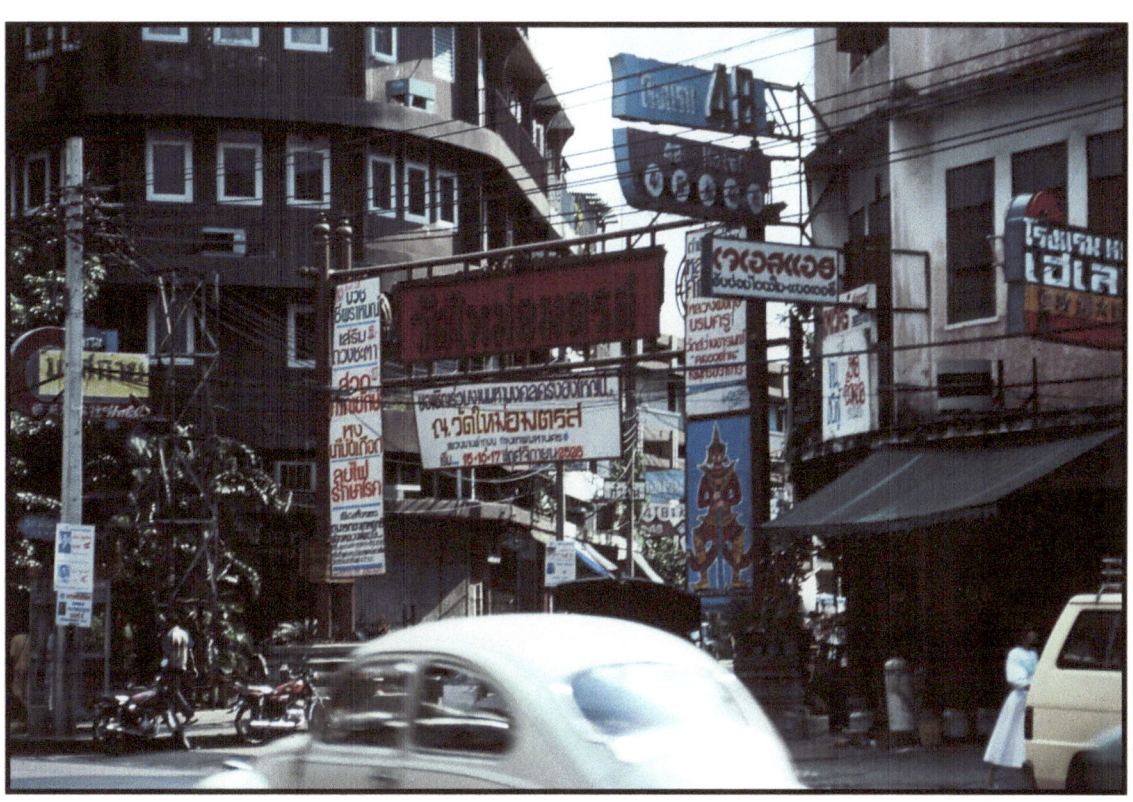

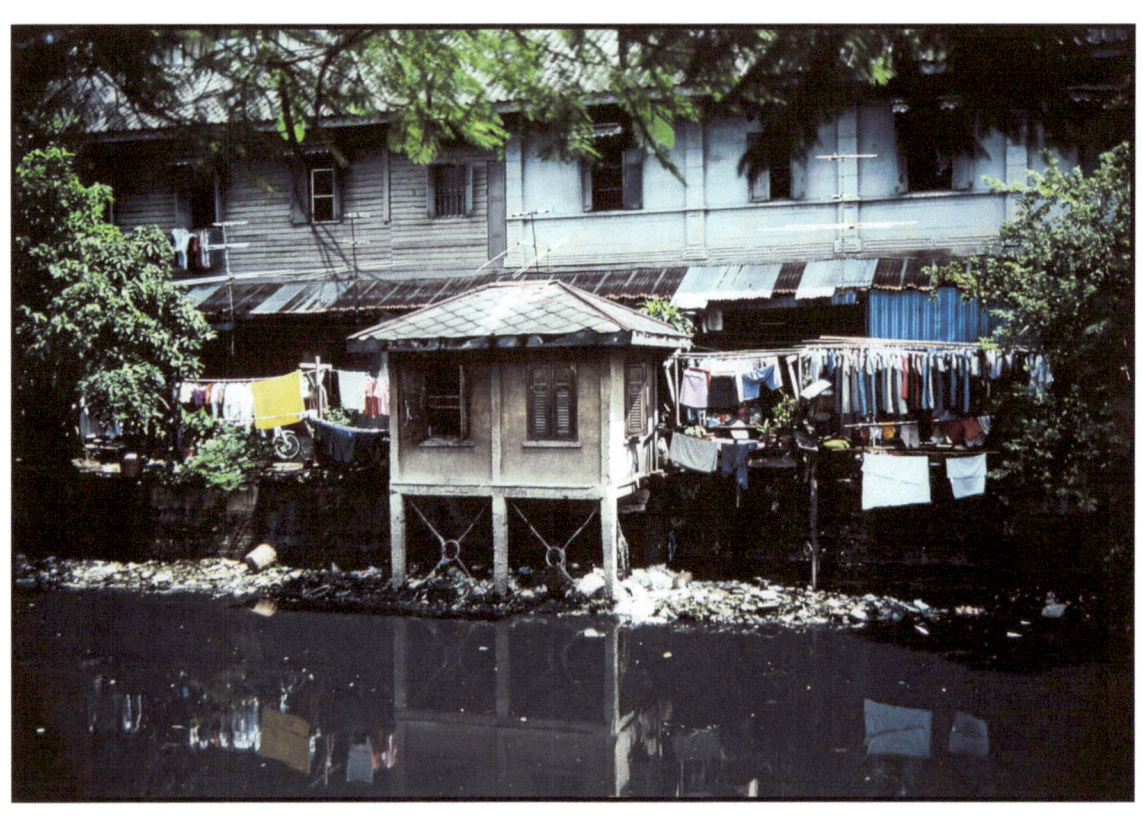

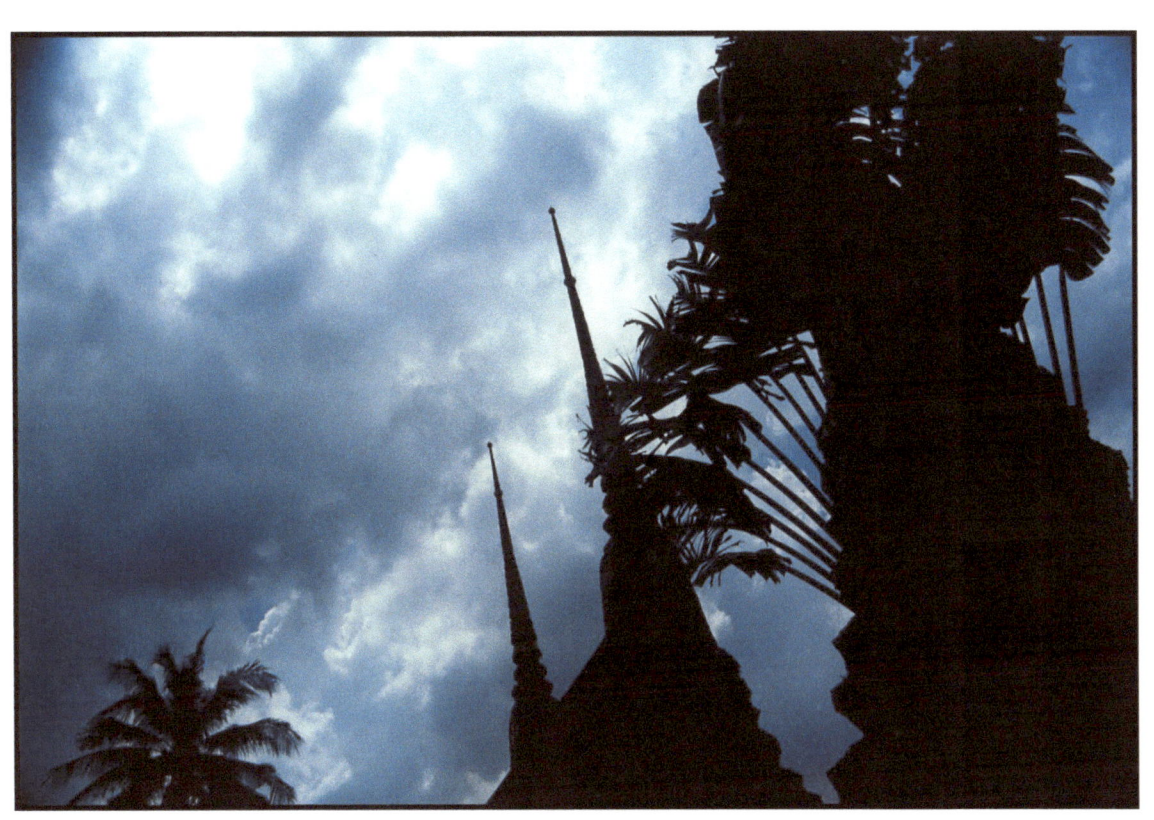

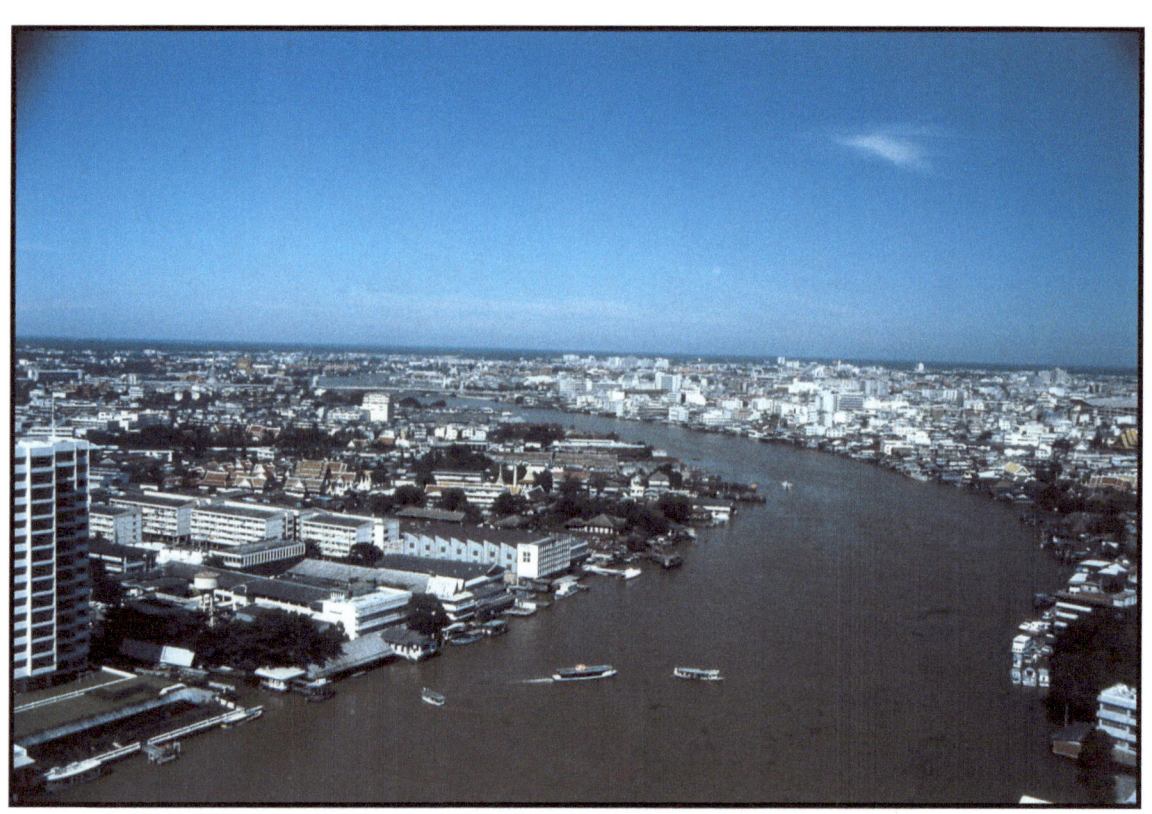

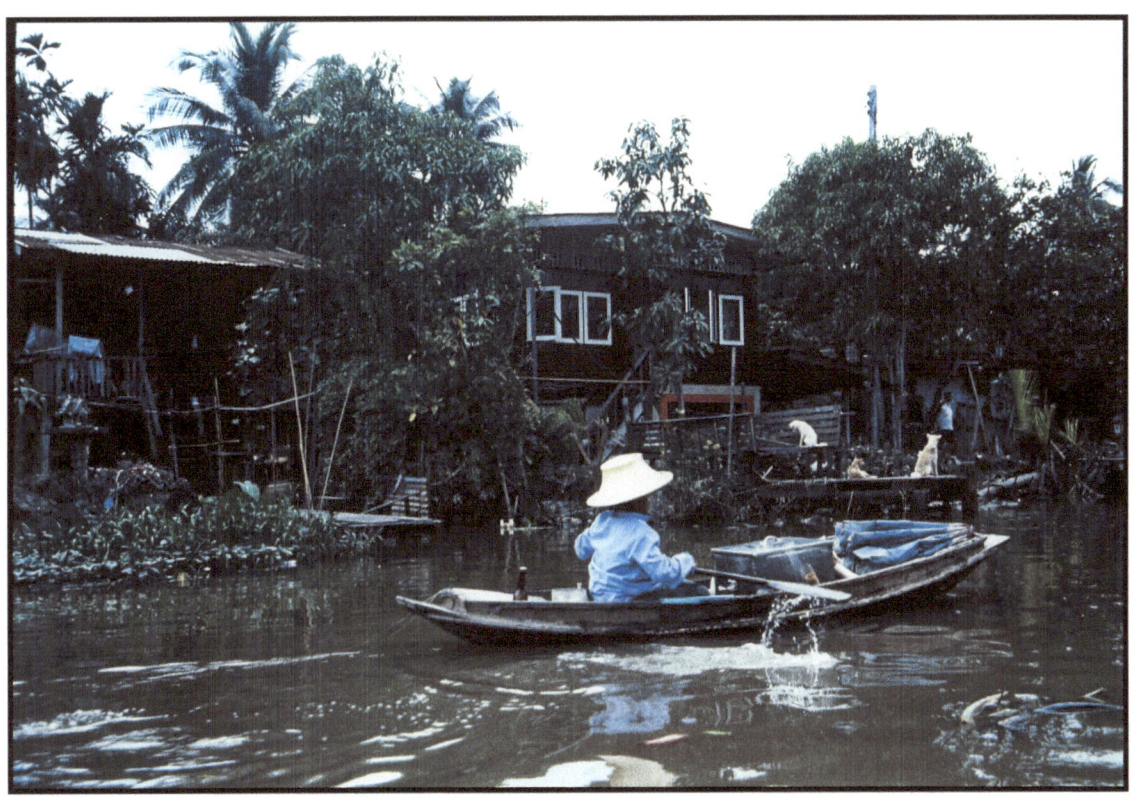

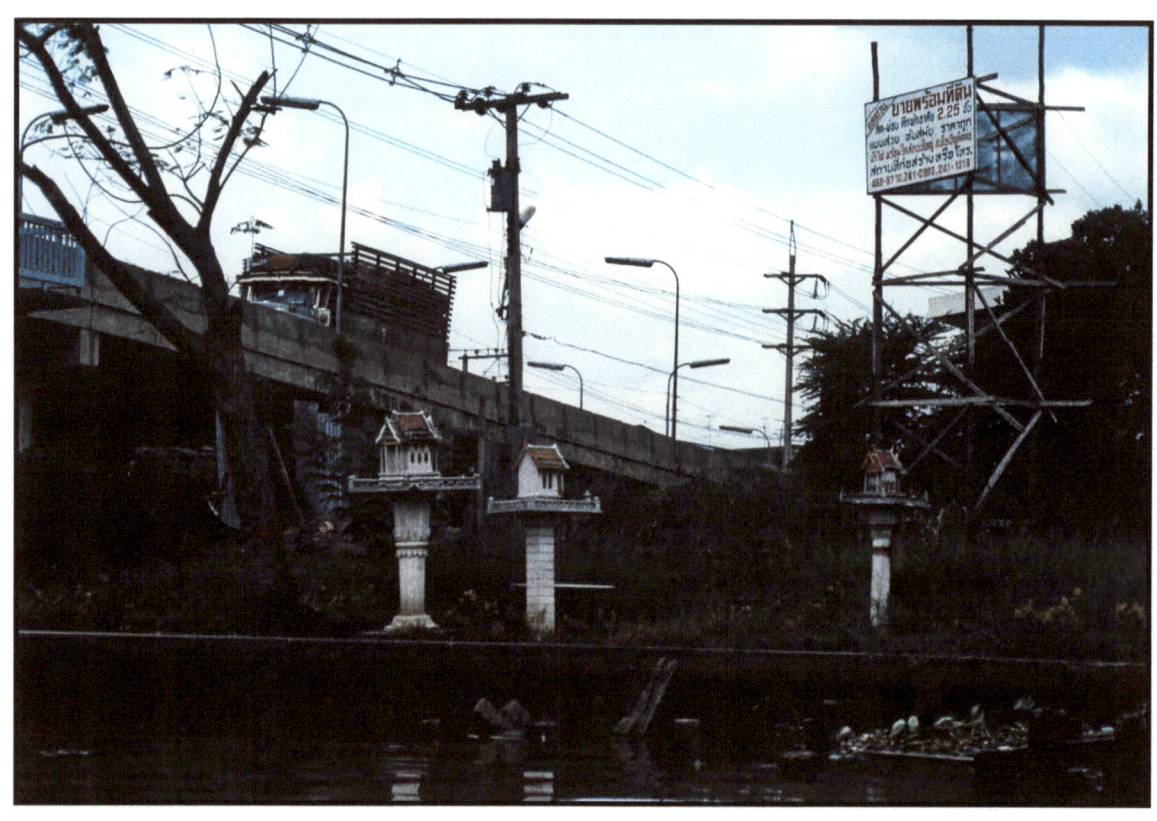

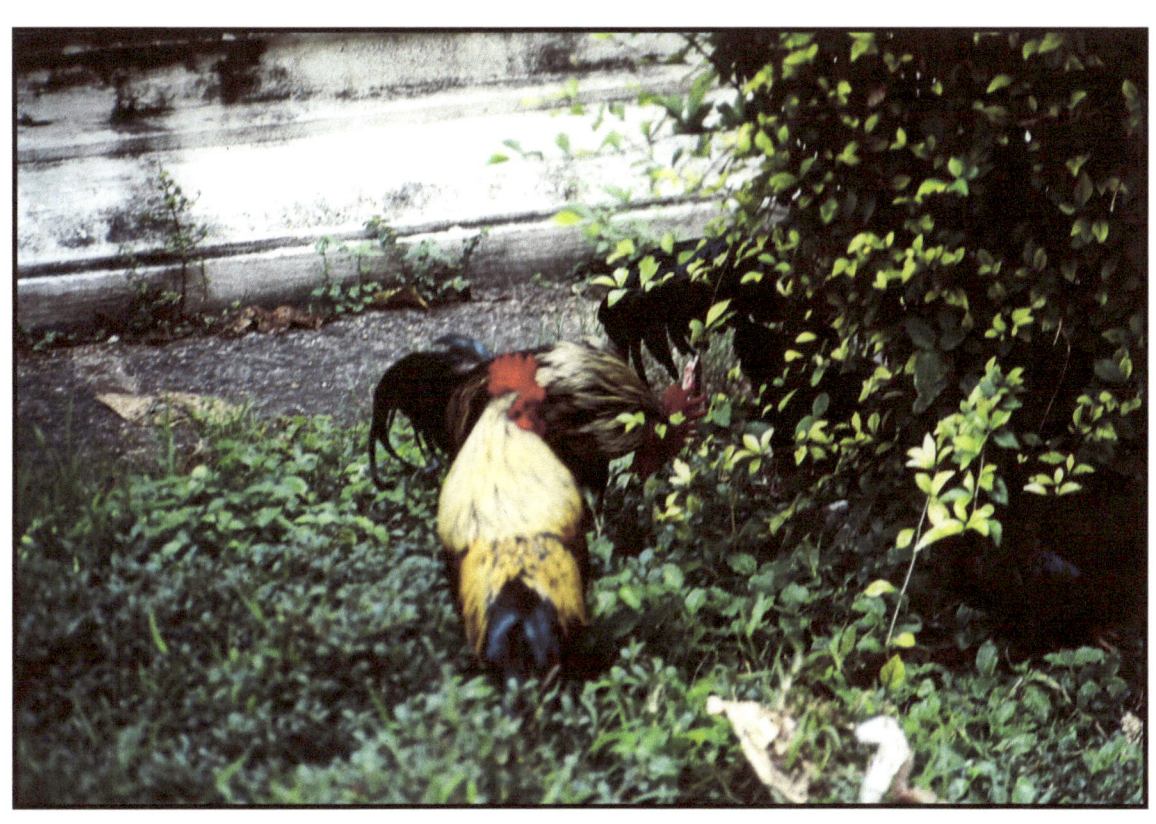

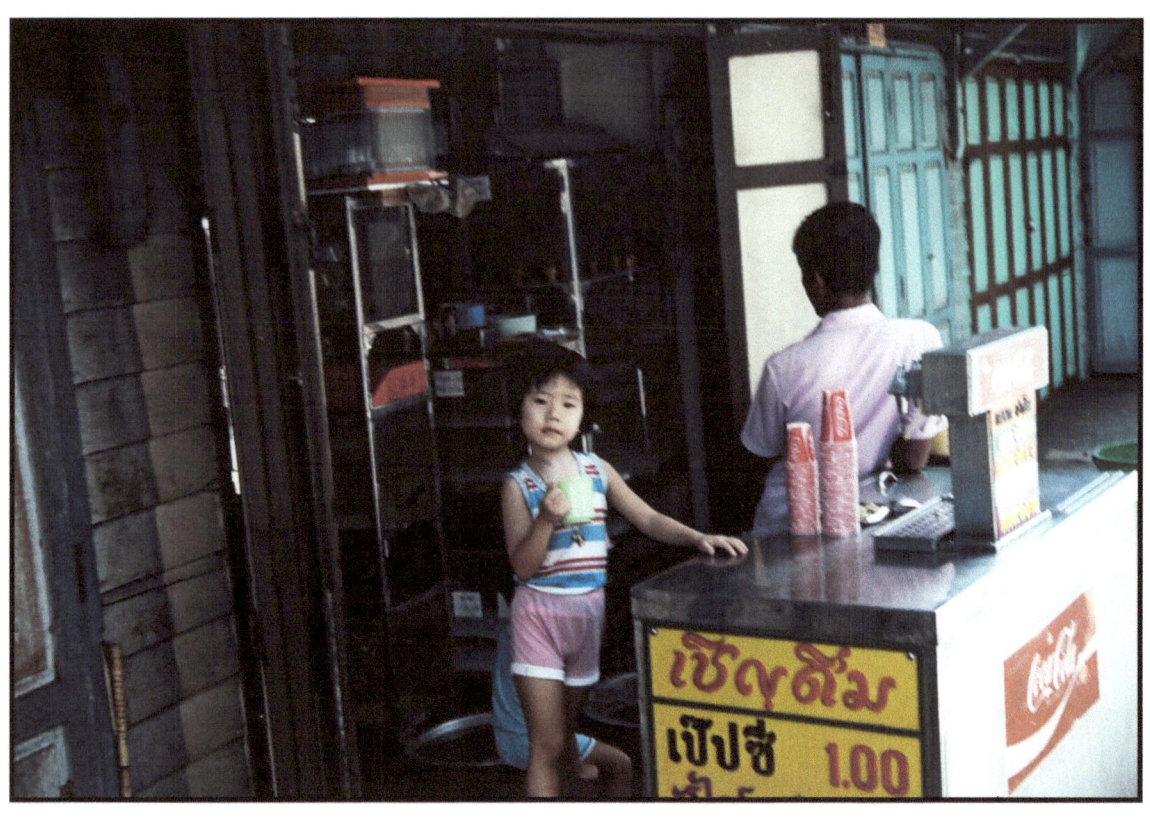

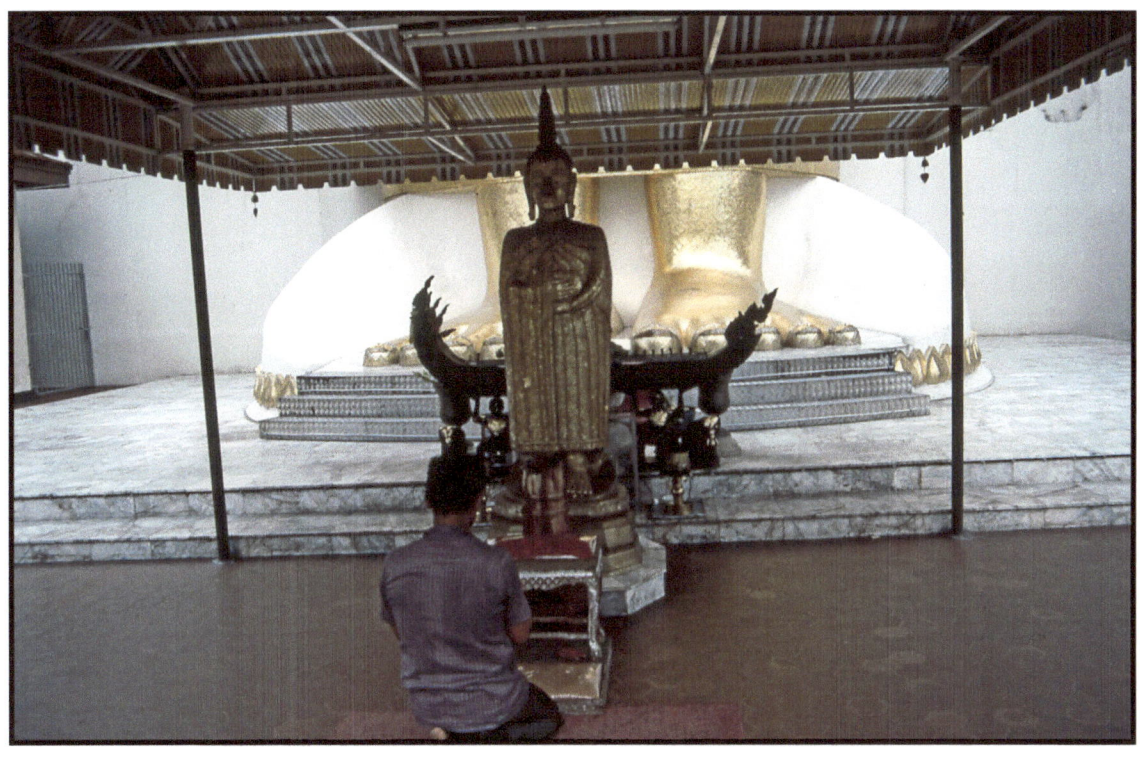

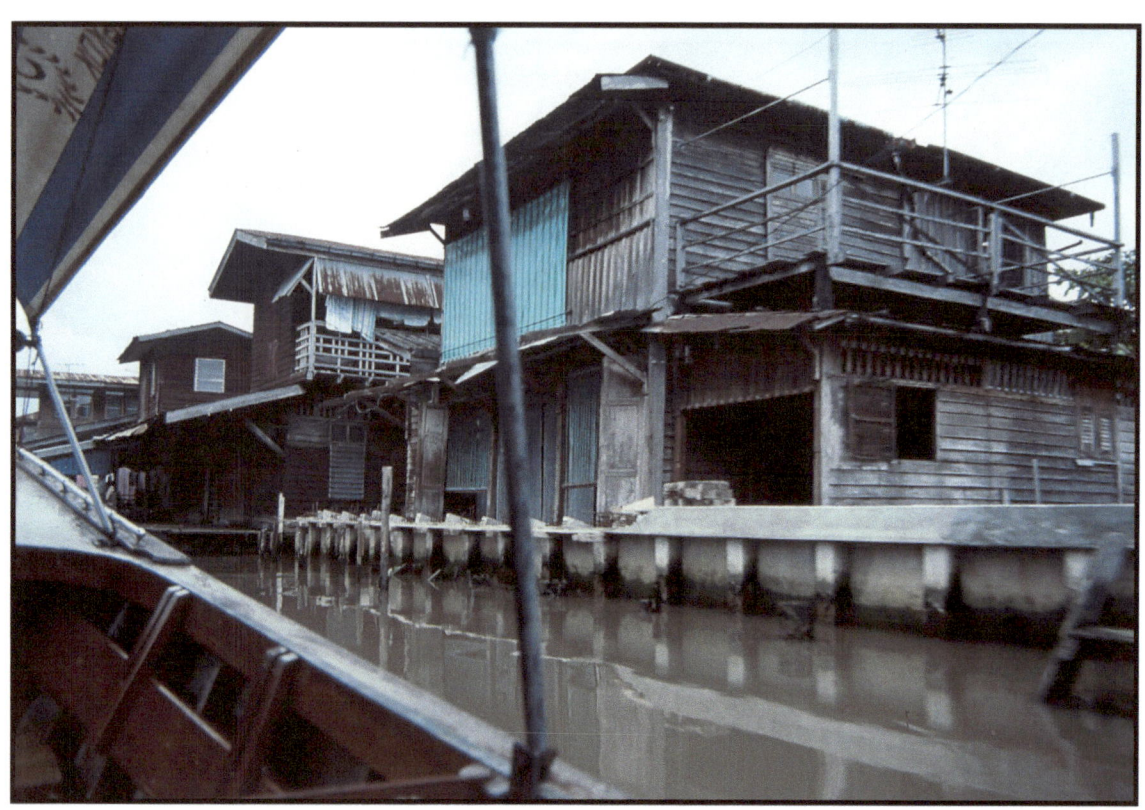

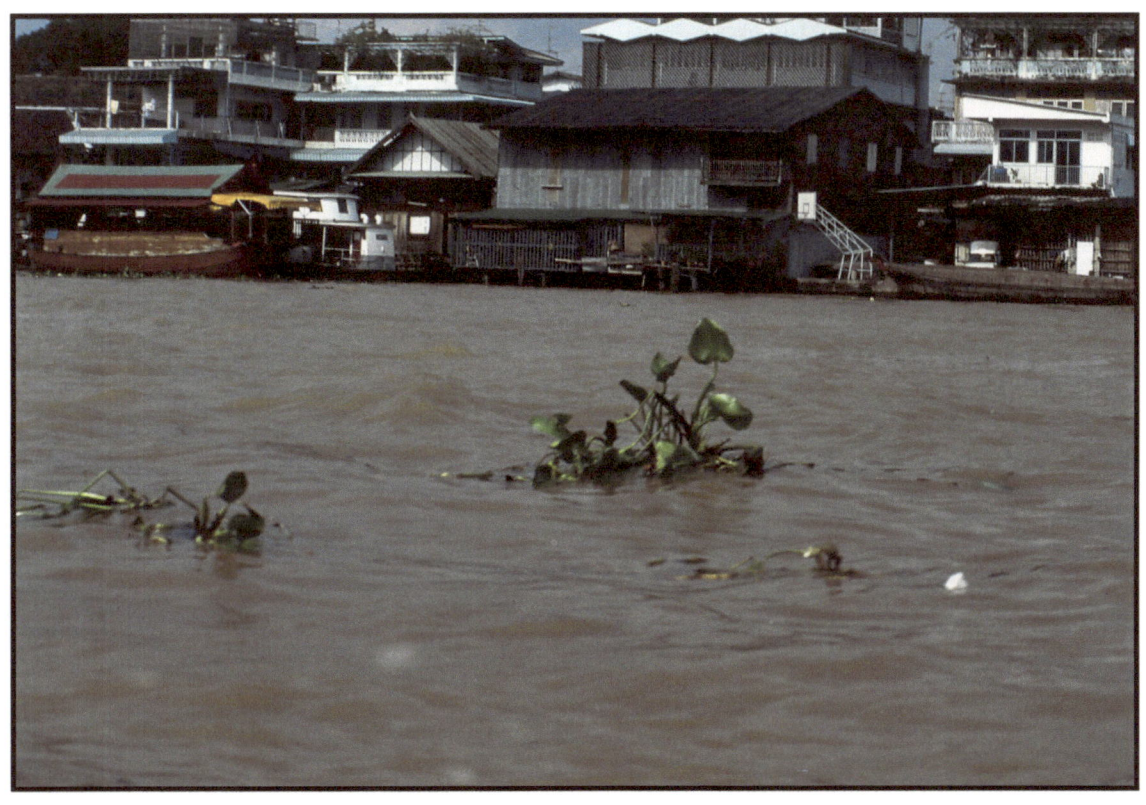

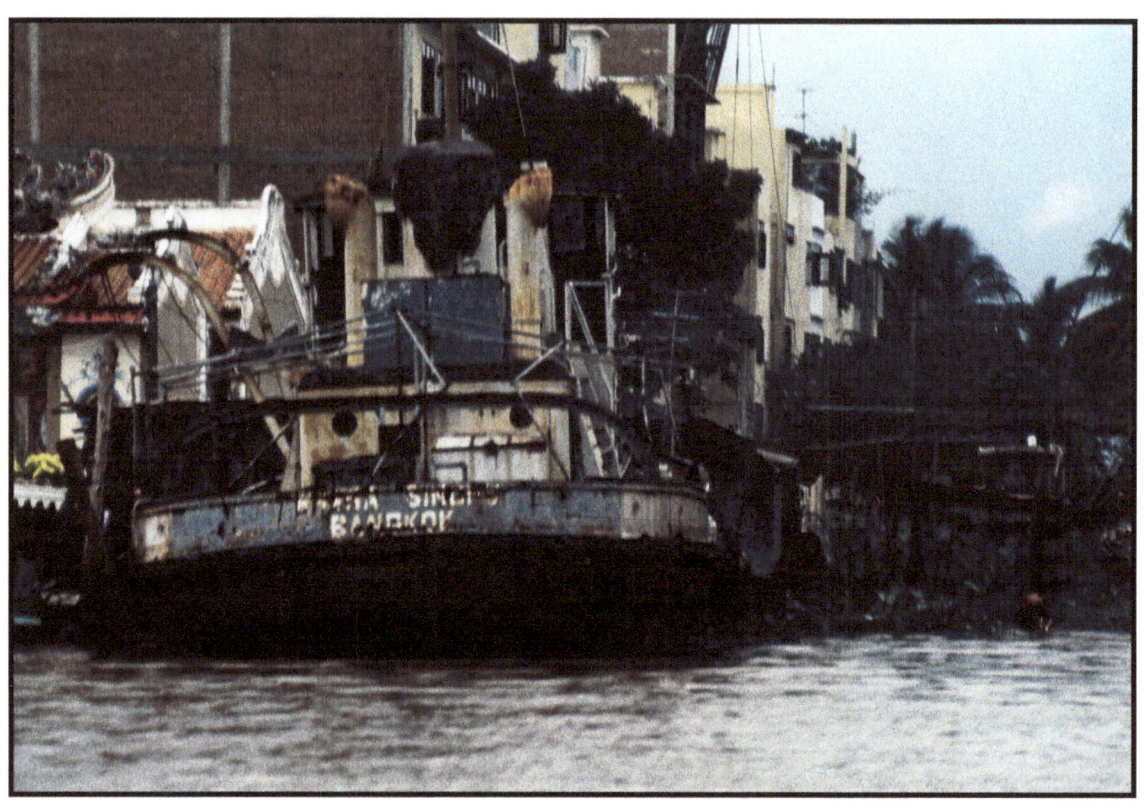

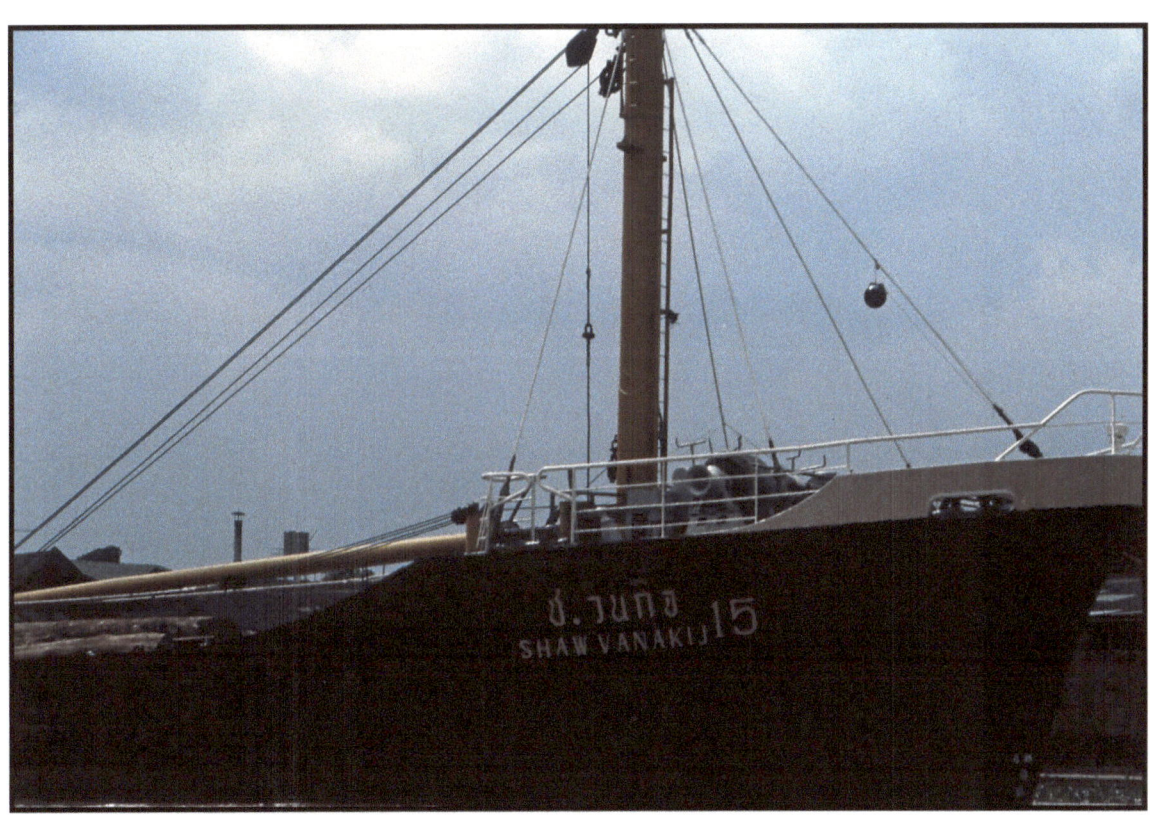

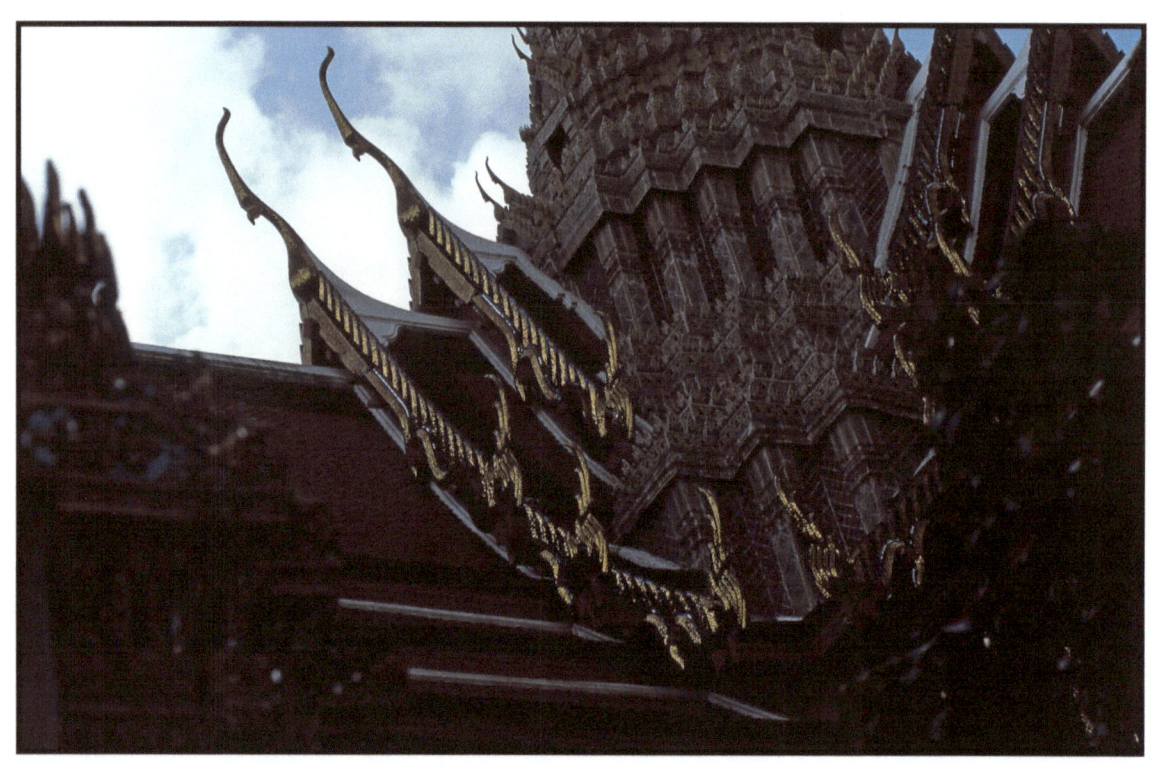

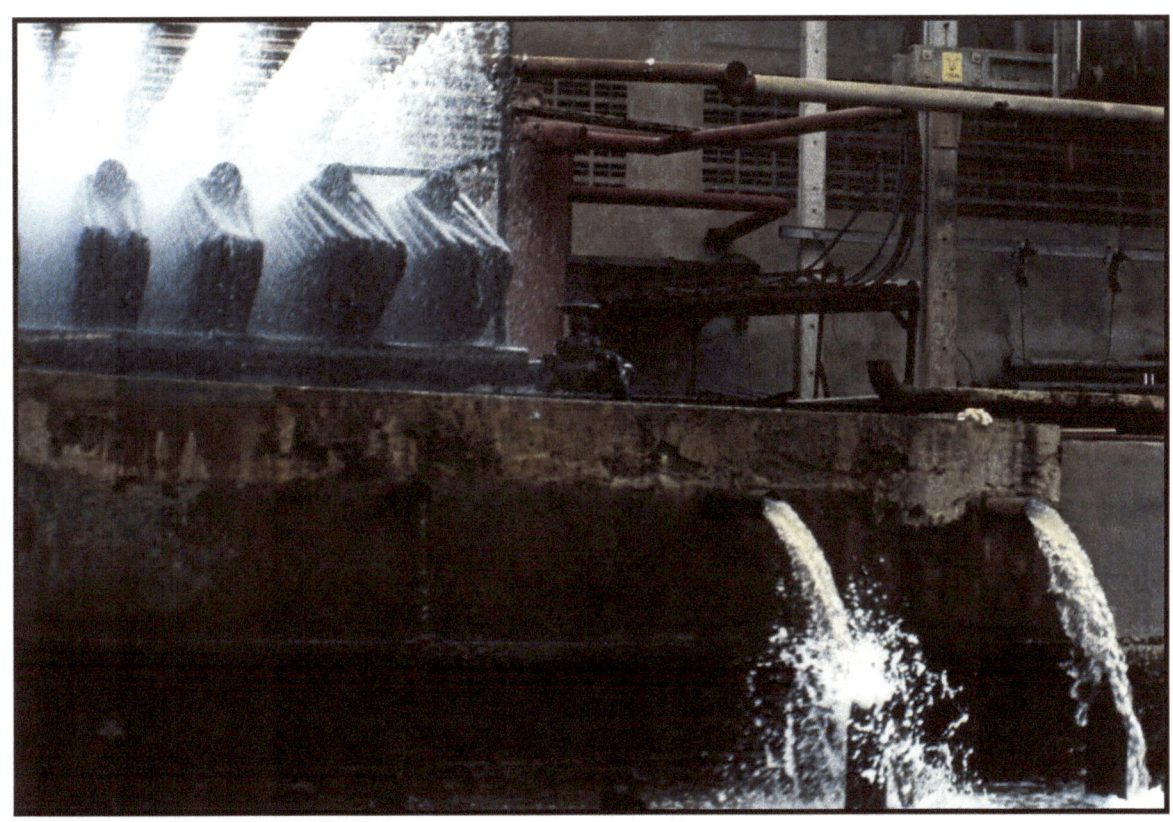

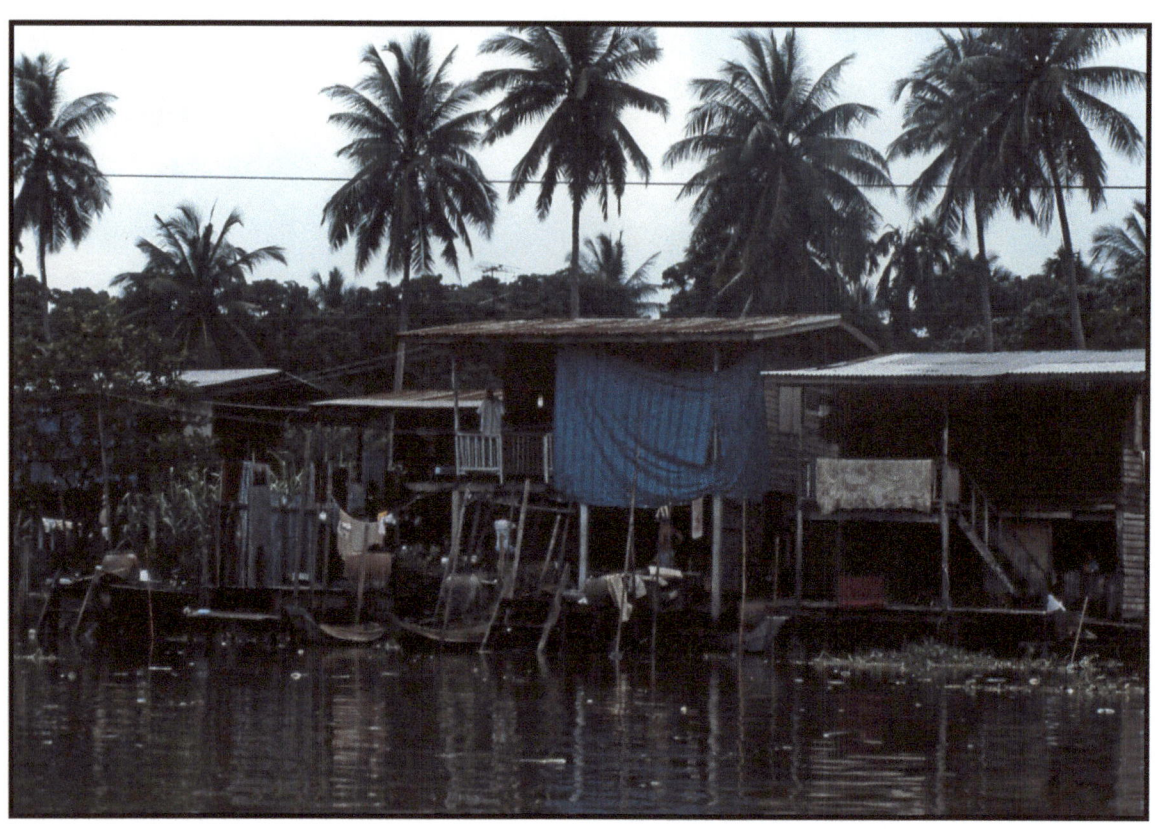

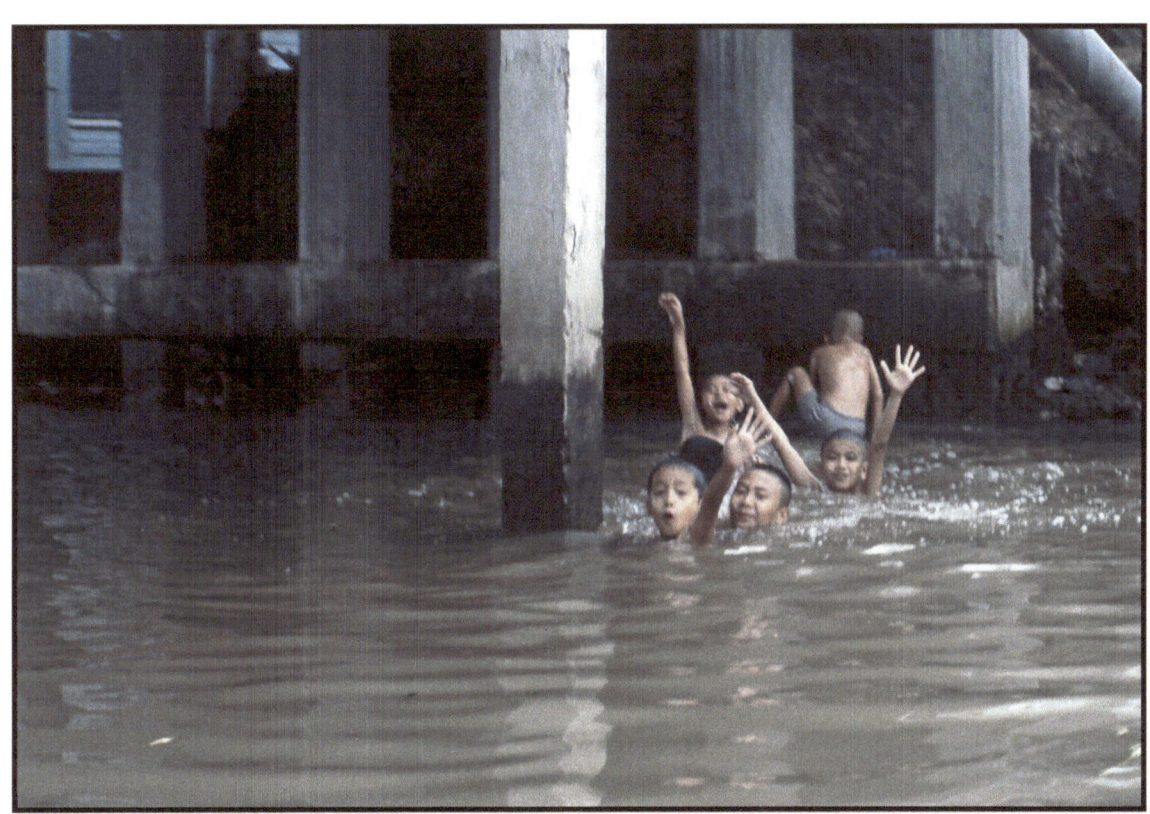

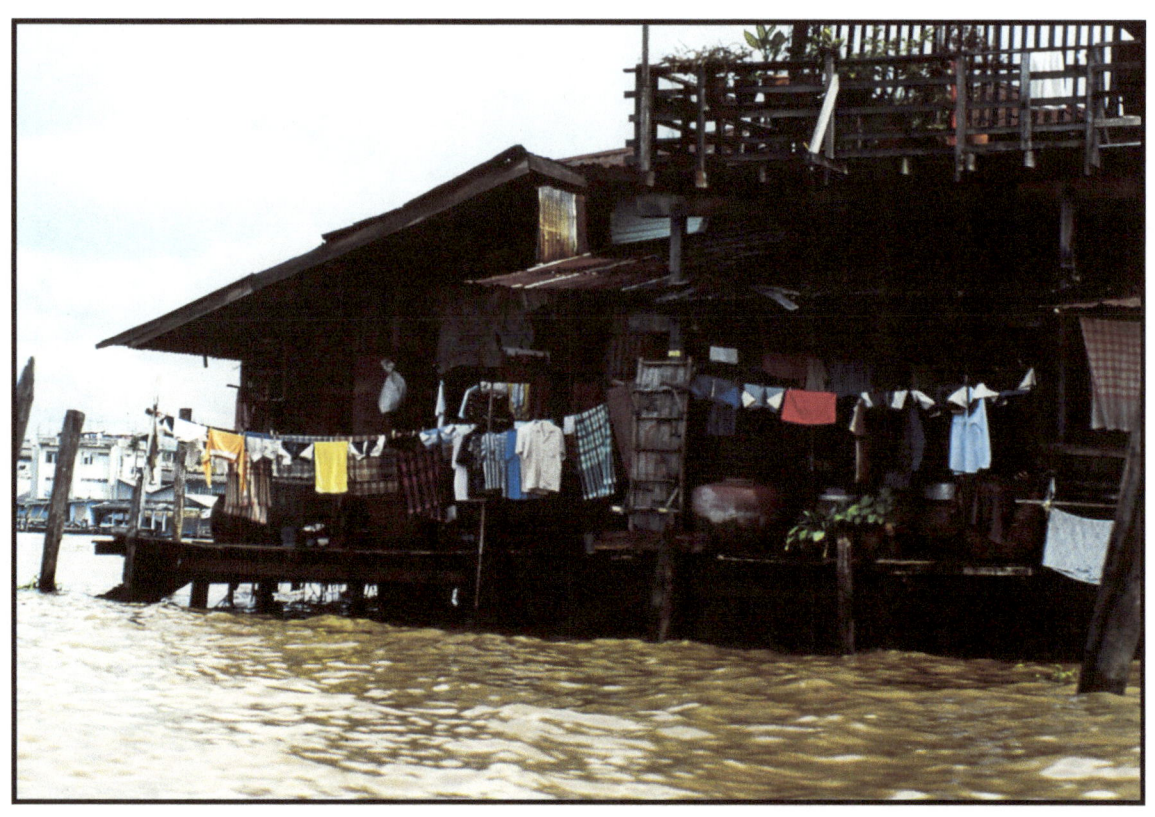

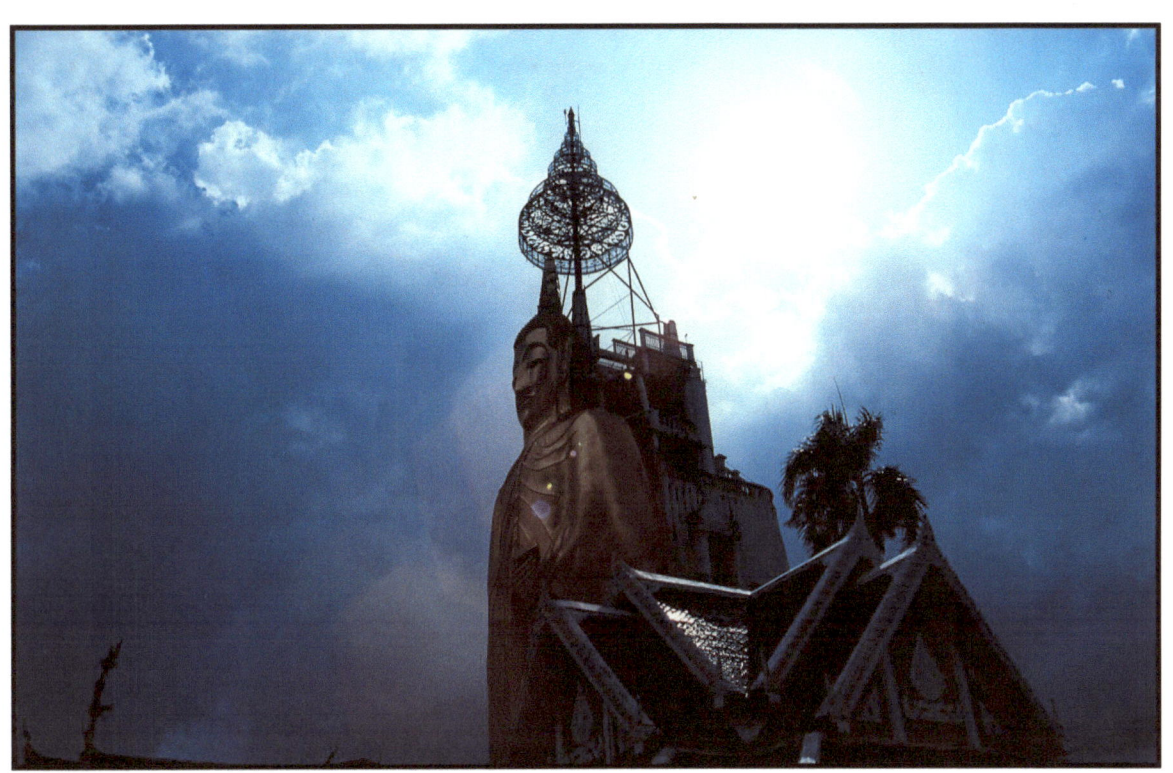

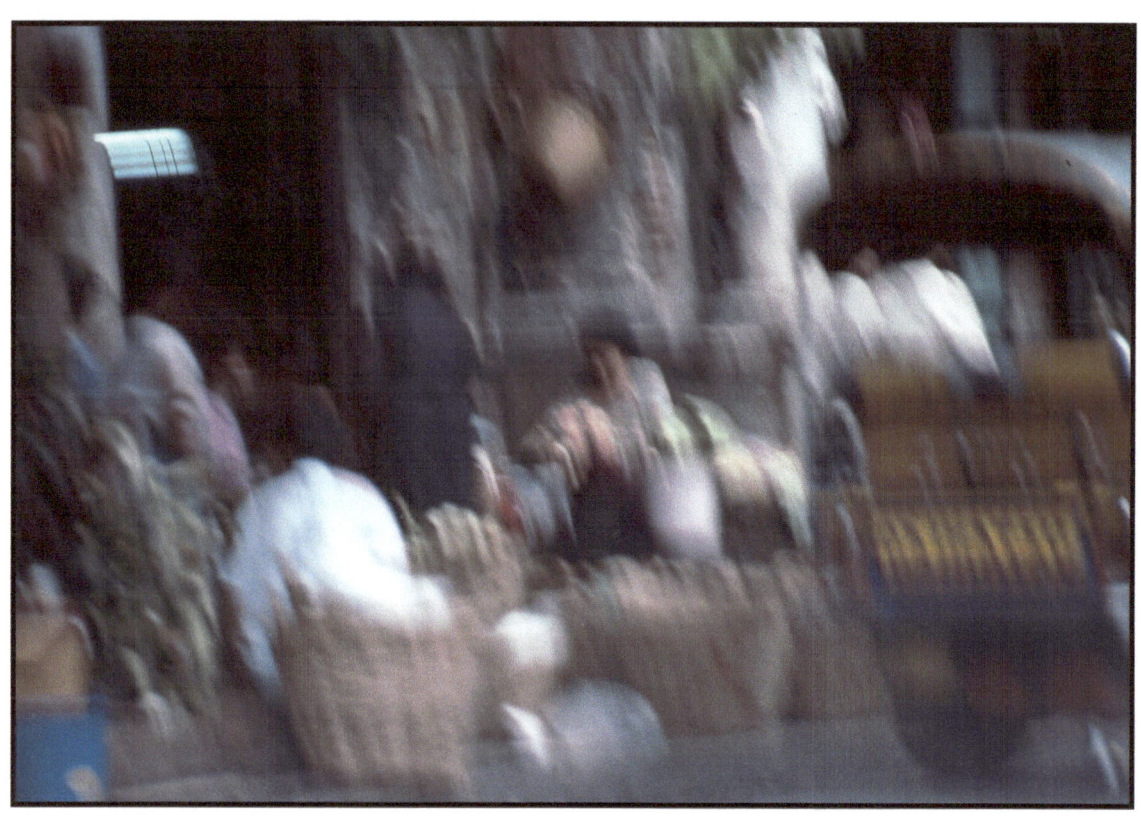

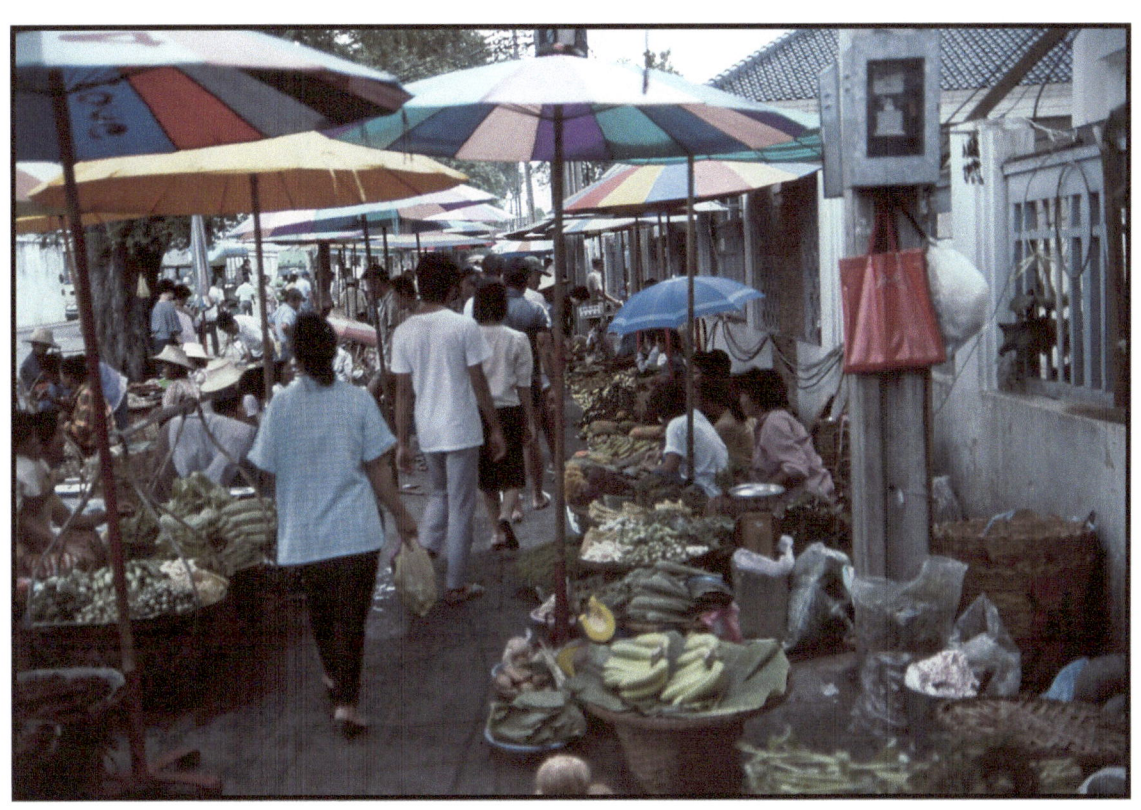

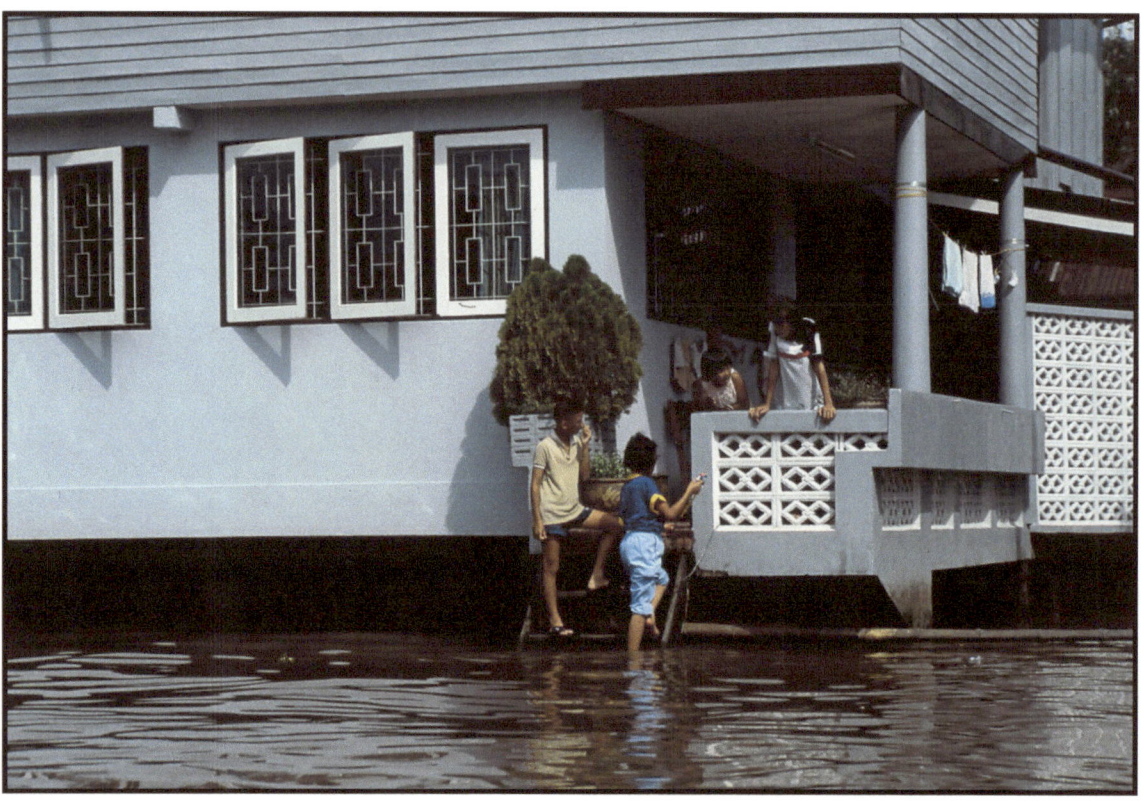

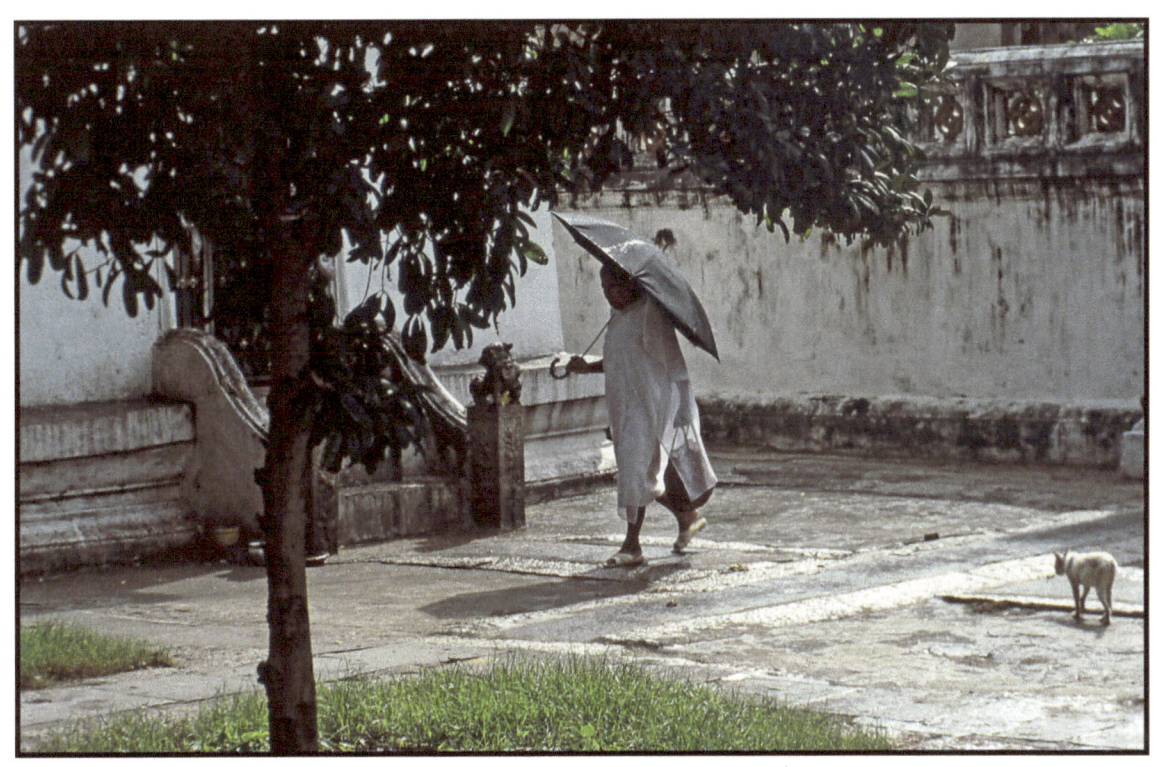

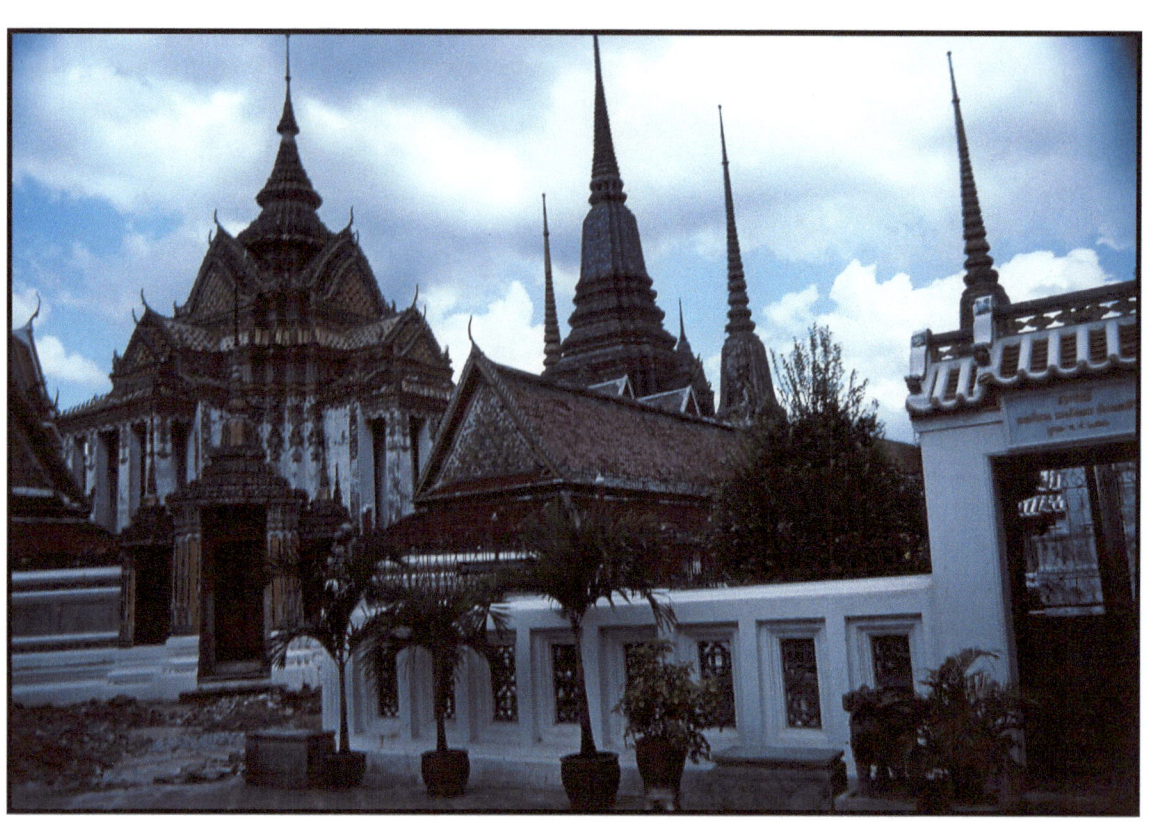

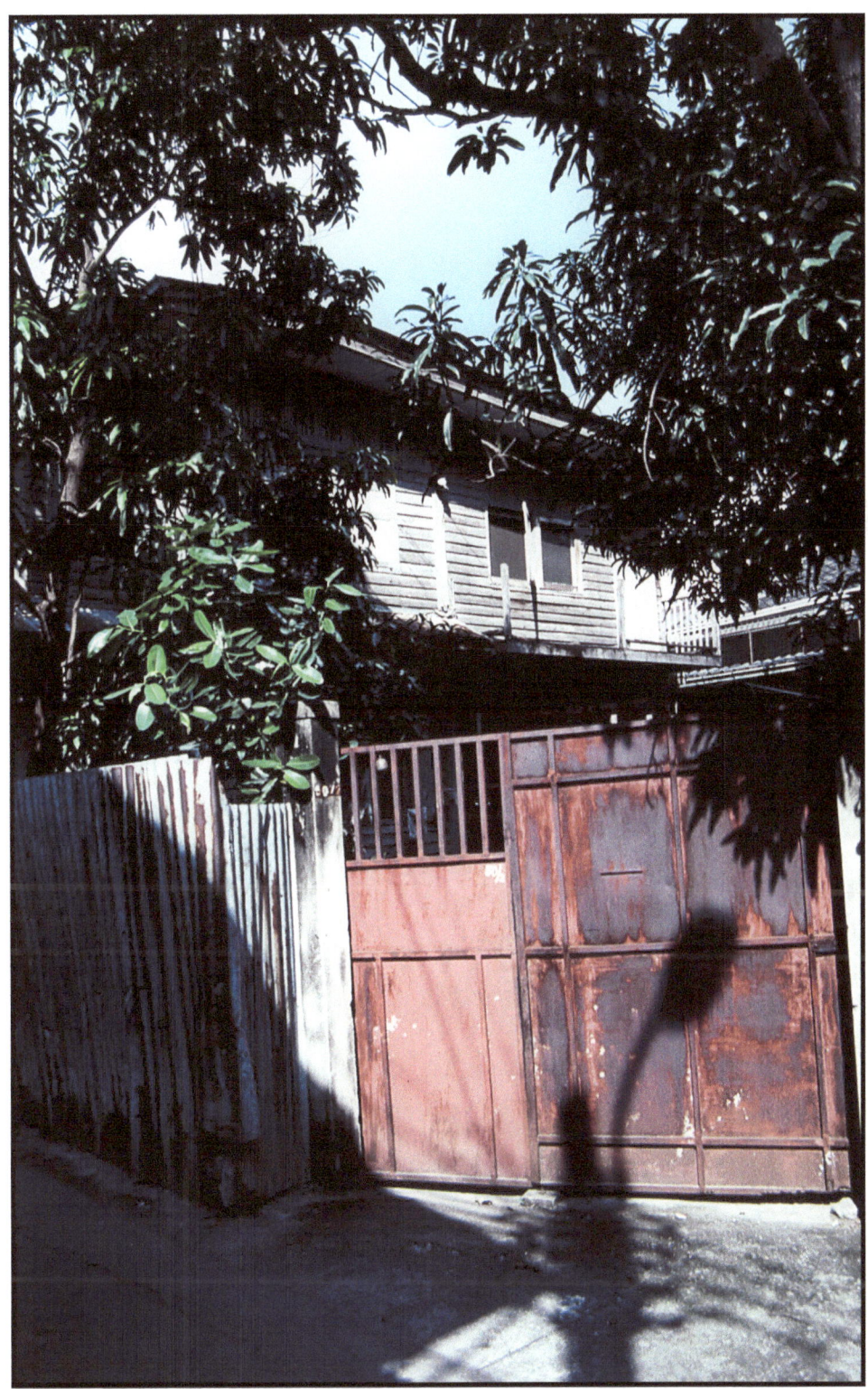

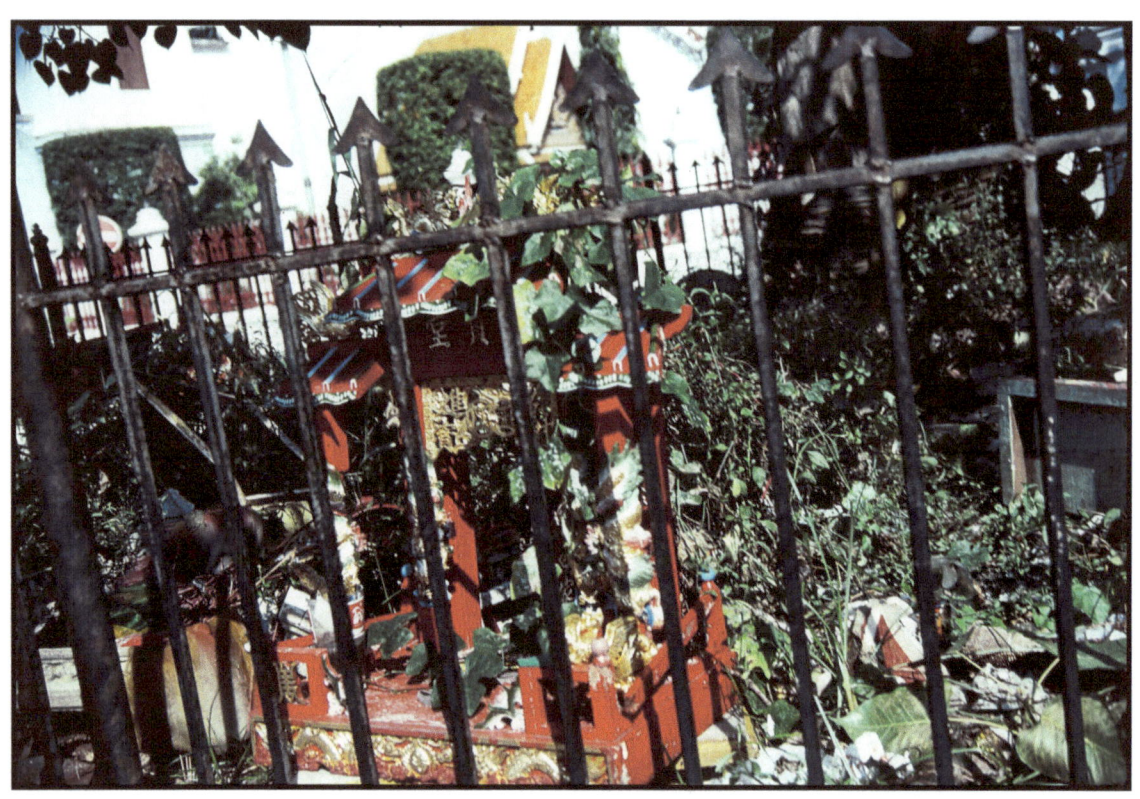

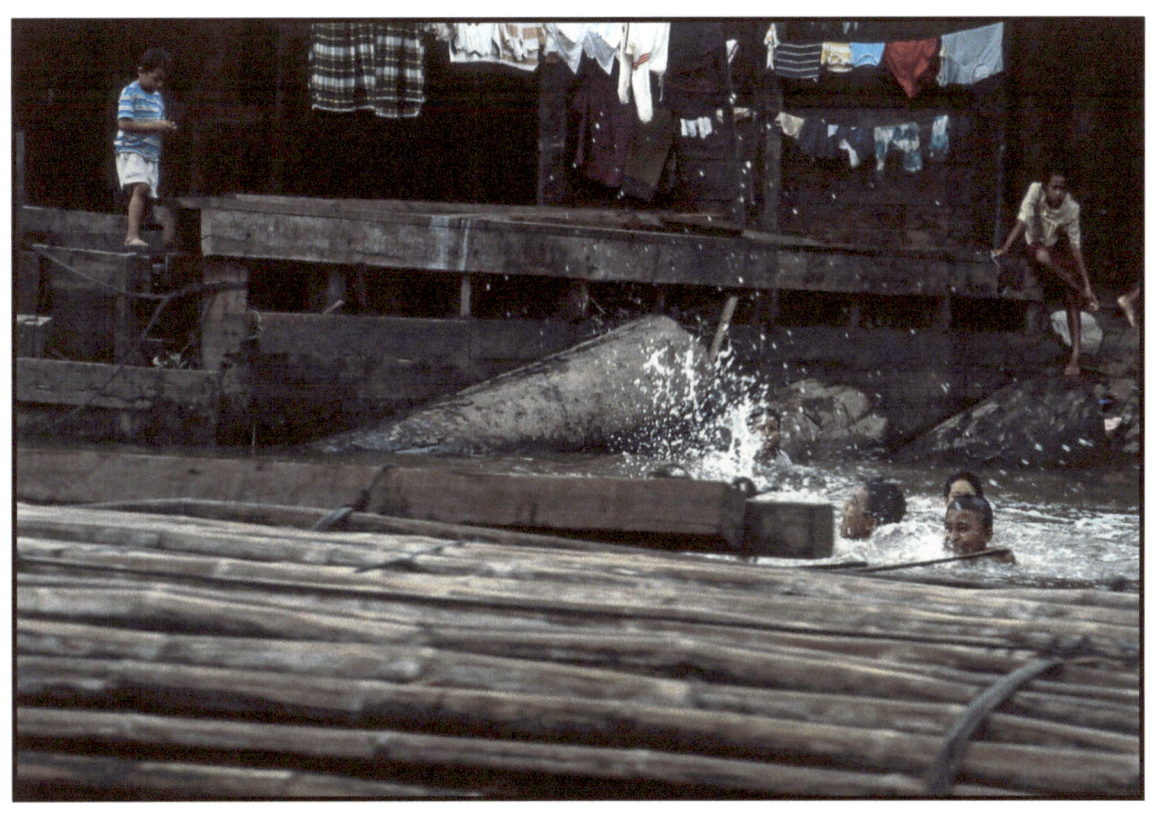

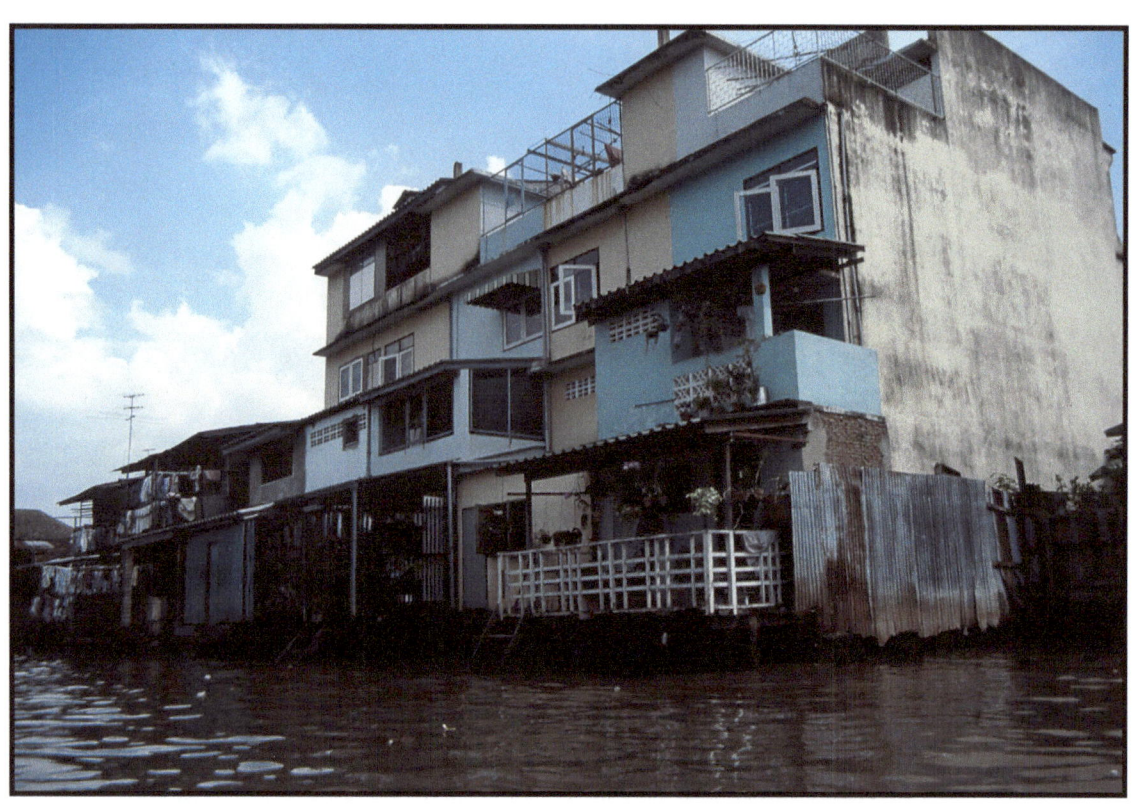

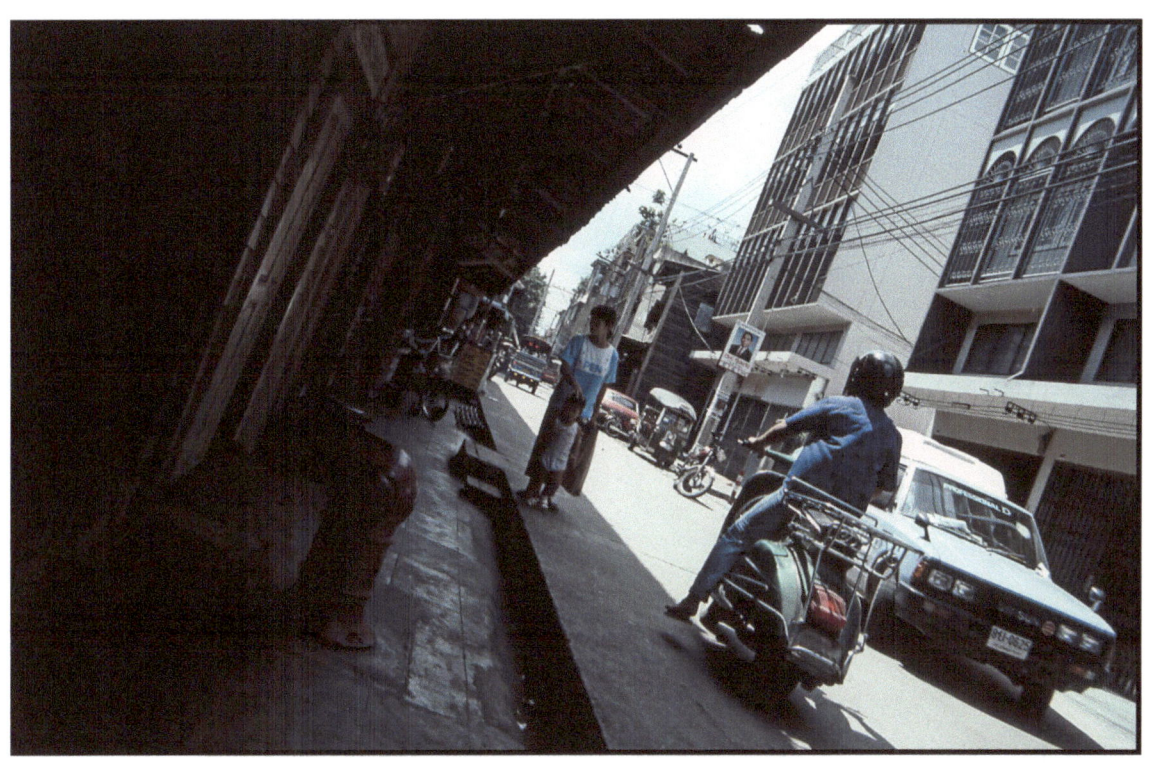

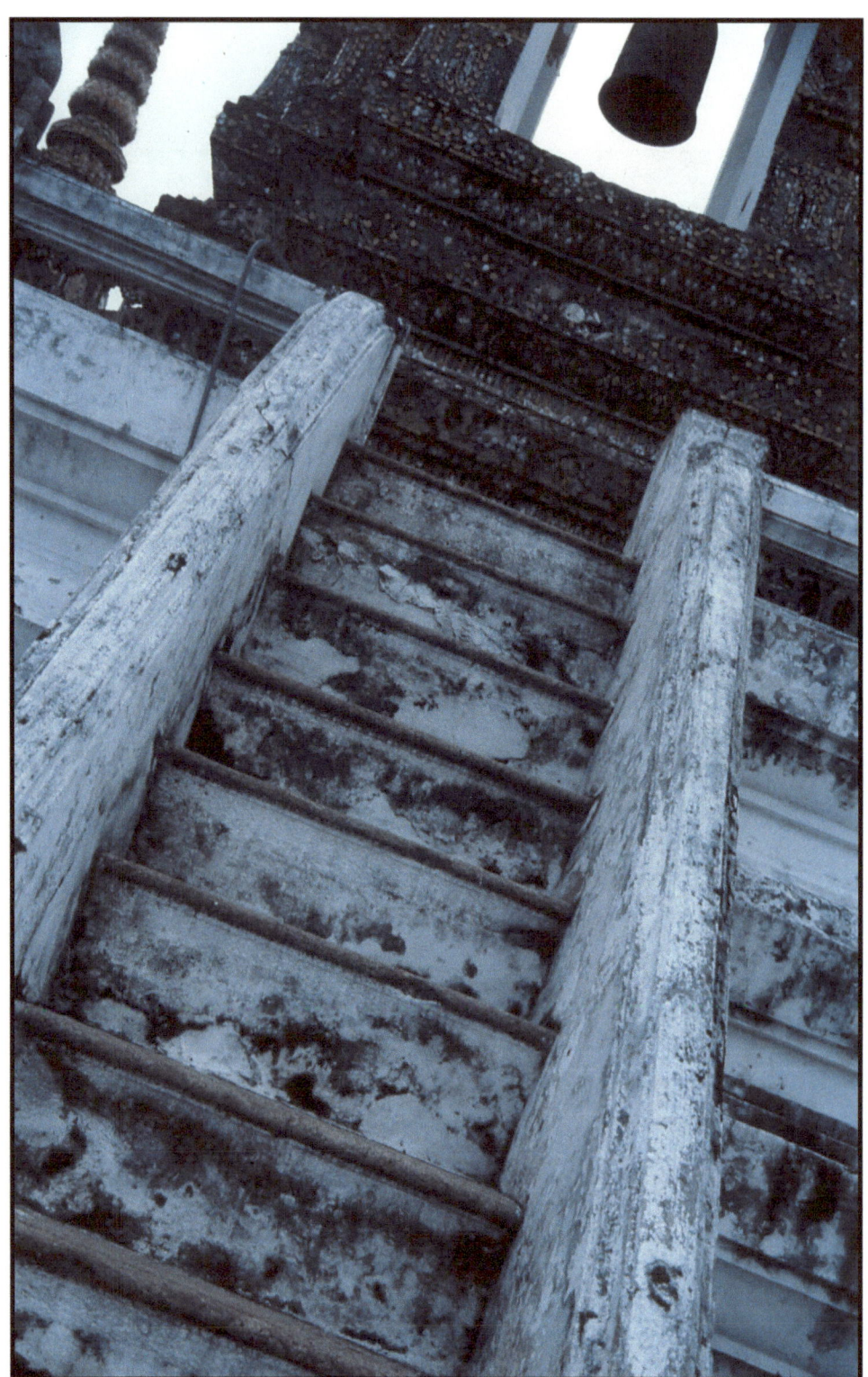

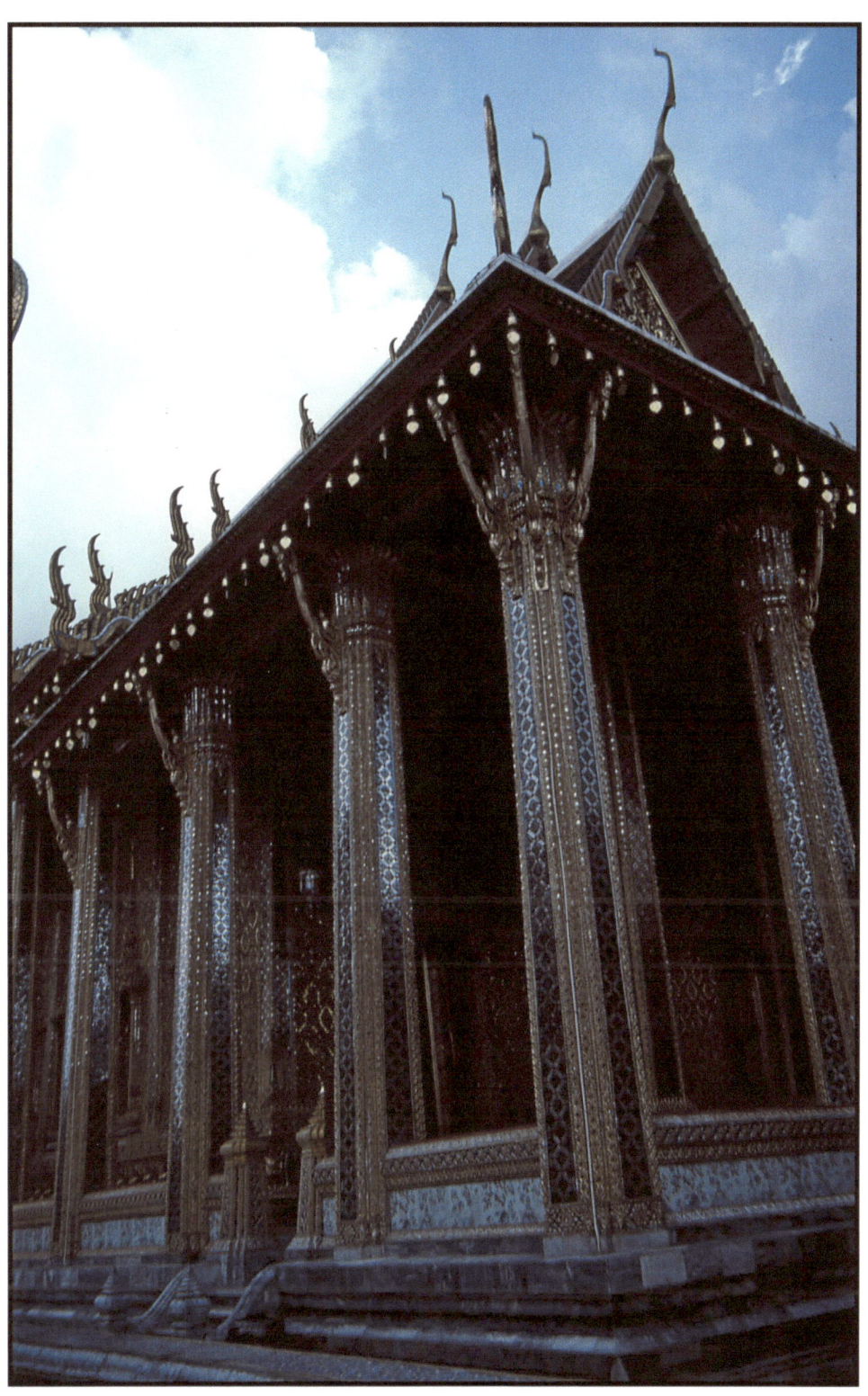

www.ingramcontent.com/pod-product-compliance
Lightning Source LLC
Chambersburg PA
CBHW051145220526
45473CB00003B/659